The Sion Grail

The Sion Grail

To Judey —
in all I friend.
I hope you enjoy
my novel.
Janet

Janet Kramer

Library of Congress Control Number:		2010916522
ISBN:	Hardcover	978-1-4568-0978-2
	Softcover	978-1-4568-0977-5
	Ebook	978-1-4568-0979-9

This book was printed in the United States of America.

Cover painting: *The Holy Grail* by Dante Gabriel Rossetti (1828-82)

To order additional copies of this book, contact:
Xlibris Corporation
1-888-795-4274
www.Xlibris.com
Orders@Xlibris.com
85233

To my children,
Douglas, Gregory, Brian and Amy

ACKNOWLEDGEMENTS

M Y THANKS TO everyone who helped during the writing of *The Sion Grail*—my writing groups, especially the Night Writers—writers Ian Graham Leask and Mary Logue—and my family and friends who read and commented on the earlier manuscripts.

And a special thanks to Doug for his patient love and support.

I am deeply grateful for the opportunity to share this story with all of you.

The Prophecy

As for you, O magdal-eder (watchtower of the flock)
O stronghold of the Daughter of Zion, the former dominion will be
restored to you;
Kingship will come to the Daughter of Jerusalem.
Why do you now cry aloud? Is there no king in you?
Has your counselor perished, that pain seizes you like that of
a woman in labor?
Writhe in agony, O Daughter of Zion, like a woman in labor,
For now you must leave the city and camp in the open field . . .
You shall go to Babylon. There you shall be rescued.
There the LORD will deliver you from your enemies.
Now many nations . . . say, "Let her suffer outrage,
let us gloat over Zion."
They do not know the Lord's thoughts nor understand his purpose;
(Micah 4:8-12)

But you, though you be from the smallest of Judah's clans,
Out of you shall come forth a leader for Israel,
One whose roots are from ancient times.
Therefore he shall give up Israel until the time when she who is in labor
has brought forth. Then those who survive of his race shall rejoin their
brethren, the people of Israel.
And they shall continue,
For now his greatness shall reach to the ends of the earth,
And there shall be peace.
(Micah 5:2-5)

CHAPTER ONE

The Collector

H ÉRCULE ST. CLAIR was in the process of repairing the recalcitrant drawer of a feathered walnut secretary in his shop, St. Clair et fils, at 16 rue des Saints-Pères, Paris, when a prospective client entered. Hércule looked up to see a tall fair-skinned, balding man. Bushy eyebrows seemed to overpower the other features of his face. "*Bonjour, Monsieur,*" he said in his normal welcoming voice.

The imposing man beckoned to St. Clair, stating, "I am a collector of *objets d'art.* I specialize in antiquities from the first to the fourteenth centuries, and I am especially interested in items that may have been brought to Europe during the various crusades. Here is my card." He handed an embossed card to Hércule. It read, "Marcel Devereaux, Antiquités, 21 rue de Sartre, Colmar, Alsace."

"I've been told that you have something of interest to me—an ancient gold chalice. They say you show it from time to time at your little events. I wish to see it." His manner was commanding and haughty. He spoke brusquely. His French was perfect, but his accent sounded Germanic.

The abrupt and surprising request bewildered Hércule. On a few occasions, he had shown the family treasure to members of the Priory at their annual ceremony, and once, in a misconceived marketing ploy, he had used the golden jewel-encrusted chalice at a shop wine tasting as a draw for a very select clientele. But he'd always told everyone that the chalice was only a copy of the original. Even the Priory members believed him.

Hércule, a much smaller, but nattily dressed man, straightened his cravat and stated firmly, "I do not carry any antique vessels, only furniture."

"You are lying! I have it from a very good source that they were invited here for a special evening and were shown a very old golden chalice. I want to see it."

"Who exactly told you that?" Hércule asked, disturbed at the harshness in his visitor's voice.

"It doesn't matter," Marcel Devereaux hedged. "It's not my prerogative to disclose that information. If you will show me the item, I will be able to verify its age and authenticity. I believe it was in May of 2008, this little event."

"Yes, I recall that event, but the item you may have heard of is not for sale. In that particular incident, a replica of a family antique was shown. As you may know, I do not normally deal in replicas, only authentic antiques, but because the item you mention is highly valued by my family, it was necessary to create a substitute for the public viewing. I have not held such an event since and do not anticipate doing so in the future. There is no such *objet d'art* in this shop. There. Enough!"

Hércule made a shoving movement with his hands as though to push this man out. He wanted to rid his shop of this rude intruder. He had to steel himself to keep from looking at the armoire in which the chalice now rested, afraid that he might draw the customer's eyes to its location. He knew the armoire was locked, but he didn't want to give this rapacious man the slightest hint of its whereabouts.

"No, I do not believe you," Devereaux persisted defiantly. He opened the drawer of a desk near him. "It is here, I know. I will find it." He moved to another cabinet.

Hércule placed himself in front of the cabinet preventing M. Devereaux from accessing it. "I am so sorry, Monsieur. You have been given incorrect information." Hércule could hear the change in his own voice, which had hardened from its initial patronizing tone. He could feel his tiny moustache twisting in agitation and derision for this rude man, but he would not let this man best him.

M. Devereaux moved about the shop continuing to open doors of cabinets as though he had not heard or did not believe Hércule St. Clair's statement that the chalice was not in the shop.

Hércule firmly shut the secretary door that Devereaux had just opened. Insulted, he spoke sharply. "As you may know, Monsieur, I am also an expert on antiquities. I do not need others to verify the authenticity of items in this shop." Controlling his agitation, he spoke almost in monotone, but there was an edge to his voice. "I thought I made it clear that there is no ancient chalice here that is for sale to anyone. If you do not believe me, then perhaps your own qualifications may be a fakery. I am about to close the shop, and I must ask you to leave."

The collector bumped Hércule St. Clair as he strode past him toward the door. Turning, he spoke in an ominous challenging tone, "We will see!"

When the door closed behind him, Hércule St. Clair quickly locked it and sank into his chair. *Sacrebleu!* How had this rude man found their chalice—their grail? Who would know of it outside his tiny and select family group? And perhaps this collector would return with reinforcements to capture their treasure. He shook with anger at this invasion of his shop and his privacy. And he was very worried.

As the Grand Master of the current *Prieuré de Sion*, he knew the history of its antique well. The Sion Grail had been in the Priory's or its members' possession almost continuously since 1188 when the leaders of the Priory of Sion broke away from the Knights Templar and formed their own secret society. As members of the Knights Templar, they were famous for their service in the Crusades where the French king sent them to protect pilgrims on their way to holy sites in Palestine and to save Solomon's Temple for the Christian world from the infidels of Islam. The Templars were said to have brought back to Europe vast treasure from Palestine including, some sources said, the Holy Grail and the Arc of the Covenant. The derivation of the Priory's extremely valuable chalice could not be precisely determined. However, Hércule had his own ideas on where it had originated.

In 1307, on Friday, the thirteenth of October, the French king, Philip IV, at the behest of the Catholic Inquisition, ordered the arrest of all Templars and subsequently imprisoned, interrogated, and tortured six hundred of them. Seven years later, their last grand master, Jacques de Molay, was burned at the stake in front of Notre Dame Cathedral. That event, Hércule thought, amused, was the beginning of our superstitions regarding Fridays numbered the thirteenth as being unlucky.

After the Templars fell from the Catholic Church's favor, the Norman branch of the St. Clair family fled to Scotland, where they anglicized the name to Sinclair—a name and a history shared by some current members of the Paris Priory.

Besieged with worry, Hércule St. Clair started looking at his options. Because of the grail's historical significance, the members of the ancient secret organization would also be concerned, he knew. Though he had long been a member and was the titular Grand Master of the Prieuré, based on his family's derivation from the first house of Frankish kings, Hércule St. Clair had little experience in how the Priory might deal with problems such as this. They had helped accomplish a united Europe, but in the last few years, the Priory's activities had been very limited . . . the membership was aging, and the crop of future leaders was dim. Hércule considered seeking the advice of the Priory's current members, but after much contemplation, he determined it best that he deal with this problem himself.

Though Hércule had locked the shop's front door when M. Devereaux finally left, within about twenty minutes, he heard someone yelling that he should open the door. He peeked from behind one of the largest pieces he had on display. Two rough-looking men were at the door. They rattled the door until he feared its glass would break. "Where's the proprietor? What the hell? It says here you're supposed to be open. We want to see the goblet Devereaux said you had. Let us in! If you know what's good for you, you'll let us in." Expletives followed.

Hércule St. Clair crept to the back of the shop and hid. He gasped in relief when the noise from the men stopped. He checked the door. Yes, they were indeed gone. "*Mon dieu*," he sighed. "What will happen next?" Sweating and shivering from this series of fearful experiences, Hércule knew he had to make some decisions about the safety of his beloved grail and soon.

Banks, yes, he knew that would be best, but he'd always detested banks and bankers. Ever since the Second World War when his money deposited in a bank he thought was safe had gone without his knowledge to support the Vichy government, which he hated. And when the Nazis had taken over, no art object in a bank had been safe. Those storm troopers stole untold treasures and took them back to Germany. Hércule had always felt safer with the chalice in his own possession. Also, the grail's mysterious powers precluded its being given to just anyone or put in just any place. He had to find an answer to this terrible dilemma.

CHAPTER TWO

Paris

THE AIR FRANCE flight attendant announced their arrival at Charles de Gaulle airport. Hundreds of weary passengers jammed the aisles, jostled each other, and pushed past the less aggressive into the terminal. Maggie Forsythe lovingly placed her mother's fifteen-year-old Paris journal and the roughly drawn St. Clair family tree into her carryall before she rose to join the others. Seeing her late mother's handwriting in the journal, so much like her own, had startled her and rekindled some of her most cherished memories. The journal had added fire to her intent to find her family here in France.

The modernity of the terminal building disappointed Maggie. She had hoped for something more "French," but then this was, after all, an airport. In the main open pavilion, brightly colored pipes swooped up and down and curled like fallopian tubes. Here she was, riding down an escalator inside a red fallopian tube. Why did she see it as a female thing? Was she feeling lusty or just frustrated with her antiquated status? Despite her looks, she had reached the age of thirty-one in this state because she'd never met the right guy, and she hadn't wanted to risk sexual involvement until it felt perfect. But this was no time to be thinking about that old canard. She was in Paris!

In the room marked "*Femmes,*" Maggie hurriedly splashed cold water on her broad forehead and high cheekbones, as she searched the mirror for signs of her long flight. Her nose was not the size of Barbra Streisand's, but it was still more prominent than she would have liked. She never thought of herself as beautiful, but she had something that made people notice her in an admiring way—like the man on the plane who seemed so interested—Israel, that was his name. "Oh posh," she said. She didn't like to dwell on her looks.

Maggie looked for a cash machine, wondering if her friend Nick would be here as he'd promised. He'd said he would meet her, but she could never count on his being prompt. She sat with her luggage in the lobby for fifteen minutes and then decided to get a taxi and find her hotel. She was headed for the exit that said "Taxis" when a familiar male voice yelled, "Hey, Maggs! Hey, Flamehead!" Maggie turned to see Nick Payne heading in her direction as fast as he could, dragging a wheeled upright suitcase with one wheel broken. He compensated his stride to match that of the disfigured suitcase as it lumped along. As usual, he looked slightly disheveled.

Nick, who was just six feet, somehow didn't look it. He wasn't a lanky type. His solidity made Maggie think he looked as though someone had set something heavy on his head that pushed his body out slightly in the middle. Maggie didn't care about that. Nick was charming, easy, and fun. His brown hair had receded slightly, but his crinkly laughing eyes and mischievous mouth took attention immediately away from his few detracting features.

He was one of the reasons for her trip. My sweet Nick, Maggie thought. They'd shared a wonderful romantic dinner at Ondine in Sausalito last week. It was then that he told her that his upcoming business trip to Paris would coincide with her trip.

Delighted, Maggie yelled back, "Nick!" Dropping her suitcase and her carry-on, she ran toward him. "I'm so happy to see you." She threw her arms around his neck and gave him a three-cheek *bise* in typical European greeting and added a warm bonus squeeze around his midsection. It was comforting to see Nick's familiar face amid all the confusion and strangeness of this airport. Maggie asked, "I thought you arrived several days ago. Why the suitcase today?"

"My lost bag finally showed up after three days. I've leased a flat near Notre Dame. I'd offer that you stay with me, but it's so tiny, I don't think you'd be comfortable there. But you must be tired. Do you have a hotel?"

"Yes. It's over on the left bank in Montparnasse. I e-mailed you the name and address before you left."

"You did? Oh, that's right, I guess you did. Darn. It's not in my head anymore."

Typical Nick, Maggie thought. He knew a million fascinating things, but ordinary and important details often eluded him.

Maggie picked up her bags. Once outside the terminal, Nick stopped an unoccupied taxi and gave the driver the address of his flat. "What's the address of your hotel, Maggs?"

Maggie pulled her confirmation sheet from her purse and read, "Hôtel de Chevreuse, 3 rue de Chevreuse." She turned to Nick. "See how easy that is to remember—the hotel and the street are the same."

Nick laughed and, looking petulant, pulled her close to him. "Don't be mean. We're here together in Paris, Ms., oops, *Mademoiselle* Forsythe." Nick closed her mouth with a more than friendly welcoming kiss. "There. We'll start from there. And boy, do you look great! Those cerulean blue eyes always get me!"

Maggie leaned back against the seat. The moment felt awkward. She was surprised by Nick's actions, but she wasn't angry. She was finally here, and she wasn't going to let any of her old hang-ups spoil it. It was 3:00 PM Paris time and a clear day. Their taxi passed fields and small farms. It didn't seem like they were anywhere near one of the world's largest cities. She leaned into Nick. His body felt comforting. He smiled down at her. "So have you made plans for the rest of the day?"

"I am tired from the flight and the time change, but I can't wait to see Paris. I'm hoping you're going to show me around tonight. I want to see all the special places. Okay?"

"Perfect. Anything you'd like to start with?"

They were passing a huge stadium now, and the country fields had been replaced with suburban housing. "What's that?" Maggie asked.

The taxi driver turned his head toward them. "St. Denis Stadium . . . pour le football."

"Football! Oh, soccer. Of course." Maggie laughed at her American mind-set.

Nick asked, "What are your plans for tomorrow?"

"First on my agenda is to find the shop called St. Clair et fils."

"I'll go with you, if I can—I'm expecting a call from one of my important contacts here."

"Second, I need to search out Black Madonna statues. Did I tell you I got a magazine assignment from *World Wisdom* to write an article on the Black Madonnas of France? I did as much research as I could in the US. Now I'm going to try to find some and photograph them while I'm here. It was a really lucky break. The statues are said to have a connection with my namesake, Mary Magdalene."

"That's great. I don't think you mentioned it before, or perhaps I've forgotten it if you did. You know me."

They passed the ugly Victorian Gare du Nord. They had been in the city for some time now, and it was not particularly pleasant looking. Maggie noticed some women idling outside the closely packed little shops.

"How do you say prostitute?" she looked at Nick questioningly. He shrugged. The taxi driver turned around and said, "*Femmes de petit vertu.*"

"*Merci, Monsieur.*" Maggie laughed. "Of course, that makes perfect sense."

The driver pulled down a narrow street and stopped. Before Nick stepped out, he kissed Maggie again. "I'll let you get settled. I'll call you in an hour or so. Take the lady to *trois rue de Chevreuse*," he said, paying the driver.

"Wait! You don't have my cell number or the hotel number," Maggie yelled out the cab window. She quickly copied the number from the confirmation sheet onto the back of her seat assignment stub along with her European cell number and shoved it into his hand. "And what's your phone number? Do you have a European mobile?"

Nick scratched his head. For a few seconds, he looked confused. He grimaced. "Yeah, I do, but I don't remember the number, and I forgot to bring the phone with me." He shook his head and said, "I'll give the number to you when I call." They waved to each other as the cab pulled away.

Ten minutes later, the cab dropped her at a small hotel one-half block off boulevard Montparnasse. "Where are we?" she asked.

"*La rive gauche. Le quatorzième arrondissement.*" The cab driver smiled admiringly as he looked up from placing her luggage at her feet. "That will be thirty-five euros, Madame."

She fumbled in her bag for a tip. "*Pourquoi?*" she asked. "My friend already paid you."

He shook his head. "No, Madame. Monsieur paid only for himself."

"I'm sure he paid for me."

The driver continued to shake his head. Frustrated and too tired to continue the argument, Maggie handed him thirty-five euros and, bags in hand, went into the Hôtel de Chevreuse. A thin woman of about forty-five with frazzled dishwater hair gave her the key to her room. "*C'est au quatrième étage.*" She pointed upward.

Four flights up a curving stairway carpeted in a garish red Jacquard pattern, Maggie found her tiny room. Stashing her bags near the bed, she immediately ran to three windows that faced onto the street and, with difficulty, opened them. This was her neighborhood—at least it would be for the next three weeks. The bustle of activity on the boulevard that crossed her street precluded it from being a quiet one. However, it wasn't teeming with tourists either. Maggie thought, I love it—the *natural* Paris.

The room was not as elegant as she had hoped, but it was reasonably priced and a convenient location. Though tiny isn't always cozy, this was. The room smelled faintly of intermingled perfumes, sweat, age, and an unidentifiable fragrance that reminded her of nutmeg. She opened all the drawers of the wardrobe, and in one she found an old laundry ticket. She peeked into the even tinier bathroom. She tested the bed's softness. I'll only lie down for a few minutes, she told herself.

She awoke an hour later. Tossing her shoulder-length, curly, red hair, Maggie moaned, "I'm missing Paris." She opened her bag and pulled out her navy hooded jacket, a pale green cotton sweater set and navy slacks and dressed for the late afternoon. Why hadn't Nick called?

Maggie had met Nicholas Payne fifteen years ago when Nick's sister married Maggie's brother. At that time, Nick, then twenty-nine, had been married himself and struggling with a young family and a career as a social worker in upstate New York. He had paid little attention to Maggie in those early days. After all, she thought, I was just a kid then. And he'd always seemed like a relative of sorts. Now, however, she was thirty-one, and though Nick was older, the fourteen-year difference didn't seem to matter at all.

It wasn't until Nick's divorce and his move to the West Coast a year ago that they really connected and became friends. The two of them discovered that they liked each other, and they had been casually spending time together since then. Maggie enjoyed Nick because he could take her on grand exciting mental voyages to places where she had never dreamed of going. He was the only one who could pull her out of the malaise that sometimes overtook her. Maggie liked the fact that Nick was a dreamer with lofty ideals and a not-too-practical approach to life, plus he had a sense of humor that made everything fun. He was a contrast to her down-to-earth frankness and honesty. Nick and I balance each other, she thought, smiling to herself.

But now, where was he? Darn! She was here—the city was waiting for her. She couldn't wait for Nick. Maggie decided she would at least walk about the neighborhood, then come back to see if he'd called the hotel.

Just as she was exiting the lobby, the concierge yelled to her. *"Madame, téléphone."* Maggie dashed back in. It was Nick. "Oh, Maggs, I've got some bad news. I've been waiting for three days to interview this psychologist who has written several papers on my research topic. He called this afternoon and said he's leaving town in the morning for two weeks, but he could see me for an hour or two yet today. I hate to let you down. I feel just awful about this."

Maggie shifted her stance. *"Merde,"* she said under her breath. She replied, "Well, sure. I suppose you must. I'll be okay. What about later? Oh, yes, I know it's hard to know how long these things will last. See you tomorrow. Bye." Oops, she thought to herself, I'm in Paris now, I should have said *au revoir,* not bye. She hung up the phone feeling disappointed, confused, and irritated all at once.

CHAPTER THREE

Hércule St. Clair

E AGER TO EXPLORE Paris, Maggie was especially intent on finding the St. Clair shop her mother had described in her journal. This was too important to wait for Nick. Her finger searched the map section of the guidebook. It didn't list all the streets. Neither did the one the concierge had given her. "Shoot!" The maps were hopeless. Irritated that one wouldn't fold, she crinkled it back together and stuck it in her shoulder bag. She remembered her mother's journal from fifteen years earlier had said the shop was on the left bank not too far from the Seine and near rue Jacob. She started walking. When she reached the river, she hung over the iron railing for several minutes watching two dirty white tour boats pass each other going in opposite directions on the wide green band of water that divided the city. Mossy stonewalls held the river to its route. Looking up and down the river, Maggie could see several of the bridges that connect Paris's left to its right.

Within minutes after leaving the Seine, Maggie veered onto a street that looked to be an area of interior design shops and antique dealers. She pulled the hood of her navy jacket up to keep the steady gray mist off her hair as she walked slowly past several antique shops, peering into windows at commodes of intricate marquetry, and what she guessed were Louis XIV or XV chairs. She stopped to look at her reflection in an ornate gold mirror in a shop window. Next to the mirror was a landscape Maggie guessed might be seventeenth century from the costumes of the strolling ladies depicted. She had only gone about six feet beyond the door to the shop when the name registered—*St. Clair et fils.*

A bell attached to the top of the door announced her entrance. A small dapper man in his early seventies looked up from a desk in a corner of the shop. "*Bonjour,*" he said, with a slight nod and a perfunctory smile. He glanced up at the slim young woman with pale skin set off by shoulder-length copper-colored hair and then resumed his reading.

Maggie moved amid the furniture, noting how elegant it seemed in comparison with what her friends would have considered appropriate for their homes. *Meubles,* she thought, reminding herself in French. The musty smell of once-damp wood and leather and the dull odor of dust pervaded the shop. The surfaces had been cleaned and polished, but the inner history of the cushions, the shelves, and the intricate carved drawers evoked past personal worlds.

As Maggie worked her way through the tightly placed furniture, she felt drawn to the farthest corner of the shop. In the dim light, Maggie stumbled over a rumpled oriental rug and lurched unexpectedly against a dark walnut armoire. Her blow threw open the outer door and one of the inner cupboard doors, jostling its contents. A large black onyx vase flew out at her. To her amazement, she caught it. Dusty white feathers that had been stored in the vase spilled around her. Maggie set the onyx vase down and looked up. Behind where the vase had stood, Maggie first saw a glow emanating from the depths of the armoire and then glimpsed its source—a gold chalice with jewels of varying colors embedded in its circular body. Without thinking, Maggie sucked in her breath and reached to touch the golden vessel. As she removed it, tingles shot up her right hand and arm. As soon as she touched it, Maggie felt instinctively connected to the chalice. She didn't understand the feeling, but she relished it.

The proprietor, who had approached her quietly from behind, said harshly, "Please hand that to me!"

Turning, Maggie reluctantly handed the chalice to the proprietor. Embarrassed, she began to apologize. "I'm so clumsy. I didn't mean to make such a mess. I hope nothing is broken. I'm so sorry." She bent to pick up the feathers. She put them into the onyx vase and set it on the shelf.

He smiled enigmatically, nodded, and said, "Nothing is harmed. Don't upset yourself. It's difficult to keep these old oriental rugs straight under all this furniture."

Maggie sighed in relief; then asked, "What is that beautiful thing?"

Hércule St. Clair paused. He looked at Maggie intently. There was something familiar about this young woman, but he couldn't place her. He wondered if he could have seen her before. Hércule held the chalice to the light and turned it slowly. He said softly, *"Elle est belle, n'est-ce pas?"*

Maggie shook her head and gasped. *"C'est magnifique!* Are those jewels real? It seems to have an aura of light around it. I have never seen anything like it before. Is it for sale?"

"No, no. This is not for sale," he said. "It is a replica of something very precious and quite old. The original was owned by my family."

"A family heirloom?"

"Oui." The proprietor carefully put the chalice back and locked the inner cabinet and the armoire with a circle of keys from his pocket. "This should have been locked," he said ruefully, "I can't believe I missed locking this—today of all days—after the upset I had yesterday." Hércule spoke to himself in sotto voce, shaking his head. "I am to blame!" He knew he was getting too old and too forgetful to have this treasure in his charge.

Maggie didn't understand his chagrin. "The name on your shop," Maggie began. "I mean—are you M. St. Clair, as the sign says? Or are you his son?" Without waiting for an answer, she continued. "I'm asking because I believe there are St. Clair's in my lineage—in my family—as well. My mother visited your shop several years ago. You may not remember. She thought we might possibly be related."

"How interesting. Yes, I am indeed M. St. Clair. Hércule St. Clair. St. Clair is not an unusual name in France—a tree with many branches." He smiled wryly, adding, "But to answer your question, there is no son. I wished for a son when I established this shop, but he never arrived."

Hércule St. Clair looked to be about her height—around five foot six—with a thin wiry build. A full head of iced gray hair set off dramatically by his olive skin. His skin was lighter than what could be called swarthy, but it appeared to Maggie as if dark genes had once held sway in his family. He wore a gray sweater vest with small watch pockets over a crisp white shirt. A red foulard ascot was knotted neatly into the neck of the shirt. Maggie thought, this man could be in a Noel Coward play—not exactly a smaller and older Charles Boyer, but very sharp. I like his looks, she thought.

Hércule St. Clair looked at Maggie with equal interest.

"I know very little of the French branch of my family." Maggie began. "I am an American."

M. St. Clair nodded and smiled gratuitously. "*Oui.* So it seems."

Maggie wondered what she could have said to give that away. She continued, "My name is Mary Magdalena Forsythe, but everyone calls me Maggie."

Hércule St. Clair smiled again. "And how did this very attractive young American woman come to think she was connected with the Paris St. Clairs?"

"My grandmother—my mother's mother—was French Canadian. We think her maiden name might have been St. Clair. My mother, Glory, came here to France to find more information about her mother's background. That was probably fifteen years ago. She died shortly after that, but she left a journal that mentioned you and your shop. She wrote in the journal that she'd talked with you. Do you recall that?" She paused, embarrassed and worried that her expectations might be unrealistic. After all, as a Paris shopkeeper with many diverse visitors would surely not remember one American from that long ago.

The proprietor interrupted her thoughts. "Madame, won't you please come over here and sit down so we can talk more comfortably." He motioned graciously to the table where he had been reading when she came in.

"Actually," Maggie laughed, "I'm not a *Madame*, I'm a *Mademoiselle*."

"Oh, *pardon*. But you know that in France once you reach a certain age, you will be called 'Madame' whether you have yet married or not. So do not take offense if you are not correctly identified by a Frenchman."

Maggie smiled ingratiatingly as he pulled up a chair for her. The chair looked so delicate that Maggie was almost afraid to sit in it. She sat gingerly. "*Merci*," Maggie said, but she wondered what he was thinking. A certain age? Was she already there? Is he thinking spinster? This was worse than the first time a waiter had called her madam.

"Now," Hércule St. Clair said, "You were saying that your mother visited this shop some years ago." Hércule St. Clair looked contemplative. "Hmmm—fifteen years ago—or thereabout?"

"Yes. She would have been about forty-five . . . pretty, with dark auburn hair . . . about my size, but her nose was different—larger—more like yours. Wait, I have a photo of her. Oh, please excuse me." She turned aside and pulled a worn photo of her mother from the pouch with her passport that hung under her sweater and handed it to him.

"*Oui*, I do remember this woman. Her hair was not as vibrant a color as yours. In fact, your mother sat exactly where you are sitting now. As I think back, I remember that she reminded me of my beloved sister. I lost my sister at the beginning of the war, and I've always wondered whether she could still be alive. When your mother was here, I didn't pursue the connection, but I've thought about that meeting many times, wondering if she might have some connection to my sister and regretting that I didn't pursue the matter at the time."

"*Vraiment?*" Maggie paused to enjoy the mental picture of Hércule and her mother sitting together as they were now.

"You recently wrote to my mother about the possibility of being related," Maggie continued. "Since she is now gone, I opened the letter. And because the idea of seeking my French heritage fascinated me, I decided to come to France to find out more about the St. Clair family." Maggie reached into her bag. "Here it is." She pulled out the envelope.

"*Oui.* I recognize the envelope." Hércule patted her hand. "My nephew Alain DuClos and I sent out several letters to names of some whom our records show might be from our original family line. In fact, I kept your mother's name and address after her visit here. I ask clients to sign my book—over there. I have signatures from visitors over many years." Hércule pointed to a book open on a small stand to the left of the door. "We could look back in the book and see if her signature is there. As I remember, she bought an item from me, and we corresponded a time or two, but then I lost contact with her. Even though I initially felt a connection with your mother, only recently did I feel the need to contact her. Perhaps it is my age, but now my need for family seems much stronger—much dearer to me."

He settled back and a distant look came into his eyes. "You know," he said, "now I remember a little detail from our conversation. Your mother said she had a daughter with curly red hair who hated to have it combed out after washing because of the snarls, so she would sing funny songs to her to distract her from crying. Was that a true story about you?"

Maggie grinned. "*Absolument!* That was me. She always sang, 'I went to the Animal Fair, the birds and the beasts were there. The old raccoon by the light of the moon sat combing his auburn hair.'" Maggie stopped singing, a little embarrassed at her outburst of song. "They probably don't sing that in France."

Hércule smiled. "It's a familiar tune. I'm sorry to hear that your mother died. She seemed like a lovely woman. And you say it was my letter to her that led you here?"

"Yes," Maggie nodded, "that and my mother's comments on meeting you."

"Well, Mademoiselle, I am pleased that you found my shop. I believe earlier you said your grandmother was French."

"Well, I never knew my grandmother," Maggie responded. "She lived in Quebec and died before I was born, but my mother often mentioned her. My father said he only met her once when they went to Montreal for their honeymoon. He said she was attractive like my mother, but very quiet—secretive, almost. Apparently she didn't speak English very well. I'm told that she changed her name to Bissette and then she married my Scottish grandfather, whose name was Fleming. She may have gone to Scotland from France and married there, then immigrated to Canada. Or she may have married twice. She . . . I really don't know a great deal about her." Her voice trailed off.

M. St. Clair nodded. He seemed to be thinking. Then he nodded again. "Yes. Just before the war you say? It is possible that we may have a family connection. I will have to look into our family records."

"Oh, would you do that?" Maggie nervously clasped her hands.

Hércule St. Clair seemed amused at her enthusiasm. "Yes," he said, "certainly. My family—perhaps *our* family—has very deep and ancient French roots. I can tell you something of the history. The St. Clair line goes back to at least the time of the Crusades, and perhaps to Christ's time. We think they lived originally in Provence and may also have lived in the province of Languedoc." Hércule St. Clair paused. He must have noticed

Maggie's tightly strung posture because he said, "Oh, pardon my manners. Perhaps you would like a cup of tea while we chat?"

"Yes, thank you. That would be very nice." Maggie began to feel more relaxed. She wanted to make a good impression.

"I will be just a few minutes. Let me know if someone comes in." Hércule St. Clair moved through a narrow door on the left.

Maggie wandered through the shop, touching various pieces, admiring the smoothness of the finish and the intricacies of the carving. She returned to the armoire where she'd seen the golden chalice. She knew the cabinet was locked, but she imagined she could still see the beauteous object. She wished she could hold it again.

Before long, Maggie heard the whistle of a teakettle. She returned to her chair, and after a few minutes, M. St. Clair returned carrying a red lacquered tray with two dainty cups of flower-strewn china that held steaming black tea. Havilland, she guessed—like her grandmother's china, which her mother had inherited and had often used at home. A real lace doily cushioned Maggie's cup from her saucer. She loved the refinement of it.

Hércule St. Clair took a gulp of his tea. "Ah, that is pleasant," he commented. Maggie nodded and followed his action.

"Now, to continue. To the best of our knowledge, the St. Clair family name originated with St. Clarus, who was said to be a disciple of St. Peter and the first apostle to Brittany. He eventually became the Bishop of Nantes."

"That sounds important."

"*Oui,* perhaps historically, but you couldn't call us sainted now. At any rate, saints or not, we can trace our family from the twelfth century to a small village east of Aix-en-Provence. Of course, most everyone lived in small villages then. That's all there *was.*"

Maggie laughed, appreciating his wry sense of humor.

The little bell on the door rang briskly. Two middle-aged gentlemen entered the shop. They spoke perfect French, but by their body build and their skin, Maggie thought they might be Italian. Hércule looked up at them and nodded. Maggie was disappointed. She wanted the story to continue. Hércule excused himself and moved to where the two gentlemen were admiring a secretary that was intricately carved with soaring birds and inlaid with what seemed to be a black ceramic substance. "Ah, yes," M. St. Clair explained, "See there is a secret compartment here behind this false drawer. The design distracts one's eyes away from the construction details." He looked to Maggie. "*Excusez-moi un moment, s'il vous plaît,*" he said to the men and hurried over to where Maggie sat.

"I am sorry, my dear, but could you come back a little later or tomorrow? Mlle. Forsythe. Was that the name?" he asked. "I love to talk about *ma famille*, but I need to attend to these customers right now."

"*Oui, bien sûr. Pas de problème. Merci, Monsieur. Merci beaucoup.* I will come back." Maggie stood. She smiled as she shook Hércule St. Clair's hand. The bell jangled again as she left the shop.

On the metro going back to her hotel, Maggie thought of the attractive man she'd met on the plane. Where was his business card? His name was Israel something. She dug into her purse and found it in a pocket. She rolled the business card between her fingers. "Hmmm, I wonder," she said. Then, instantly, she made up her mind as to what she would do. She would continue to see Paris on her own. It was simpler this way.

"Well, Mr. Israel Hawkins," she said, tapping the business card, "I think I'll wait a day or two before I call you."

CHAPTER FOUR

Israel Hawkins

ISRAEL HAWKINS GLANCED into the hall mirror as he left his hotel room. Thick, rigid, curly hair, the color of weathered cedar conquered his head, offering no possibility for movement or change. He reflected that his forty-six-year-old face paid homage to his Jewish legacy, but the eyes were not typically Jewish in their shape or spacing, sunken under deep brows and set apart like gray-blue pier glasses above high cheekbones. An older colleague at the university—a woman—had once told him that he could have been an ancient Persian warrior.

Israel wanted to see if the mirror showed any change in expression or lift to his face from the recent wonderful news. After all, because of having just won an international book award for his latest study of Renaissance European history, he had been feeling unabashedly happy of late. No, he thought, the face is the same—too much Mr. Jew and not enough Mr. Goy. Well, the French won't care. He chuckled to himself.

His mother, Golda—he'd loved her name—wanted him to *feel* his Jewish heritage, but, as a marital compromise, she had raised him in a liberal Protestant tradition that better fit his father's upstate New York family traditions. Yet under his mother's influence and like the land of his name, Israel was always striving to be more.

When he was young, his name had been difficult. He'd asked his mother many times why she'd named him such a name. She was a first-generation American born in what is now Israel, and she'd told him that she just wanted to hear the sound of her native land often to keep from feeling homesick. Now, after forty-six years, the name seemed to fit. Names! Hell! Nothing could be less important.

Hawkins ran his fingers through his resilient hair, remembering the vibrant redhead who'd sat next to him on the flight to Paris. She was gorgeous. What an attraction he'd felt to her. Of course, he'd embarrassed himself by letting her in on his secret—his damned fear of flying. Why did he have to let it show? But she'd been wonderfully sympathetic and helpful when the plane started jerking. And she seemed really interested when he shared his knowledge about the Cathars and the Templars. They had that connection too. Too bad he didn't know where she was staying here in Paris. Another dumb move, he grumbled to himself.

As he left the hotel, he decided to walk to the Centre Pompidou on this glorious spring day. Near the Pompidou, he stopped at the Café Beaubourg. He loved its art nouveau atmosphere. When the waiter approached, he asked, "Was this built in the twenties or thirties?"

"Oh no, Monsieur, the building is much newer than that," the waiter said. "The building was built within the last twenty years. That's *very* new in Paris, but it's been designed and furnished to look like something from the thirties." The café's interior reminded Israel of the setting for a film noir, with tall blond elegant women in sleek low bias-cut gowns swaying to cool jazz, their cigarette holders drooping, and tuxedoed croupiers settling bets in the back room. Israel loved the mystery and the style of that era. Even in the late morning, being there made him feel debonair.

He sipped his espresso and pondered his wonderful luck. Yes, it *was* mostly luck. He shrugged his shoulders to release the tension in his neck. The action seemed to remove any vestige of self-doubt, and at the same time it allowed him to react to the strength of the coffee—definitely a head-clearer.

Sometimes he wondered how he had become a successful historian with a background like his. He had done reasonably well in school and he'd had some lucky breaks—like the job at Michigan and, of course, marrying Emily—that had seemed lucky at the time anyway. Emily! God! He wished there were an answer to all her mental problems.

Em's father had been a professor at the University of Michigan when he'd been there in grad school. He was such a wonderful, creative man—a Renaissance man—one of those exceptional people who made his way out of life's strictures to where he truly wanted to be. His life was like a fairy story. Imagine an English literature teacher becoming an astronomer just because of his interest in stars. Israel knew it was unlikely that such a thing would happen today—now you had to follow serious scientific academic disciplines virtually from childhood. Israel had loved him. He sighed and looked at the murky stains in the cup's bottom.

A magpie cawed from a rooftop close by—a not uncommon sound in Paris. Israel looked up. The black-and-white bird reminded him of tickling a neighbor kid's nose with a crow's feather in Michigan. Ann Arbor 1990s . . . warm summers, long glorious autumns, short but memorable springs, and everlasting damp winters . . . friends . . . challenges . . . academic politics . . . Emily's loveliness and her fragility. Had he left too soon? Should he have tried to hold on? The questions were always there, but he knew he had done his best to live with her under the circumstances. Still, he regretted having to end the marriage.

But this—Paris—was a different world, one he thought he could claim as his own—well, along with five million or so French and a few hundred thousand tourists. Oh, what the hell! It felt like his at this moment. Israel inhaled the dank, stale smell of spilled wine and snubbed cigarettes in the air that still pervaded the café this morning. It turned his stomach. Still, these smells were Paris too.

CHAPTER FIVE

St. Clair et fils Encore

AFTER A WONDERFUL night's sleep and two of those delicious croissants with *café au lait*, Maggie took the metro to the rue du Bac station. It was close to eleven in the morning when she exited from the station into the clear morning light. She wondered if M. Hércule would be at the shop at this hour.

The shop looked different in the clear brightness of the morning than it had in yesterday's shaded afternoon light. Its age seemed more obvious, like a mature woman without her makeup. Layers of peeling bottle-green paint on the molding around the windows exposed a metallic gold undercoat. Frayed edges of the red canvas awning escaped from its tight roll. This must have been a very elegant place in its day, Maggie thought. But even today it looked perfect to her just as it was.

She stepped into the shop. The bell announced her. "*Bonjour,*" she called a bit timidly. She was about to make a similar entreaty in a louder voice when Hércule emerged from the pantry where he had made their tea the previous afternoon.

Brushing crumbs from his vest, he looked up. Seeing Maggie, he smiled. "*Bonjour, Mademoiselle. Bienvenue.*"

Maggie responded politely. "*Bonjour, Monsieur St. Clair.* Are you busy?"

"No, indeed not. This has been a very slow day. I was just having a morsel to tide me over until dinner."

Maggie looked at him expectantly. "I was hoping you would continue your stories about the St. Clairs. I am interested in the family motto—the one on your stationery."

"Ah yes. '*Et in Arcadia Ego.*' *Alors.* The Latin can have different meanings, depending on who is doing the interpreting. Do you know about Arcadia? It was supposedly located in the central Greek mountains. I don't know if the place really exists, but from the Renaissance on, poets and artists used Arcadia to symbolize a peaceful, rustic or pastoral setting where one could live a happy, simple life—sort of the opposite of bustling Paris. Arcadia was considered a paradise on earth—picture in your mind green mountains and gentle shepherdesses minding their flocks on the hillsides. Literally, it means 'And in Arcadia I am,' but the verb is understood—so we say, 'And I am in paradise.' There are other interpretations. You will also find the saying on the St. Clair plot in the Cimetière Montparnasse."

"How interesting. I must go there," Maggie commented.

"That saying goes back to a time in Languedoc near the Pyrenees when our people were Cathars. Do you know about the Cathars?" Hércule asked.

"Only a little."

Hércule St. Clair pointed to the chairs where he and Maggie sat the previous afternoon. "Why don't we sit? Can I get you something, Mademoiselle? Some coffee or tea perhaps? Or a cognac?"

"It's a bit early for cognac, but I'll try it," Maggie said, taking the same chair she'd sat in earlier.

Hércule St. Clair returned with two small glass snifters. Once settled, Hércule began, "The Cathars were a free-spirited religious sect. They were prone to independent thought, and they were tolerant of the Jewish and Moorish cultures in nearby Spain. Actually, they were too open-minded, especially when it came to criticizing the hierarchical Roman Catholic clergy. That was their downfall."

Hércule took a sip of his cognac and continued, "The Cathars lived simple humble lives. Itinerant preachers, called perfecti, preached their Gnostic message to the Cathari peasants as they worked in the fields. The Cathars believed they were each vessels of the same Holy Spirit as Christ."

Maggie interrupted. "Vessels of spirit. I like that image."

"You'd probably also like the fact that Cathar women were valued and treated as equals and that children were taught to read the Bible, especially the book of John. Girls had the opportunity to become as educated as boys and could become preachers of the faith."

"That's amazing for those times. Some parts of the world are not that advanced today," Maggie commented.

Hércule nodded, "*Vous avez raison, Mademoiselle.* Education threatened the church's control, and in those days the Catholic Church was everything—they held complete political and ecclesiastical power over their subjects' lives, and the common man's beliefs had to conform to the church's. Although the Cathar religion taught that good and evil vie for power in our lives, it differed from Roman Catholic beliefs and practices. The Cathars believed God could speak and work through them individually. They believed they did not need to go to confession or to mass to hear God's message. Also, they did not pay the corrupt and wealthy Catholic bishop's surcharges for their crops. This angered the clerics. In the end, the Catholic Church considered the Cathars heretics and killed them all."

"Heretics? Because they didn't pay the church tax or go to communion? That doesn't make sense to me. I believe that God works through each of us. Were their beliefs and practices documented?" Maggie asked.

"The Inquisition destroyed almost everything there was."

"*Pardon*," Maggie hesitated, and then continued. "I always thought that France was a Catholic country. You speak so—so critically. Are you not Catholic?"

"Yes. I was brought up in the church, but we French are realists. And because of my family's ancient Cathar history, perhaps some of that Gnostic philosophy has stayed with us over the years. Of course, some French are still truly obedient to the church, but, for the most part, we see it like the British monarchy—a wonderful tradition that is part of our culture. We French are very independent. We follow our own judgment. We are not lambs."

I'll bet you're not a lamb! Maggie thought. Hércule St. Clair seemed forthright in his opinions. She liked that.

"One can still visit the ruins of many of the Cathar castles in the Languedoc area in the Pyrenees," Hércule said. "Perhaps it would be of interest to you to go there to see for yourself."

"It would indeed," Maggie said.

The small and intense man's tiny moustache wiggled slightly as he spoke. He continued. "I don't know if it's true or not, but the family legend is that our chalice was spirited out of Montségur castle, a Cathar stronghold, which was known as the Grail Castle. The Inquisition killed hundreds of thousands here in France, and the siege at Montségur was their attempt to annihilate the entire sect. My St. Clair forebears and one or two others were virtually the only survivors, along with our grail.

"The church did so many terrible things in those days. It's disgusting!" Maggie said angrily.

Hércule nodded. "*D'accord.* I agree."

"I'm curious about the bejeweled golden vessel I saw yesterday. Is it very old?"

"Yes, indeed," Hércule answered.

"You said it was a replica, but it certainly looked valuable. Where is the original? I would think it would be in a museum. If those jewels are real, it must be extremely valuable."

Hércule St. Clair looked about nervously, although there was no one else in the shop. He was at a loss as to whether he should explain his little lie or not. But he felt inexplicably close to this young woman—as close as he felt to Alain whom he'd known since childhood, despite the fact that he had only just met Mlle. Maggie—and the moment felt right, so he said, "I told you that you saw a replica. However, *hier,* you, Mlle. Forsythe, had the unusual honor of seeing the Sion Grail—the St. Clair family treasure."

"And of course, you are right." He added, "The chalice would be better protected in a museum. But even museums have thefts. And it is only here temporarily until I find a new and much safer place for it. I keep it close to me because it is important to me. I like to be the one in control—to know its exact whereabouts." Hércule's eyes misted as he said this: "It is silly perhaps, but the way of an ornery old man."

"So," Maggie asked, "could your chalice be the true grail, the grail that Christ used in the last supper or the grail used to capture his blood after the crucifixion?"

"Oh, my dear. That we cannot know." Hércule St. Clair raised his eyebrows. "It is interesting though, is it not?"

"*Eh bien,*" Hércule reached again for Maggie's hand and smiled while looking intently into her eyes. "I am pleased that you've found me, Mlle. Maggie. Very pleased, indeed. Now, where did I leave off?"

"You were telling me that the chalice I saw might have come through the Cathars."

"Ah, yes. You have a good memory, my dear. At my age, I sometimes forget. But not the history, not the old times . . . that I do not forget." He smiled as he reached to finger the silk ascot at his throat.

"I read something recently that hinted that there was a link between Mary Magdalene and the Cathars. I feel a connection with her because of my name. Do you know anything about that?" Maggie asked. She tried to remember where she'd read this—perhaps it was through one of her sources on the Black Madonna.

"Yes," Hércule began, "She is said to have preached in the south of France in the first century, but her Christian message differed from that of the hierarchical Catholic Church that St. Peter founded. The Cathars believed in Mary Magdalene's version."

Before Maggie could ask more, the bell on the door rang heartily. A shabbily dressed and dirty faced little girl of perhaps eight years marched confidently toward them holding several roses. She stopped directly in front of Maggie. "*Une fleur pour Madame?*" she said as she shoved one of the roses into Maggie's hand. Maggie was startled by the child's determined and aggressive manner. She laid the rose on the table at her side and fumbled in her purse for money. When she looked up at Hércule, he shook his head.

His voice sounded cross as he spoke to the child. "*Assez, ma petite!* Not today. Leave now!" He handed the little girl the rose, took her by the hand, and began pulling her out of the shop into the street. He made a shooing motion with both his hands as he shut the door. Just before the door shut, the child lifted her frayed skirt and stuck out her bare bottom at him. Hércule grimaced. Maggie suppressed a giggle. Hércule looked at his watch, pulled keys from his back pocket, and locked the door.

Maggie was perplexed at his behavior.

Hércule spoke emphatically. "These foreigners! Some of them are gypsies. They have no manners. I hate rudeness," he said, "and the flower is a trick so that they can pick your pocket while you are distracted."

He motioned toward the door. "I've locked up for the lunch hour. Now we won't be disturbed again." He turned on a nearby lamp. Its amber fringed silk shade added a mystic glow to the room. They settled back into their chairs. Maggie sipped her cognac, enjoying the mixed scent of aging leather, dust, and faint mildew that pervaded the shop.

"Some of the family came to Paris shortly before the French Revolution. They became coopers and learned the wine trade. One of the brothers, Pierre, hid the treasured family chalice deep in a public well to keep it from being confiscated by either the revolutionary ruffians or the royals. The spot was so obvious that virtually no one, including the king's men, thought to search for it there. When the revolutionary fervor died down and life could be lived without threat, Pierre and his brother, Jean, removed the chalice one night and returned it to the family's care."

"Did I mention that the Sion Grail has a history of danger?" Hércule asked.

"Sion? What's that? You didn't call it that before," Maggie said.

"Oh." Hércule hesitated, "I can explain. It is rumored to have come from Solomon's Temple on Mount Zion. There is your *Sion*."

He reached nervously to again check his ascot, then continued, "According to the family legend, many of my forebears lost their lives over this chalice. The chalice passed from brother to sister to cousin and back across familial lines—greatly desired by everyone—the cause of many family squabbles and even death between some of the jealous caretakers. So we suspect that lovely chalice somehow drew disaster to those who had it in their possession. Yet to others, it did not. Who is to know why?"

An audible yawn escaped from Maggie's lips. Hércule stopped immediately. "But you are tired, my dear Mademoiselle, are you not? I have been noticing your eyes for some time. They do not focus as well, shall we say?"

Maggie's eyelids felt like lead despite the fact that it was still early afternoon. Although she'd been trying to absorb every word that Hércule was saying, her exhaustion from jet lag had out-maneuvered her wits.

Hércule said, "Enough of an old man's stories; enough for today. You need to rest, my dear."

Groggy from the cognac, Maggie got up unsteadily. She held out her hand. "When you have time, I would very much appreciate it if you could check the family records about my grandmother. Do you mind?"

"No, no. I already have suspicions as to who she is, but I want to check some things. We will see. Can you come back tomorrow? I should have some answers for you then. Here is my card. You can stop by any time that is convenient."

"*Merci beaucoup.* This has been delightful."

"*Mon plaisir.* It is not often that I have a strikingly pretty young woman visit me. Do you need me to call you a taxi? Or I can walk you to the metro."

"*Merci, mais non.* The metro is only a few blocks. You have already done enough."

"*Non.* I insist on walking you to the metro." Hércule St. Clair slipped on a jacket and closed the shop's door behind them. The bell's parting ring ushered them into the warmth of midday.

CHAPTER SIX

Mélisande

"*B*ONJOUR!" ISRAEL GREETED the man who was sitting at the next table at the Café Beaubourg. The man nodded, smiled, and responded in kind. After a few minutes, the Frenchman caught Israel's attention. He nodded toward the stairs. Israel, puzzled, looked in the direction of his nod. A woman who looked to be in her early twenties was confidently flouncing up the stairs from the lower level ladies' room. She flung her head so that her hair rearranged itself in perfectly cut blond layers that moved in unison from her crown and eventually hugged the nape of her neck. He recognized the precision of the style, and he could guess the cost. In his world, this kind of elegance wasn't important, but he couldn't help admiring it, like anything of beauty.

He saw her ask the waiter something and then head directly for his table.

"Hi!" she said. She held out her hand. "Sandy Winters. Mind if I sit here? The waiter said he thought you were an American, and I need to speak English for a change. I'm semi-brainless from trying to constantly conjugate French verbs."

The shock of being forced out of his reverie into the new reality of this chirpy American woman was unsettling. Israel, a little taken aback, hesitated before agreeing, "No, I don't mind."

"God! This is the coolest place. I *love* those moving sculptures in that fountain over there, especially those crazy lips!" Sandy Winters pointed to the view out the window.

Israel wondered if he could endure this much enthusiasm this early in the day. His lips pursed into a tight, precise line. He didn't really feel like participating in frivolity at the moment. However, he didn't have a clue as to how he could maneuver an escape or protect himself from involvement in his tablemate's enthusiasm. After listening for fifteen minutes to the young woman's machine-gun description of her recent sightseeing in Paris, he broke in, "Is your name truly Sandy?"

Despite, or perhaps because of, his years in academia, Israel disliked most preppy things, including nicknames. One look at the woman's startled face told him she found his remark rude.

"I, uh, only meant is Sandy short for something?" Israel said quickly, trying to recover from his gaff.

Cautiously, she responded. "Yes. My highbrow mother named me for Mélisande from the opera *Pelléas et Mélisande*. Have you ever heard of it? It is hard for people to *get* Mélisande, you know, especially the other kids—when you're young." She grimaced, but then shrugged in a carefree sort of way, apparently ready to get back to her Paris stories.

Israel laughed, thinking: *As though she isn't young now.* Her flair and humor pleased him. "Mélisande is a truly beautiful name. I prefer it to Sandy."

Israel, though pleased he had made an adequate recovery, chided himself: Sometimes, Hawkins, your smart-ass attitude causes trouble. You enjoy your cleverness too much. He shook his head. He knew this was not one of his better qualities.

They talked for more than an hour, mainly about the young woman's European adventures with Israel adding his own observations on the places she had seen. As they conversed, Israel found himself surprisingly soothed by the lightness and insignificance of her conversation. The contrast to his usual intensity was relaxing. Maybe this is what I need, he thought. And she seemed impressed that he was a historian. He could always use a little admiration.

He said, "I don't know about you, but my body can't absorb any more caffeine." Israel shook his hands wildly. Mélisande Winters laughed and started shaking hers too. He showed her his watch—already past one. "I'm hungry. The best antidote for this condition is food. How about taking the metro over to Montparnasse? We could lunch at La Coupole. It's where Ernest and Alice B. and Ezra and Scott and Zelda and the gang used to go for lunch—that is if they ever ate!"

For a second, Mélisande looked confused. Then she smiled. Israel watched her reaction. He couldn't tell whether she understood his comment about the people Gertrude Stein called the Lost Generation or not. But given her rapt attention to everything he said, he would have been surprised if she'd said no.

Within ten minutes via the metro, Israel Hawkins and his new acquaintance went from the fourth to the fourteenth arrondissement, arriving near the restaurant he'd suggested. La Coupole, which didn't really have a cupola at all, had always fascinated the historian in Israel Hawkins. When it opened in the late twenties, it had been the hangout of Miller, Rhys, Hemingway, Pound, and miscellaneous philosophers, intellectuals, and Russian refugees. Today, it was simply an elegant place to eat. The thirty-two original paintings that decorated the restaurant's columns remained, but the aura of Bohemian life was gone. Now, there was no distrust of the middle class, no humorists holding forth, and no one getting very drunk.

Their lunch was pleasant but spare by American standards—a piquant salad, a small hard roll, some paté for the roll—all artistically presented with curlicues of carrot and lemon peel over the salad, and bits of candied violet over the desserts on the dessert tray. Quality over quantity—the ever-present difference that Israel loved about France. The light wine he had chosen was very cold. It relaxed him. As they opened a second bottle, he began to tell her about his youth. He felt happy.

When he thought back on it later, he remembered enjoying the pleasant banter and playing the suave experienced Parisian visitor for his young acquaintance, yet knowing all the time this wasn't the real Israel Hawkins.

After the waiter presented him with the bill, a flash of burnished red hair interrupted his concentration. He caught a glimpse of the woman who had been next to him on the plane. She was laughing in apparent delight at her male companion's *bon mot*. Israel caught her eye for a brief moment. It left a memory in his mind of the sun emerging from darkening skies tingeing everything with gold.

CHAPTER SEVEN

La Coupole

DURING THEIR LUNCH at La Coupole, Maggie told Nick about the previous two afternoon's adventures at M. St. Clair's shop where she saw the amazing St. Clair antique chalice.

"How did you find the St. Clair et fils shop?" Nick asked.

"I remembered some of the directions from my mother's notes, so I just started exploring an area near the Seine. I was amazed I found it so quickly. Maybe I'm clairvoyant." She laughed.

"That's it! I'll be your barker and we can join the circus!"

"Stop it!" Maggie grumbled. "You're always teasing me."

"Yup, and I always will, because you're loopy."

"Am not."

"And how did you find the fancy chalice once you entered St. Clair et fils?"

"I walked right to it . . . as if I were drawn to that corner of the room. Something just propelled me. I tripped on a rug and slammed into an antique armoire. The door flew open, a vase flew out at me, and there it was." Maggie demonstrated catching the vase.

The waiter brought the bill, and while Nick was paying, Maggie looked away for a moment and caught a familiar person in her peripheral vision. "That's strange," Maggie commented.

"That's what I've been telling you." Nick grinned broadly.

"No. I'm not talking about that. I just caught a glimpse of the guy who was seated next to me on the plane from San Francisco to Paris. He's here in the restaurant with a much younger woman." Maggie shook her head, "You men—you're all the same."

"Huh? What are you talking about? I'm not like that." Nick's face wore his most hurt look.

Maggie laughed at his contrived expression. "I know. You aren't like that, and I appreciate it very much."

Still, seeing Israel Hawkins again was intriguing. "Nick, I'm going over to say hello," she said.

Maggie dodged quickly between the tightly spaced tables and headed toward the couple. Waiters bustled by and jostled her, corks popped and glasses clinked at tables as she passed. She hadn't noticed all this noise before. The coffee machine seemed to be hissing loudly just to irritate her. She glanced back. Nick was following her.

Seeing her, Israel stood.

"Israel?" she asked, though she knew the answer.

Israel reached his arms out to her and grabbed both of her hands in his. "I'm delighted to see you again. I recognized you immediately when you came in." A voltaic surge ran through Maggie's arms and settled in her chest. She felt breathless.

The young woman at the table looked at her with a curious expression.

Maggie nodded to the woman explaining, "We sat next to each other on the plane from San Francisco."

Israel released her hands. "You look wonderful. It seems Paris suits you." He pulled out a chair and motioned to Maggie. "Please join us."

"No. Thank you. I'd like to, but we were just leaving. I wanted to . . ." Maggie felt suddenly and inexplicably insecure. She wondered why she'd even started this. "Just to say hello," she murmured. Then, despite her refusal, she sat down in the proffered chair.

Nick arrived at the table just as Maggie sat down. Israel stood and offered his hand. "Israel Hawkins." He motioned to the young woman. "This is Sandy Winters . . . from Philadelphia."

Maggie reached across the table and shook Sandy's hand. "Maggie Forsythe." She motioned toward Nick. "And this is my good friend, Nick Payne. We're on our way to a cemetery." That must sound ridiculous, she thought, suddenly embarrassed.

"Nice to meet you both," Nick said. Then, tapping Maggie on the shoulder, he said, "Come on, Maggs, these people don't want to talk about the dead over lunch." Maggie stood up. She didn't really want to leave, but she had no reason to stay.

Nick turned Maggie and steered her toward the door. They began walking, but before they'd gotten ten feet, they heard Israel's loud voice, "Wait!"

When he reached Maggie, Israel tugged lightly on her sleeve. She turned. "I couldn't let you go without thanking you for your kindness yesterday on the plane. I'd like to repay you, at least in a small way, by treating you both to dinner or a nightcap at one of my favorite Paris restaurants. How about the Café Marly tomorrow night about nine? The four of us." He whipped two cards from his coat pocket. "Here's my Paris address and phone. Just let me know if that—or another day—would be convenient." He handed one to Nick and one to Maggie. He pressed it hard into her right hand. A soft heat from the card lingered in her palm.

CHAPTER EIGHT

Le Cimetière

AFTER LUNCH AT La Coupole, Maggie and Nick walked through the Luxembourg Gardens. By the time they had reached the main gate to the Cimetière du Montparnasse on Boulevard Edgar-Quinet, Maggie questioned the wisdom of having had wine at lunch. She felt more jet lagged than she had yesterday.

Nick seemed to sense Maggie's exhaustion. He asked, "Do you want to rest before we start on this?"

For Maggie, the sight of what seemed like miles of statues, onyx vaults, and narrow cemetery plots and pathways felt suddenly strangely energizing. She responded, "No, I want to look for a St. Clair plot."

The cemetery was huge—forty-seven acres of family gravesites in no particular order. As she began walking down the rows of monuments near the main gate, Maggie spotted a note held down by two small stones on a plain cement sarcophagus. She picked it up. It read, "Dear Simone, I came to see you again today. Rest in peace."

"Nick!" Waving the piece of paper, she called to Nick, who was standing nearby looking over the map they'd gotten from the gatekeeper, trying to come up with a scheme for attacking the maze of aisles. She showed him the note.

"Look at this! Someone left a note to Simone de Beauvoir, as though she might arise from her grave and read it. She's buried right here," Maggie said, pointing, "next to Jean-Paul Sartre. Amazing. The French *are* different. Americans wouldn't write a note like that."

"I would," Nick commented, "especially if it was your tomb, dear Maggie."

Maggie laughed, punching Nick's arm. "I'm not dead yet!" Maggie carefully put the note back on the vault.

The cemetery map was hard to interpret. Maggie and Nick decided to systematically work their way row upon row looking at the familial headstones and markers. They split up to cover more territory.

Maggie's enthusiasm to find the St. Clair plot began to sag in the heat from the afternoon sun and the heavy sweet fragrance of the budding trees. Then she heard Nick shout. "I've found it! Maggs, get over here!"

The gravesite was in division twenty-six, not far from that of Guy de Maupassant, the writer of ironic tales of misplaced romance. The St. Clair plot was similar in size to the others, but without the photos, the plastic flowers, and the personal items that filled so many other gravesites. At the center stood a genderless, granite heraldic angel blowing what must once have been a horn. There were large headstones for "Pierre Emanuel" and "Jean Ignace." Smaller stones announced that Mireille, Maryse, François, and Etienne were among the St. Clairs who had retired to this resting place. Two were above ground in more auspicious sarcophagi; the rest were buried beneath the sparse grass interspersed with purple and yellow pansies.

"Look at these dates, Maggs. This one, Horace, was born in 1610. If these are your relatives, Maggie, they are *really* old!"

Maggie decided not to acknowledge Nick's stupid joke. Her attention was focused on the markers to the rear of the trumpeting angel. Within minutes, she called excitedly to Nick who was investigating the writing on the stones in the front of the gravesite. "Nick, come here!"

Nick obeyed. "Help me with this," Maggie commanded, struggling to right one of the fallen headpieces now lying on its side. She looked down to see mossy stains from the stone on her white tee shirt and wrinkles in her linen slacks from crouching. "Agh," she groaned as the stone she had partially lifted fell back into its original position.

Nick rolled up his sleeves and, with a quick flourish, flexed his left bicep.

"Okay, Superman. Thanks for coming to my rescue."

"You know I'd do anything for you, Maggie," Nick said. "Seriously," he added. Nick knew this was important to Maggie, and he didn't really want to appear the clown.

Together they hefted the broken granite piece so its backside was to the earth. As they turned it toward the light, they could see a carved outline in the granite of two bears holding a banner with wording, which read, "*Et in Arcadia Ego.*"

Maggie caught her breath. "It's the *same* family shield and motto my mother drew in her notes, and it's the same emblem that was on the stationery of the letter Hércule sent to my mother. This must be my family's plot," she said triumphantly.

"This phrase seems incomplete," Nick said as he touched the words to see if he could feel where something might have been chipped off at the end. It is odd, really. Literally, it means 'And in Arcadia I.' Maybe the verb is just understood—like, 'And I am in paradise.' That would be fitting for a gravestone. But my Latin is rusty, so there could be other interpretations."

"Correct," Maggie said, "I asked Hércule about the motto. He agreed with your translation. Oh, I wish I'd brought some paper. I'd like to do a rubbing of the motto with the bears. I'd like to compare it with the one my mother did on her last visit. I'll bet she was in this exact same spot." Maggie grabbed Nick's hands. "You know, Nick, I feel like the world is singing: 'You're home, Maggie. You've found your ancestors.'"

That evening, Maggie and Nick had cocktails in his second-story flat. As they stood on the balcony looking out toward the Seine, they heard sounds from the apartment below. Nick looked puzzled. "There hasn't been anyone in that apartment since I arrived."

A tall balding man appeared on the terrace below them. He called into the apartment in a harried voice. "*Un apéritif. Vite! Vite!*" A shorter and younger man with a handsome face and a darkly tanned complexion appeared carrying a tray with two glasses and a bottle. The two sat opposite each other just within their view, talking in hushed tones that occasionally erupted into angry exclamations. The taller and older man remarked, "Damned selfish fool. We'll see who the idiot is."

CHAPTER NINE

Records

AFTER LEAVING MAGGIE at the metro station, Hércule St. Clair remembered he had forgotten to lock all the shop cabinets. He hurried back. His mind fastened on the charming young woman who had just entered his life. It had been so long since he had thought about things of the flesh, but Maggie slipped unwilled into his consciousness. He knew it was ridiculous for him to be thinking about her that way, despite his good health. He *was* seventy-five after all. Her enthusiasm for his storytelling had flattered him. "Silly old fool," he said aloud, shaking his head and laughing.

Yet this had been the most satisfying day that he had experienced in months. No. Years. He liked his sedate life most of the time, but Mlle. Forsythe's company had created an explosion inside him. It felt surreal. What was it those Chinese were always talking about? Oh yes, *chi*—silly word—but he liked this new feeling of the life force flowing through him.

After his wife Mireille's death, Hércule had often felt lonely. He remembered that when she was there in the shop with him, it seemed that she softened things. She made the shop feel like a home. And today . . . today, he felt her presence as though she was still here.

Hércule washed the snifters in the pantry sink and began walking through the shop, putting items back into their correct places. He stopped in front of the armoire where his family's treasured chalice was temporarily stored. Without hesitation, he unlocked and opened its doors, pushed aside the vase that shielded it, and gently pulled the chalice toward him. This was not a replica. He had used that as a clever ploy with that nasty collector. There never had been a replica. As he'd told Mlle. Maggie earlier, this was the Priory of Sion's grail.

Even in the dimness of the shop as Hércule raised the chalice, it seemed to hold a certain light that was more than just the reflected glint from its golden exterior. The chalice sent waves of energy up and down his arms. He had forgotten how powerful it felt. As he held it, Hércule wondered if his recent attractive young visitor had been able to sense its power. It struck him that if she were of their family she might have that same ability to sense its energy. Also, he'd wondered about this when she had first discovered the chalice. She'd seemed drawn to it.

The forceful man who had so rudely visited him yesterday came to mind. What was his name? Devereaux. That was it. The name stuck in his craw. He knew he had to do something immediately to assure the safety of the Sion chalice from this man and those threatening thugs he had so far successfully ignored. He sensed this man would stop at nothing to get the grail.

Hércule pulled an aubergine-colored velvet bag from a nearby drawer and laid the chalice lovingly in it. He decided to move it to a locked drawer in a secretary-desk. It was good to vary the location. Up until this recent threat, Hércule had kept the grail safe for the last thirty years. *Je suis fier de ça*—proud, really proud.

"*Merde!*" he said, almost inaudibly. "I do not want to give up the family treasure, but it must be considered. I will have to find a much safer place before too long."

His brother Horace had left the grail in Hércule's care along with the house in the Madeleine section of Paris when he died. Hércule thought about the other members of the Priory, whom he usually saw annually at the ceremonial reunions he had hosted at either the shop or his home. Should he give the grail to his brother François? No, he is older and much less wise. It is too late for him. And it's too late for Didier Rousseau and Hélène Cocteau. They have less sense than I. They couldn't deal with someone like this Devereaux fellow. What about Alain DuClos? He's younger, and he's bright enough. But he takes too many risks. Alain's friend Thérèse has ties to the Priory, but I doubt that her family line has been proven. And the others, like McLaren and Jean Desmarais, he just didn't trust them—especially not McLaren. Someone named Hawkins had recently written in response to his letter, but he hadn't even met him as yet, so he couldn't be considered.

What if Mlle. Forsythe is truly one of us . . . *une vrai St. Clair*? He had felt so comfortable with her, and he sensed that she felt so with him. "I must know," he said.

It would not be difficult to find the answer—all the family records that he had been able to collect over the past years were in his small but comfortable house. He would go there after stopping at his favorite brasserie for a meal of bread, paté, salad, and veal cooked with oil, butter, and garlic. He could have prepared it himself at home—he loved to cook—but he had not gone to the market today, what with the visit from Mlle. Maggie, and he was tired. He deserved to have others wait on him tonight.

When he opened the door to his home, Hércule said loudly, "*Je me suis ici.*" He spoke to the empty house out of habit. He believed the spirit of his wife, Mireille, was often present here as well as in his shop.

Hércule changed into more relaxed clothes—his dressing jacket, sans cravat and sweater vest. He loved being precise. He loved dressing for the moment. He despaired that this sort of dressing was becoming a lost art. But he knew it was an art that he possessed, and it pleased him.

The family records were stored in an unused upper room. The sight of boxes upon boxes might have stymied another, but Hércule knew exactly where to look. His search would begin in the box labeled "1938." Mlle. Maggie's story on her first visit had intrigued him, because his sister, Hélène, had been missing since before the war. They'd searched for her after the war, but to no avail. Wherever she was, she may have married and changed her name. He knew there'd be old photos in one of these boxes. They wouldn't necessarily show a connection to Maggie, but perhaps there'd be something, some clue that could connect them.

He pulled out several black-and-white photos turned sepia from age. Hélène had been the oldest of his three sisters. She would have been seventeen in 1938 and still at home. He remembered her as bossy, though fun too. She'd always found his hiding places, but never let the others know. In the photo, her beautiful long auburn hair was pulled back from her face into braided loops pinned tightly over her crown. The old photos brought tears to his eyes. Oh, what fun they had had before the war. It had been a lovely time. Maman and Papá had been so happy together with their brood. Then it all changed. The children were separated and sent to live with relatives where it was safer than in Paris. Hélène, almost ready for university, had stayed in Paris.

Hércule found another photo of Hélène. She was dressed in a white dress and hat and wore lacy white anklets and high-heeled ankle-strapped shoes. It might have been her birthday. There was a striking resemblance to the photo Maggie had shown him of her mother. The nose, the set of the eyes, and the high cheekbones were the same. The nose, especially, was the giveaway. St. Clair women were often disappointed when they inherited the hawkish family beak; though through personality and other becoming facial features, most were still considered attractive. If Hélène was Mlle.

Maggie's grandmother, why didn't Maggie have the family nose? Of course, she had her father's genes too.

Perhaps his nephew Alain could check the Canadian death records through the Internet using the names Mlle. Maggie had mentioned. That would tell them for sure. He decided to phone his nephew.

"Alain? Yes, I know it's late, but I have a rather urgent request. Could you check the Canadian death records on the Internet for a Hélène Bissette or a Hélène Fleming? She probably died in the fifties or sixties. Yes. She could be my missing sister. Call me back if you find anything. I will wait. *Merci.*"

Hércule mused, Could Hélène have gone to Scotland to visit their relatives there? And then the war broke out—perhaps she couldn't get back. Did she marry there? Then the couple may have emigrated to Québec because the language would have been easier for her there. But why wouldn't she have contacted her family here? Perhaps there had been a family argument that he wasn't privy to. Hélène was pigheaded. Or could she have encountered problems because of being a member of the *Prieuré de Sion*? They were a larger group then, and they had worked for the French Resistance during the war. Oh, why hadn't she called or written them? What a loss to both of their lives!

Hércule brought the box down the stairs into his living room for further study. He hadn't looked in these boxes for many years and perhaps he'd never bothered with the contents of this particular box. He sat reading and thinking about the delightful red-haired woman that had sat before him not two hours before, when the phone rang. Hércule rushed to it.

"Alain?"

"Yes, I've found your sister. She's listed as Helene St. Clair Fleming. She died on October 22, 1965."

"*Vraiment?* Oh, if only we could have found her earlier. Think of the years we could have had together." Hércule's eyes filled with tears. "*Enfin, maintenant* at least we know. I am happy that we have finally found Hélène, but so sad that I missed sharing her life."

"Would you like me to print this out for you, Hércule?"

"*Oui*, print everything out and bring it to me as soon as you can. *Merci beaucoup, Alain.* You have helped me to solve a dilemma."

Hércule hung up the phone. Smiling broadly, he said, "*Incroyable!* She had her facts right. Mlle. Forsythe is truly of the French St. Clairs. My own grandniece! This pleases me."

After an hour and a half of poking through delicate, musty papers, he found a family memoir book with a dried rose between two of its pages. He would make a copy and give it to Maggie at one of her visits. He believed it would please her to have something from her French family, especially something of her grandmother's. Hércule decided he would tell this lovely young woman of their family connection immediately, but he would wait until the appropriate moment to share the book and photos that would introduce her to the French side of the family.

Putting the dusty book aside, Hércule felt a chill run through the room. "Who's there?" Hércule asked. "Horace? Mireille?"

He heard the early May wind squeal as it cut around the corner of his house. He looked out the window and saw it ruffling the curtains of his neighbor's slightly opened window. Usually, he paid little attention to such things, but perhaps tonight it meant something. Perhaps this was a sign that Maggie Forsythe had been sent to him by forces unknown to assist him in his current dilemma. It was an arresting thought.

CHAPTER TEN

The Cheval Glass

MAGGIE SPENT THE next morning at the Musée d'Orsay. The former Victorian train station made her feel as though she were moving back through time. She imagined herself living in the late nineteenth century when Paris was at its most brilliant. The soft light filtering through the heavy metal grillwork of the arcade seemed to Maggie the perfect setting for the impressionist artists' portrayals of turn-of-the-century bourgeois life and the difficulties of the French working class. The museum was not crowded. For several minutes, Maggie felt isolated from her real twenty-first-century self.

After viewing the impressionist gallery, Maggie settled in the restaurant on the first floor to have tea and *glace à la crème*. Fan-shaped wafers perched at the side of the tulip glass and curled dark chocolate shavings covered the vanilla ice cream. A bearded man, whom any casting director would have hired to play Sigmund Freud, sat stirring his demitasse and watching her from his seat near the windows. Maggie let the warm tea turn the cold ice cream in her mouth into streams of sweet silky richness that flowed down into her throat. It made her think of Proust and his madeleines. She wondered what Nick would think of such decadence in the morning.

While he was busy working on his project, she was free to do whatever she felt like during the day. It was great having Nick's company, but she had begun to feel that she really didn't need his presence to feel capable of handling any situation that might arise. She felt a certain power in being in Paris alone as mistress of her own fate.

As she left the d'Orsay, Maggie decided to make another impromptu visit to St. Clair et fils to see if M. St. Clair had found any documentation of her grandmother's family connection. When she entered the shop, though everything looked just as it had been before, somehow it seemed too quiet. Something felt different. "Hello?" Maggie's voice quavered a little, as though she were trying to get the pitch right. She looked around warily, like an animal sniffing out her territory.

Now louder, "Hello." Though there was no answer, Maggie wended her way toward the armoire where she had seen the beautiful golden vessel on her first visit. She concentrated on pulling in her tummy so she would fit between the heavy furniture pieces wedged closely together in the small shop. She heard a rustling in the front of the room and turned.

"*Ma chère Mademoiselle?*" It seemed more of a question than a greeting. She recognized Hércule's cultured diction and the warmth his voice had evoked on her previous visits. Though Hércule's face wore a worried look, he nodded and smiled as he greeted her. "My dear, I'm so glad you came in today. I have wonderful news for you."

Maggie said, "Really? You have checked on my grandmother's connection?"

"Yes. My nephew verified through the Canadian records that your grandmother is indeed my sister Hélène who disappeared in 1944. I am your uncle—your great-uncle at that." He paused and looked to Maggie for her reaction to the news. He thought a bit guiltily now, that perhaps his earlier slight infatuation with her had really only been a hint of their family relationship.

"*Mon oncle!* Wow! That's marvelous. I'm flabbergasted. I suspected, but I didn't dare let myself really believe. Oh, this is wonderful!" Maggie rushed to Hércule and hugged him so hard he fell slightly backward.

Hércule straightened up and pulled back, dusting himself off. With a slightly embarrassed cough, he said, "Yes, my dear Mademoiselle. I am surprised, though happy too—very happy indeed. I could not wait to tell you of our connection."

"I have so many questions about my grandmother. What was she like as a young girl? Her personality? Was she studious? What did she look like? Do you have photos of her?

"*Bien sûr.* I found them in my attic last night." Hércule reached for a file at a nearby desk. He pulled out two photos and, grinning, he handed them to Maggie. "This is how Hélène looked in 1940, and this is the two of us on her eighteenth birthday."

Maggie held the photos lovingly. "Oh, I can see the resemblance to my mother. They both have that nose. I've always been glad I didn't inherit it, but they were both beautiful even so. Do I resemble her?"

"Yes, mostly in the shape of your face and the setting of your eyes."

"Thank you so much, M. St. Clair. I'm thrilled to see these." As she reluctantly handed them back to Hércule, she asked, "Could you have copies made for me?"

"It would be my pleasure, Mlle. Maggie. I hope we will have many times to talk about your grandmother and our childhood together."

"I appreciate the time you spent with me yesterday. It meant a lot to me."

"*De rien,*" Hércule said as he bent down to kiss her hand. "I enjoyed our talk very much myself. To have a charming young woman eating up my every word, as they say, is rather nice, you know."

Maggie was surprised, almost embarrassed, by Hércule's chivalrous attentions. "I do have a very specific question," she said. "Before I left the States, my father mentioned a possible family connection to a line of French kings. Can you tell me anything about that?"

Hércule looked startled. "Hmmm, yes," he said after a moment. "Won't you come and sit down." He motioned to Maggie to follow him to the chairs where they had sat on her previous visits. "Yes. There is a connection. Your father was correct. As a St. Clair, I inherited membership in an organization that stems from the first line of French kings, the Merovingians. They would be considered crude by today's royal standards, but they have a unique history. We descendants are proud of our ancient heritage, but after eight hundred years, it would be foolish to consider my relatives or myself royalty." He asked, "Would you like to know a little more about my life?"

"Of course. I'm very interested," Maggie answered.

"Being descended from a line of kings has not made my life particularly exciting. In fact, I've led rather an inconspicuous life. I graduated from the Sorbonne in art history with high honors. I married well—a lovely woman. My wife, Mireille, was the daughter of a diplomat who had tours of duty in Tunisia, Algeria, West Africa, and the United Kingdom. The constant disruption of her education and her childhood friendships didn't serve her well in her growing years, but later, I think she was very happy to live a cosmopolitan and uninterrupted life as a Paris shopkeeper's wife." He reached for Maggie's hand and held it gently. "We lived quietly and happily for twenty years. We had no children, but our lives were full enough with the business and our brothers, sisters, nephews, and nieces. Then my wife died unexpectedly. A congenital problem that resurfaced in midlife took her, leaving me a new and lonelier life to execute by myself."

"I'm sorry about your wife," Maggie said softly. He was such a dear man.

"It's been a very long time now." Hércule's response was matter-of-fact.

Maggie commented, "These must have been lonely years."

Hércule looked at her intently. He dropped her hand as he began to speak again.

"I am going to share something rather troubling with you," he said. "I have received a threat to the safety of the chalice you saw yesterday."

"Oh, no!" Maggie gasped. "Is your life in danger?"

"*Oui, c'est possible*," Hércule looked down and then caught Maggie's gaze again.

"Oh my gosh! Why would anyone threaten you?" Maggie asked.

Hércule jumped up. His voice wavered in agitation, and it seemed to Maggie that he was so keyed up that he could barely get the words out. "A very unsavory man who claimed to be a collector of antiquities came into the shop yesterday after you were here. He demanded to see the St. Clair chalice." He began to pace back and forth in front of her. "Of course I refused. But there are always people who desire wealth or notoriety." He pulled a handkerchief from his pocket and spit into it. "Disgusting people!"

This was a different Hércule than Maggie had seen yesterday. He seemed so distraught.

He continued, "Our chalice has known trouble and danger before. This is a new version of an old recurring story. I hoped those days were past, but apparently danger still lurks."

Hércule sat down again and took Maggie's hand. "You were right yesterday when you wondered why I hadn't gifted the chalice long ago to the Louvre or the Cluny, or found some other safe home for our treasure. I should have. But Hércule St. Clair has the confidence and ridiculous pomposity to believe that he doesn't need that. No!" As he paced back and forth, Hércule waved his hands in the air. Maggie could see droplets of sweat forming at Hércule's hairline, and his face had grown ruddy in his distress.

Hércule's tirade was hard for Maggie to follow. She waited for him to finish.

Then Hércule stood again, stomping as he spoke. "That rude man wants the ancient chalice that has been the *Prieuré de Sion's* for years. He called me again today. I refused to speak with him!"

Maggie interrupted. "What was that you said? The *Prieuré de Sion*? What is that?"

"Did I say that? I hadn't meant to say that. Please excuse me. I am speaking out of turn in my excitement. We can discuss that later."

Then he continued, "At any rate, I don't know how this unpleasant man found out about our chalice, but I fear that he will stop at nothing to get it. I must hide the grail. It can no longer be here at the shop—not even for a day. I must think of some way to keep it safe."

Maggie watched Hércule intently. A grail? Even before the family connection was firmly established, in her own romantic way, she'd begun to think of Hércule as her newly found relative and of the chalice, with its circuitous and dangerous past, as her own mysterious treasure, but she'd never imagined it to be a grail.

Hércule stopped pacing and sank heavily into the other chair. "Pretend, dear Mademoiselle, that you are my priest and hear my confession. The grail was being cared for by another Priory member until the day before your first visit. I felt it was safer with me than with him, so I demanded that he turn it over to me. I hid the chalice here in the armoire temporarily, as you saw it. There." He pointed in the direction of the piece. "Of course, it is normally locked, but occasionally I slip up—as I did on the day of your visit. I was planning to transfer it to my lock box at Crédit Lyonnais when they opened, but I hesitated to do that. In the last thirty years, it has always been in the hands of a Priory member—not in banks or museums. I do not trust the banks or bankers." Hércule paused. "Your finding the chalice was very disturbing to me. I have begun to realize my frailties, and I have begun to question my ability to keep our precious treasure safe."

Hércule St. Clair stared at Maggie as though lost in thought. "And then there was the note."

Maggie asked, "Note? From whom?"

"I don't know precisely. It appeared mysteriously over there on that sideboard just in the afternoon." He pointed to the large heavy piece to their right. "There were several people in the shop at about three, which is unusual. I was showing two Swiss gentlemen the Louis XV table. Right there." He pointed again. "I noticed a short middle-aged man browsing in the area of the cabinet where you saw the grail. I asked if I could assist him. He only smiled, shook his head, and said, "*Non. Merci.*" Then he left. There was a woman in here, too. I could smell her perfume long after she left. It could have been any of them, I suppose. Shortly after that, I found the note."

"What did it say? Do you think it relates to the man who threatened you?" Maggie could hardly bear the suspense.

Hércule pulled a carefully folded piece of thick cream paper from his pocket. He read slowly. "*Aujourd'hui, St. Clair est libre. Le soleil sourit sur la rue des Saints-Pères. Mais l'ancienne merveille sonne faux à la bataille. Le nouveau veut être la concierge. La vrai famille doit protéger son histoire. Prenez garde! L'ours vous assistera.*"

As he read, Maggie translated from the French in her head. Today St. Clair is free. The sun smiles on the street of the Holy Fathers. But the ancient marvel sounds a false battle cry. (Or does that mean sounds out of tune?) A new one wants to be the concierge. (Why the concierge? Perhaps it means the guardian.) The true family must protect its "history" (or protect its "story"). Beware! (L'ours? She pondered the sound, not connecting it with an English word. Finally, it clicked: the bear.) The bear will help you.

He held the paper out to her. She read it again for herself. What could it mean? Where had she seen a bear recently? It came to her—on the letterhead and at the cemetery. She said, "How very odd. Do you consider this note a threat?"

"No. Threat is a bit strong. The note is more of a warning for me to be careful. However, I believe the St. Clair chalice is in danger, as am I. I must find another hiding place for it before"—his voice trailed off. "I need to find someone whom no one would suspect." As he said the words, the look on his face changed.

Suddenly Hércule threw his head back and laughed. When he spoke, his voice held a new decisiveness. "*Inspiration!*"

Maggie smiled as she thought to herself how certain English words become more meaningful when given the French pronunciation. He continued, interrupting her thought, "I have an idea." His sharp, dark eyes looked appraisingly at Maggie, as though he might be going to make an offer to purchase something. "I have been contemplating this for the last several days since we met. Here is my idea. What would you think, Mlle. Forsythe, of becoming the new temporary caretaker of the St. Clair chalice?"

Maggie, startled, could hardly think. Did Hércule really mean what he had just said? She felt a tingling at the nape of her neck. Me? In her confusion, she couldn't get her thoughts translated to her tongue. She could only repeat what Hércule had said, "The new temporary caretaker?"

"I know." He patted her hand. "It is a surprising idea. Even to me. But the more I think it, the more I say it out loud—it could be perfect. No one will know that you have any connection to my family or me. You are an American tourist, yet definitely not ugly like some." He paused and smiled at his little joke. "Who would suspect?"

"Do you think you could find a safe place to hide our family treasure for just a day or two? I hope you can convince me that you can." Hércule looked longingly at her.

Maggie felt suddenly confused and frozen in place. Her confusion must have shown, as Hércule quickly apologized. "Oh my dear, I see that

I haven't given you time to absorb this. It is the St. Clair way. When the thought arrives, we say it. I apologize for being so abrupt."

Maggie laughed—the St. Clair way. This gentleman and his family entranced her. She wanted to help and be a part of all this, but she hesitated. "I don't know if I could help. This is my first visit to Paris. I hardly know my way around the city. I wouldn't know where to hide such a thing or how to keep it safe."

The shop bell jingled. Hércule pushed Maggie gently in the direction of the door where he had gone to make their tea on her first visit. "In there," he said abruptly. She found herself in a narrow room similar to the pantry in her grandmother's kitchen. It had leaded glass cupboards, where packaged biscuits, tea, and perfectly placed china looked out at her from behind the glass doors. She waited quietly. She remembered that Nick had said his apartment had a small hidden safe in it, probably left from the days of the Nazi occupation or after the Bolshevik revolution sent wealthy *émigrés* to Paris. Nick mentioned it the other night, but she hadn't seen it yet. Would that be secure enough? Even if it were a secure safe, this would still be a terrible worry.

This challenge felt very foreign, but Maggie sensed that something exciting was happening. Suddenly, like the sky opening above her or the infamous light bulb in a cartoon, Maggie understood. That's it! At home in San Francisco, no one would have asked her to do such a thing. No one at home ever expected her to take responsibility. Someone else always took over. In that moment, it became clear to Maggie how others had catered to her and stifled her at the same time.

Hércule entered the pantry saying, "Just a picker. Henri Diamond. He comes by fairly often to look over what I have. He negotiates buys for his clients. He was here yesterday, too. That's a bit more often than usual." Hércule looked puzzled by this, but motioned Maggie back into the shop.

They sat again. Hércule continued. "I hope I didn't frighten you earlier when I spoke of danger connected to possessing the chalice and the rumors that it has special powers. After all, despite its age and value, we both know that in reality, it is just a beautiful object like any other." He wasn't being exactly truthful, but he felt he had to finesse this issue.

Maggie nodded her agreement. Realistically that had to be true. Yet the prospect of caring for this auspicious vessel was frightening even if it couldn't put her in physical jeopardy.

"I assure you," Hércule continued. "This would be very short term—perhaps a day or two at the most until I can devise another Priory sanctuary for it. I just can't lose our family treasure to this man or his ilk!" Hércule lowered his head remembering the old prophecy that decreed that the grail must stay within the Priory family's care. He waited for Maggie's response.

Slowly, Maggie said, "As I consider it, I believe I do know of a possible safe place for the grail. I will do it. I will help you," Maggie spoke quietly, but resolutely. "After all, we're family."

"*Merci, Mlle. Maggie. Merci beaucoup!*" Hércule's voice sounded positively joyful. He reached across and enclosed both of her hands in his. Then they discussed Maggie's plans for hiding the chalice. Maggie told him the she could not keep it at her hotel, but that her friend Nick's flat had a small safe in it. That sounded good to Hércule. No one would suspect Mlle. Maggie and her friend Nick would be even further from suspicion. He had never been to the shop. He had never even met Hércule. "*Bon. Très bon.*" Pleased with himself, Hércule thought, at least we can keep that Devereaux at bay temporarily.

He pulled a card from his breast pocket. "Here is my card," he said. "On the back is my mobile number where you can always reach me or someone close to me. You must tell me if anything changes with regard to our beloved chalice." This time his voice was firm and resolute. He stood and moved to the chalice's new location. Maggie saw that he wasn't heading for the armoire. Surprised, she followed him. Hércule's fingers massaged the group of keys in his pocket until he felt the right one. He unlocked the secretary drawer, removed the ancient chalice from its bag, and placed it in Maggie's cupped hands.

Maggie felt the vessel meld into her hands, as though it was a part of her. She imagined this must be like holding one of those prehistoric rocks that can communicate the details of its history. As she held the grail, in her mind, Maggie saw a mountain with a castle at its peak and a woman with brown braided hair tied with interlocking blue ribbons. Under her wool cloak, she carried a baby on her left hip, and in a secret pocket was the hidden chalice.

How unusual, Maggie thought. The vision disappeared when M. St. Clair took the Sion Grail from her and began to wrap it securely in layers of soft cloth and then finally he returned it to the aubergine-colored velvet bag.

"I need to finalize this before more customers appear. Please give me your address and hotel phone number or a mobile phone number if you have one—any numbers where I can reach you."

Maggie gave Hércule her address and mobile phone number. As she left, he said, "I will contact you very shortly to retrieve the chalice."

"The chalice stays in St. Clair hands," Maggie said, smiling mischievously.

Hércule's tense face relaxed into a grin of recognition and release. "Indeed!" He said, smiling back at her. "And I will be back to you within two days at the most to keep you apprised of our next step."

As she left the shop, Maggie glanced at her reflection in a long framed mirror mounted on swivels that stood next to the Louis XV armoire. Seeing herself in the cheval glass, Maggie noticed that there was something different about her—an indefinable change—but one that she liked.

CHAPTER ELEVEN

A Hiding Place

AS SHE LEFT the shop, Maggie's thoughts were on her new possession. She looked about to see if anyone could have seen her leave the shop. She saw no one. She would have to be on guard at all times now.

The chalice was secure at the bottom of her black nylon day bag, covered by her guidebooks and maps. She clutched the bag. The chalice bumped her hip as she walked, reminding her of its presence. Her concentration made her oblivious to the quiet footsteps behind her. Where could she safely hide the chalice? Ahead of her, Maggie saw the onion dome of St. Sulpice. A fountain bordered the drab, discolored stone church. Flocks of pigeons circled the fountain, pouncing greedily on crumbs thrown by locals onto the cobblestones. Scaffolding disguised one side of the ancient church. Maggie decided that a bit of churchly solace might be just the thing in this moment of fear and indecision.

A dirty-looking beggar sprawled at the entrance, hat in hand. "What are *you* doing here?" he demanded in a surly manner. "*Je veux voir l'église,*" Maggie responded matter-of-factly. He surely wasn't going to get any money if he talked to people that way, Maggie thought. She pushed past him and entered the church. Ancient dampness and mildew mixed with the burning wax of many candles assaulted her nose as she passed the frescoes in the first chapel and moved on toward the nave with its enormous pipe organ. She eased into one of the wooden folding chairs in the nave. Though she didn't often pray, Maggie felt compelled to quietly ask for guidance as the steward of this antiquity.

The large ornate gold candlesticks on the altar made her think of Jean Val Jean. As she moved her index finger over the outline of her bag, she wondered if the chalice had been in this church before. She imagined revolutionary citizens praying here for the freedom of a nation unfairly ruled by a series of hedonistic kings. Then, ironically, she remembered that she'd once read that it was those very revolutionary throngs that sacked St. Sulpice of its valuables and renamed it the Temple of Victory.

Perhaps two-dozen people were walking here and there in the church's halls. Others sat silently fingering their rosaries or whispering their prayers. Maggie held the bag close to her body with her right arm. She couldn't get over this unexpected responsibility that she'd been given. She was pleased to be able to help Hércule St. Clair and her newly discovered French family, but the awful burden of this was mind-boggling. Maggie looked around suspiciously. Though nothing untoward was going on, Maggie sensed danger here. Something silky, perhaps a sleeve, brushed the back of Maggie's hair and her shoulders. Startled out of her reverie, Maggie shivered. The faint scent of L'Air du Temps remained in the air around her. Maggie turned quickly. For a second, in the strip of bright light from the opened door, she saw a woman's form. Then it disappeared. Was someone following her?

St. Sulpice didn't feel welcoming or even comfortable. Maggie found no solace here, only a sense of fear that seemed to rise like a chill around her. So clutching her precious cargo, she left the church. The gray haze had lifted. The sun shone through the water spraying from the St. Sulpice fountain, anointing the pigeons and creating prisms of rainbow colors on the courtyard. Even the grimy church walls glinted a bit in the sun. Surely this was a good sign. Though she knew Nick's apartment wasn't far, spent by emotional excitement and unsure of her route, Maggie hailed a cab. As her taxi neared the Seine, the water seemed greener than the day before—another good sign, she hoped. Maggie looked back. The light had changed, and the cars following her were delayed by the traffic *gendarme's* signal. She breathed a sigh of relief.

The cab driver let her off at the nearest cross street to Nick's apartment. Maggie approached the nineteenth century stone building at 77 rue de Beaune near the Quai Voltaire. Its thick stonewalls looked so solid, so sturdy, so safe. Maggie felt glad to be here. Under the hanging wrought iron lantern, Maggie punched in the code for Nick's flat, and when he answered she said, "Hi, it's Maggie." She heard a door open and then descending footsteps. She hoped Nick would agree to help her hide the chalice.

Nick opened the door and, smiling broadly, hugged her, saying, "Hey Maggs! Welcome to my little *pied à terre*!" Maggie followed him up the stairs.

Nick's apartment's tiny foyer was barely a yard wide. It opened into a long and narrow high-ceilinged room with tall windows. A narrow wrought iron balcony surrounded two of the windows. The room was sparsely furnished with a mix of furniture styles that spanned half a century from late nineteenth to midtwentieth—the majority of the furniture being from the latter era. None looked recently upholstered. A former closet, closed off by an extra-wide brocade drapery, had been converted into a utility kitchenette and a second larger closet was now the *toilette*. The once elegant structure had at some time apparently been chopped up into small units.

"I can see why you didn't invite me to stay here, but it does have a certain charm," Maggie commented.

"I told you. Not much extra room, but Rudolph Nureyev once lived just down the street, so it's definitely prime real estate now. Let's hear it for shabby chic!" Nick joked, giving Maggie a second warm hug that encompassed the black bag. "Hey! What's in there? That's an interesting shape—bumpier than your Paris street map. Why don't you set that bag down? It seems to have become a part of your body." He looked at Maggie quizzically. "Did you find a unicorn's horn at the flea market? Or maybe you bought a pair of fancy Ferragamo hiking boots."

"No," Maggie laughed. "You're way off the mark." Maggie hesitated. Despite her fears of breathing a word about the chalice to anyone, she needed Nick's help. Her hotel room wouldn't be safe and his apartment might.

Nick said, "What's the matter? You look frozen all of a sudden. Can I help?"

"Well, there's good news and there's bad news," she said. She set the bag down and told Nick the story of her visit with Hércule St. Clair—the joy she felt on learning of her French family connection and her trepidation about her new assignment as temporary keeper of the St. Clair grail. She ended by saying, "The responsibility for this valuable antiquity scares me shitless! But I felt I had to do this for Hércule. He has been so welcoming to me. Will you help me find a safe place to hide it?"

"That's awesome." Nick shook his head in amazement. "I mean, sure. Let's see it."

Maggie removed the guidebooks and maps. She carefully lifted the thick velvet pouch from her bag and unfurled the layers of soft white suede cloth that Hércule St. Clair had wound loosely around the vessel. She held it up to the late afternoon sunlight that shone in from Nick's windows. They inspected the chalice together. There was plenty of evidence of usage and wear. However, the sun's rays seemed to give each golden dent and scratch a momentary healing as it glistened there before them. Rubies, emeralds, and sapphires were set in artistic patterns circling the curved gold cup. Only one jewel was missing from the intricate setting.

For seconds, neither Nick nor Maggie spoke. Then, a long hushed whistle emerged from Nick's lips. "This beauty can almost talk."

"Do you think this could actually be the cup that Christ used?" Maggie asked.

"Gosh," Nick answered. "You're asking the wrong guy. You'd need an expert or two or three to answer that. Actually, I doubt that Christ would have had anything this splendid. I'd expect some pottery cup, not this. But who knows? There were artisans who worked in gold and precious jewels even before Christ's time. Look at the Egyptian treasures they've found."

"A devious and rapacious collector is after this chalice, though Hércule didn't tell me who. That's why Hércule is afraid to keep it in his shop—even for a day or two. The collector threatened him. Hércule felt the collector would not know or suspect me," Maggie said as she began to replace the chalice in its velvet bag.

"I don't like this one bit, Maggie. Someone could have seen you at the shop and followed you here. We could be mucking around in something really dangerous here," Nick said. "It might not be at all safe to have this. Hércule's got his nerve dumping this valuable antiquity on you! I think you should just take it right back to him. That's my advice."

Maggie could see that Nick was distressed.

"I can't let Hércule down, Nick. I have to do this. You told me the other day that you'd found a small safe in this apartment, probably left from the days of titled *émigrés* who left Russia with their jewels when the Bolsheviks took over. Can you show it to me? Will this fit in it? It's just for a day or two, Nick," Maggie pleaded. "Nick, you're the only person in all of Paris that I can trust."

They discussed their options for some time. The chalice had to be easily accessible in case Hércule contacted Maggie for its return, but she obviously couldn't carry this valuable antique with her on her daily ventures in Paris. Neither felt that Maggie's hotel room was safe, since maids and other hotel staff had access to it. Depositing such an item in a bank might draw suspicion since they had no local reputation—and it was only going to be for a day or two.

"This is supposed to be a secure building," Nick said finally. "I don't like this, but—What the heck? I can't think of a better spot at the moment."

The safe was old and rusty. Nick had discovered it in a cubbyhole under the bathroom sink hidden by a false cabinet door. Placed on its side, the chalice fit perfectly. They made cotton stuffing cut from the lining of one of the apartment's old drapes to fill the corners of the rusting twelve-by-ten-inch metal box. The small straight key left in the lock stuck and didn't want to turn, but Nick dipped it in a little olive oil and it worked. Nick pulled the key out and jiggled it in front of Maggie's face. "Who gets the honor?" He asked. "You," she said hesitantly. "I would like to be in control, but this is your place, so you'll have to be the guard."

"No," Nick said, "you may need to have access to the grail, so I'm going to hide the key in this almost empty aspirin bottle in the medicine chest." He dropped the key in the bottle as Maggie watched.

"Oh Nick, you're such a wonderful friend! You've saved me again. You can't imagine how nervous I've been about this whole thing. I thought I'd die just getting this fabulous thing here. I kept imagining people were following me. I took a cab from St. Sulpice just in case." Maggie sighed in deep relief from the emotions of the day. Nick held out his arms, and Maggie rushed into them, enjoying a feeling of warmth and safety she hadn't felt since she left the US. Nick was such a joy.

Hércule closed and locked the shop's door a bit early that night. He was tired from all the stress of the day, but he was pleased with his decision to give the chalice to Mlle. Maggie. He smiled to himself. She was such a charmer. Yet he wanted to talk with Mireille about these recent disturbing happenings. He heard an unfamiliar noise—a scuffle of shoes on the carpets, as though someone had tripped. He turned to see two men approaching, one from the street side and one from the inner side of the shop. Where had they come from? He saw no one before he had locked the door, but he knew the tall armoires and the dim light offered plenty of hiding places.

Aghast, Hércule was about to yell out when one grabbed him from behind and put a rough hand over his mouth.

"Forget it, old man," he said under his breath. "You don't stand a chance with us. We're going to find out where that chalice is."

The two quickly gagged him and bound his hands behind his back and half-lifted half-pulled him out of the shop and into a waiting car.

CHAPTER TWELVE

Unicorns

MAGGIE STOPPED AT Nick's flat the next morning to check on the chalice. "How's our baby?" she asked.

"Sound asleep like all good babies," Nick assured her when he saw Maggie's worried look. "Where are you off to this morning?" he asked.

"I thought I'd browse through some of the haute couture houses—Dior, Chanel, Hermes, St. Laurent. Want to come?" Maggie asked.

"No way. What a bunch of high-priced baloney! Think of the hungry people you could feed instead. God, it makes me sick to think of those society types gratifying their egos and their up-the-social-ladder competitiveness with all that frippery. Who needs $500-shoes? That's insane!"

"I know how you feel. The costs are ridiculous. But this is France's biggest export business. They call it *le luxe*. Don't you believe in capitalism? Paris isn't exactly the third world, you know!"

"Well, it's not that far away from here." Nick's voice had a serious undertone. He was challenging her beliefs, as he often did. Maggie picked up her bag as though to leave.

"I'll babysit our cherub," Nick said. "But I'll see you in a couple hours at the Cluny. It's in the Latin Quarter. I want you to see the Cluny's collection of medieval art and tapestries."

Nick and Maggie met at two o'clock that afternoon at the Musée de Cluny in the Latin Quarter. They climbed to a semicircular room on the second floor where five large medieval tapestry panels were displayed. According to the descriptive placards, each panel was a representation of one of the five senses. In the first panel, called *Sight,* a lion and a unicorn flanked a lady dressed in late fifteenth century style. The lion held a red banner with three white *fleur de lis* on a diagonal dark blue band. The unicorn raised the lady's skirt and rested his hooves in her lap; his head was reflected in the mirror she held. Maggie gasped.

"What's wrong?" Nick asked.

"I forgot to tell you," Maggie said, "I had a tarot card reading before I left." Maggie paused. "I was told to watch for unicorns. And here we are standing in front of a unicorn—and a beautiful Renaissance one at that."

"I suppose your tarot card reader knew about these tapestries." Nick was obviously being sardonic. His comment irritated her.

"Don't spoil it for me," Maggie said. "It's magical to have the prediction come true." Maggie backed up so as to have a full view of the tapestry.

"The colors in the myriad tiny flowers are so rich, and I love those sweet animals sitting there," Maggie paused. Surprised, she added, "Somehow it feels sensual." She wished she could touch the lush soft yarn, but she knew that was not allowed.

Nick commented, "This was meant to be sensual—carnal even. The unicorn's horn is a phallic symbol . . . you know, a symbol of virility and manliness." Nick clasped his hands in front of his crotch and looked skyward.

Maggie couldn't help laughing. "Oh, sure! I suppose you're the expert in *that* department!" It seemed a natural response, but then she was immediately sorry. She hadn't meant to make fun of Nick. She hoped he wouldn't take it that way.

A museum guide and a crowd of sightseers moved into the room and surrounded them. The guide began explaining to the group: "Unicorns have been pictured since the Bronze Age. If you go to the Dordogne region of France, you will see unicorns in the ancient cave drawings there. The unicorn drawn by early man may have been an antelope without the perspective of both horns, but more likely it was an imaginary creature. Greek and Roman fables claimed that it was virtually impossible to capture this ferocious animal unless you could lure it to the side of a virgin. Then, as it slept with its head in the virgin's lap, it could be taken."

There it was again—the damned virgin thing. No matter where she was, the reminders followed her. Maggie whispered, "There's something erotic going on in this scene." Just talking about eroticism gave her a rush.

She looked up at Nick. Sometimes, Nick's suggestive nuances made her wonder if he wanted more from her—like his furtively kissing her in the cab back from the airport. He wasn't usually like that, and Maggie didn't understand what had changed. She wished he'd be more direct about his feelings.

Behind them, the guide was continuing. "The style of this tapestry is called *mille fleur*. They say that experts can identify each of the herbal flowers shown in our tapestries. Tapestries were used to tell stories. Some believe this scene could have religious significance. At the beginning of the Renaissance, in folklore, the unicorn was a mystical symbol for Christ, as was the lion. You've heard him called 'the Lion of Judah.' This tapestry could be the telling of a classical story of the sacred king, portrayed as a unicorn, proposing marriage to the love goddess."

The love goddess? Maggie thought. If the unicorn is Christ, who is the love goddess?

As they passed the fifth panel, Nick grabbed Maggie's hand, pointing. "Look, Maggs. Now this is really unique. See that tiny red *X*. I read about that. The red *X* is a device artists used during that period to show their sympathy for Cathar beliefs."

Maggie noted a brown rabbit seated at the foot of the damsel in the tapestry playing with a red *X*-shaped flower.

"We know what the rabbit symbolizes, don't we?" Nick laughed. "And that holly tree over there has to have a mate to produce berries."

Maggie didn't respond. Nick was teasing, but she wished this procreation thing didn't have to keep coming up. "Ha-ha," Maggie said sarcastically.

"But I do know that the red cross was also the symbol of the Knights Templar." Scanning the crowd in the room to make sure no one could hear, Maggie whispered to Nick, "Nick, did I tell you that Hércule told me the St. Clair family line descended from the Cathars? And he said our golden chalice may have come from the Knights Templar. And here we are seeing this beautiful tapestry with a Cathar secret right in front of us!"

Then suddenly it dawned on her that if the unicorn, the lion, and the fair maiden were mystic symbols for the sacred king and the love goddess, then the love goddess had to be Mary Magdalene, whom the Cathars believed in and whom the Gnostic gospels claimed to be Christ's closest apostle. These beautiful tapestries could be visuals in secret religious code of the Christ and Mary Magdalene story.

As her eyes scanned the five tapestries, Maggie saw them with a new sense of their specialness. She leaned back and shook her head in awe. She was definitely supposed to see this.

CHAPTER THIRTEEN

Judgments

WHY HADN'T M. St. Clair contacted her? Two days had passed and no word had come about the grail. Maggie was tempted to go back to the shop to see Hércule, but she was afraid of being seen there. She just had to be patient and trust that all was well. She also knew that she needed to get on with her research on Paris's Black Madonnas.

Nick had completed his most urgent business and nothing had occurred to cause them any new worries over the safety of the chalice, so they decided to do a day-trip by train to Chartres Cathedral to see its famous sixteenth-century Black Madonna, called Our Lady of the Pillar.

At the SNCF Montparnasse station, they entered a first-class compartment. Two couples were already seated. Both appeared to be Americans. Just before the train pulled out, a short man in his fifties entered the car. One couple looked to be late forties. They said they were on a two-week cathedral sightseeing binge. Both had grown up in Minnesota and been transplanted to California. The man appeared serious as he commented that despite the fact that they were from California, they were moral people.

Realizing he meant it, Maggie grew angry. After all, she was from California and wasn't she a moral person? "How can they make character judgments by state?" Maggie whispered to Nick. His face had reddened, and she guessed he was suppressing a retort.

Unable to restrain himself, Nick whispered back: "I guess that makes us slimy California slouches, doesn't it? I call them the JJ and the JJ."

"What?" Maggie asked.

"The judgmental jerk and the judgmental jerkess," Nick whispered.

Maggie couldn't help laughing. She tried to keep her laughter low and unnoticeable, but the California couple glared at them.

Nick began a conversation with the other couple seated directly across the aisle. The man, a retired Presbyterian minister from Indiana, looked to be in his eighties, his wife perhaps ten years younger. They were on their way to revisit the Normandy beachhead where he had fought in WWII and to organize a reunion of what remained of his command group. Maggie and Nick enjoyed the couple's stories, including one about a daughter-in-law who had written the screenplay for the movie *Thelma and Louise*.

Other than a cursory glance when he first entered the car, they paid no attention to the fifth person until he came forward with a slight limp and stood in the aisle leaning on Nick's seat with his back to the younger couple. The man was about five feet six inches tall. A prominent nose parted pale green, close-set eyes, partially hidden by small metal-rimmed glasses. His voice was soft—like rippling papers—yet authoritative.

He bowed slightly to the older woman. "Madame," he said, "I overheard your story about the movie *Thelma and Louise*. How very interesting. The movie's show of female power enthralled me, but I did not so much care for the violence. However, that is the way with many films today."

All nodded their heads in agreement, and the minister's wife thanked him. The man smiled. "Let me introduce myself. Henri Diamond." He shook their hands. "Henri Diamond," he said again as he bowed to Maggie and shook her hand and then Nick's. "Are you all going to Chartres to see our cathedral?"

The passengers nodded again.

"You will find many stories at Chartres . . . they are built into the cathedral. I go there often—every month or so." He smiled. "I hope you enjoy your visit. We will be there soon." Henri Diamond returned to his seat.

Maggie watched him as he stopped to introduce himself and chat for a moment with the couple from California. His name seemed familiar, but she couldn't think where she'd heard it.

"Different kind of guy," Nick said.

Maggie nodded. "I liked him, though. There was something about him that made me think of Bilbo Baggins in *The Hobbit*."

As they left the train, Maggie said to Nick, "What a contrast!" She nodded toward the two couples ahead of them. "I know I do as much labeling as the next person, but I wanted to smack that ex-Minnesota guy when he said that *he* was 'moral.'" Nick put his arm around her and hugged her as they laughed. They headed up the hill from the station arm in arm.

Nick nudged Maggie as they stood at the cathedral's entrance. "Look, Maggs," he said, pointing to signs of the horoscope that were carved close to the heads of Catholic saints all around the doorframe. "There are layers and layers of belief systems in these old cathedrals that apparently changed as the building's construction continued over many years. What the church now decries were, evidently, in other times, acceptable beliefs. Many pagan beliefs were eventually Christianized."

As they entered the cathedral, an Englishman lectured animatedly to a group of young college students gathered around him. Maggie and Nick stood in the background and listened. The Englishman discussed the story behind one of the windows. He mentioned that the Knights of the Order of the Temple were the financial force behind the construction of the great Gothic cathedrals in France, and that previously unknown esoteric principles of mathematics and engineering learned from Islamic or Judaic sources in the Middle East had allowed this new type of construction. The Englishman noted that guilds of stonemasons were formed to actualize the Templar's designs. He added that one of the Templar's tenets was harmony between masculine and feminine energies in all things, and that the Templars expected their splendid cathedrals to restore the feminine principle to the world.

Nick nudged Maggie, "Boy, that didn't get far, did it? Look at the Catholic Church today."

Maggie didn't respond. Her mind was on the recurrence of the Knights Templar in her life and with their handiwork here. The staggering size of the cathedral's broad nave impressed her; its arches had to be over one hundred feet high. But under the Gothic dome, even with all the stained glass windows, the light was dim, especially as one entered from the bright sunlight outdoors. As Maggie's eyes adjusted, toward the center of the church and to her left, she saw a splendid array of candles that formed a contrasting glow to the dim light.

Nick tapped her elbow. "Maggs, I'm going down to see the crypt."

"Maybe I'll join you in a few minutes. I want to look at this." She pointed to the candlelit shrine.

"These old cathedrals are loaded with spirits. Don't get spooked now." Nick kissed her on the cheek and disappeared into a doorway to her right.

Maggie approached the shrine where rows of tall tapers vied with vigil lights for prominence in their dedication to the small wooden statue of a dark-skinned woman dressed like a Moorish princess in a dress of flowing gold-embroidered silk. She held a babe in her arms and wore a golden crown. Maggie sat on one of the wooden benches. Her first real Black Virgin—and very unlike the statues of the Mother Mary she had seen who always seemed to be dressed simply and in blue.

She felt something special here, as though a soothing presence had joined her. Maggie was content to rest and allow herself the privacy of her thoughts. Why have I been given this ancient chalice? She asked. Has Hércule been honest with me? I feel so alone with all this responsibility. She twisted her hands. Why do people who aren't honest and trustworthy show up in my life?

Nick had always been honest with her, but she recalled other men who didn't mention that they had wives until they let something slip. "God!" The loud oath escaped her. The sound of it echoed back and forth through the hollowness of the open space between the cathedral's ancient walls. She looked guiltily around to see if anyone had heard her.

Once during one of their in-depth talks, Nick told her that he believed each person in our lives, especially those who are important to us, mirrors back to us who we are. At that moment, Maggie glimpsed the California cathedral-bingers following behind the Brit-Chartres-whiz and his entourage. The couple's presence gave her a second angry charge. She hated righteousness of any kind.

If Nick's theory were true, did that mean that she too was judgmental? The idea began to bother her. She looked up at the Black Madonna. There was something in the statue's visage that calmed Maggie. She heard the words, "The grail is here to teach you, my dear. Cherish it." Who spoke? There was no one in sight other than the statue of the black virgin.

As Maggie rose to leave the shrine, she realized her anger and worry had disappeared. She felt cleansed. She lit a candle, bowed her head, and said quietly, "Thank you."

CHAPTER FOURTEEN

Henri Diamond

MAGGIE MOVED BACK into the nave of the cathedral until she was directly in front of the Mary Magdalene window—a story of the woman's life in red, green, yellow, and brilliant blue glass, as seen through the eyes of the fourteenth-century artisan who designed the window. The afternoon sun sharply outlined the rainbow story. Maggie tried to interpret each colorful frame by the stories that she knew about Mary Magdalene . . . washing Christ's feet with her hair . . . the waiting at the tomb . . . holding faith with the other women below the cross at the crucifixion . . . meeting the risen Christ outside the tomb. Those she knew. She didn't have the background to interpret the other frames.

A voice directly behind her said, "*La Pauvre!* Mary Magdalene was so misjudged." The words reminded Maggie that she had just been judging and possibly misjudging the people around her. She turned to see Henri Diamond. He held a Chartres guidebook and was gazing at the gleaming storytelling panes before them. He wore the same gray wool newsboy cap that she had noticed on the train. He spoke with an unusual accent.

"I agree," Maggie said. "I don't think anyone ever understood this woman. What she must have felt. She knew so much. To know Christ!"

Henri Diamond nodded. "Indeed. From what I know about Mary Magdalene, she was an extraordinary woman for those times. Many believe she was the thirteenth and only female disciple. To have been that and Christ's favorite—I mean—that's truly exceptional. It is unfortunate that Mary Magdalene is often thought of as a prostitute, rather than as the rightful feminine protagonist of the Christian story. I don't understand why women today, in this age of feminism, aren't naming their girls Mary Magdalene to honor her."

Maggie laughed. "Funny you should say that. That's my name." She held out her hand. "Mary Magdalena Forsythe. Everyone calls me Maggie."

Henri Diamond laughed heartily and shook his head in disbelief. "Are you, as they say, putting me on?"

Nick joined them as Maggie was telling Henri that this was her first trip to France. Nick said, "I slipped into the bookstore. There are a couple books there by that Chartres expert." He pointed to the Brit, who was now lecturing to another group of tourists. "His name's Malcolm something. The clerk said he's here most every day."

"Oh, that is Malcolm Miller," Henri indicated. "He has made Chartres his life's work. He lectures all over the world on this cathedral and on medieval architecture. You would be fortunate to hear his lectures. However, I believe his last tour today has already started."

"I wish we'd known that earlier," Maggie said.

Nick laughed and said, "You know, I can only hear so much British accent before I suddenly want tea." He looked to Maggie. "We passed a *salon de thé* on the way up here. What do you think?"

"That's a great idea. Let's have tea. Would you join us, M. Diamond?" Maggie offered. She was enjoying this clever man.

"Henri Diamond is pleased to accept." Henri responded with the same little bow that he had given her on the train.

Before they left the churchyard, Henri pointed out the lopsided look that the differing spires gave to the cathedral. "The tower on the left is called the Old Tower, the *Clocher Vieux*. It is in the Romanesque style and a very simple version of the Romanesque at that." He pulled out his guidebook. "Finished in 1160, it says. The tower on the right is called . . . can you guess?"

"The New Tower?" Maggie ventured, laughing. "It *is* very different."

"Right you are. The *Clocher Neuf* was built in the sixteenth century. It's in the flamboyant style. This cathedral was rebuilt many times. There were at least five fires that destroyed its previous incarnations."

They headed for the village of Chartres and found a delightful *salon de thé*. Dried flowers hung from open beams. Blue baskets filled with sachets of lavender, and rosemary sat atop circular tables covered with lace cloths. The window was filled with napoleons, madeleines, and lemon cakes.

As they waited for their tea, Henri Diamond addressed Maggie. "I saw you sitting at the shrine to Our Lady of the Pillar."

"Yes," she said, "She felt special to me. Thoughts came at me out of my past while I was sitting there. I didn't really want to remember them, but, in a way, it was helpful. I felt cleansed afterward."

Nick looked surprised at Maggie's personal confession to a man they'd only just met. "I should have been there with you, Maggie," Nick said apologetically.

"No, Nick. I needed to be alone," Maggie said.

Henri Diamond spoke: "Many people feel the European Black Madonnas are very special—very comfortable to be with. They evolved from earlier beliefs in the mother goddesses, such as Cybele and Isis. And there is a connection to Mary Magdalene." Henri continued, "Some historians believe that the Black Madonna was especially symbolic to those early independent worshippers who followed the way of Mary Magdalene—a more personal way of worshipping without having to bow down to the priest's skirts or the Pope's ring or the clergy's demands for money. Some say the Black Madonna represents the dark Egyptian maiden who accompanied Mary Magdalene to France."

The proprietress brought their tea and sweets, and Henri Diamond asked, "Are either of you aware of the *Provençal* legend about Mary Magdalene? As Americans, you may not be aware of this."

Maggie and Nick shook their heads.

"The Provençal legend alleges that Mary Magdalene came to Marseille on the Mediterranean coast in a rudderless boat along with Mary Jacob, the mother of James and John; and Mary Salomé, the sister of Christ's mother; and Sarah, a young dark-skinned Egyptian girl, who may have been their servant. Some versions also include Martha and Lazarus. The group left Palestine in about 40 CE to flee the persecution besetting the early Christians. Mediterranean winds blew them to port near Marseille. Martha and two of the Marys on the ship remained in that area, as did Sarah. A tall impressive statue of Ste. Sarah can be found in a gypsy town called Les Saintes Maries de la Mer in the Camargue, near Marseille. It is the largest and possibly the most famous of all the statues of the Black Madonna in Europe. Gypsies throughout Europe worship Ste. Sarah. Every summer in July, the gypsies converge on Les Saintes Maries de la Mer and carry the Black Madonna en masse out to the sea that brought the celebrated group to France."

Maggie asked, "What happened to Mary Magdalene? Did she stay in Marseille with the others?"

"Mary Magdalene was said to have eventually gone to the Haute Provence, a higher, more mountainous area near the city of Aix-en-Provence. She was accompanied by one of the other early Christians on board the boat, a man named Maximime. It is said that Mary Magdalene lived in a cave high in the massif there for thirty years. A Dominican monastery was built close to the cave. It looks as if it is suspended from the cliff. It is a steep climb to the cave, but masses are offered each day there amid statues of the crucifixion and a pietà of the Magdalene holding Christ's body. A reliquary there holds what are reportedly some of Mary Magdalene's bones. Crowds of people make pilgrimages there on her feast day, July 22."

Maggie laughed. "Wow! That's my birthday. My father named me for Mary Magdalene when he saw my red hair and blue eyes. He had admired a painting of the Magdalene in the Louvre on one of his visits—a Botticelli, I think."

Nick commented, "I didn't know that, Maggs. What a neat connection."

"Indeed. It appears you were aptly named, my dear." Henri Diamond continued: "There is also a church dedicated to Mary Magdalene in the village below. It is very old, and though the exterior shows its eight hundred years, the interior is quite lovely. The village is named after St. Maximime, Mary Magdalene's companion."

Henri paused and then asked, "Would you be interested in seeing that area? I would be happy to show it to you."

"I think Maggie is already scheduled," Nick said.

Maggie understood that Nick was being cautious about this strange man who had befriended them, but she couldn't stop herself from saying, "Oh, I would *love* to go there . . . to see that."

Refreshed, the threesome left the tea shop and hurried to catch the next train. They continued their conversation on the train ride back to Paris. When their train reached the Paris station, they exchanged phone numbers and promised to be in touch very soon.

Nick pulled Maggie aside as soon as Henri Diamond had left. "Are you sure you want to do this, Maggs? You don't know anything about this Diamond guy."

Maggie squeezed Nick's hand to reassure him and explained, "I know this is a little unusual, but who knows where it could lead? I feel that a part of my journey here is to search for my namesake. Maybe Henri Diamond is to be my guide. He certainly seems harmless."

CHAPTER FIFTEEN

Rendezvous at Café Marly

THEY RETURNED TO Nick's flat to check on the chalice. Maggie said, "I'm so disappointed that we haven't heard from Hércule. What could be wrong?"

"I'll bet he's just searching for an alternative safe place for the grail. I'm sure you'll hear from him soon," Nick said. "But if you'd like, how about I go over to the shop and check it out? No one could connect *me* to the St. Clairs."

Maggie said, "I don't think that's a good idea, Nick. I guess we'll just have to wait and see what develops. There hasn't been a problem with this place so far. So let's cross our fingers that all is well."

"Okay," Nick said.

Maggie had been thinking about Israel Hawkins. She hadn't seen him since their lunch at La Coupole. She said, "Well, now that's decided, I have an idea for tonight. Why don't we call Israel Hawkins and arrange to meet Israel and his date for an after-dinner drink?"

Nick looked dubious. "I guess. We don't have anything else planned."

When she called, Israel Hawkins mentioned that they could meet at Café Marly in the Louvre. Maggie was delighted—this was a chance to wear the expensive black cocktail dress her father had slipped into her luggage as a surprise. She knew the dress would make her feel glamorous.

They entered the café from rue de Rivoli at the far end of the museum. En route, they passed glass-enclosed ancient statues of Greek and Roman gods illuminated dramatically against the venerable Louvre walls.

Inside, the Café Marly's sleekly modern interior surprised Maggie. She leaned toward Nick and whispered, "This place feels a little disorienting—it's such a contrast to the ancient Greco-Roman art treasures we just saw." Adjusting to the dim lighting, Maggie's eyes took in deep red faux-finished walls, small black lacquered tables and chairs, and the sparse crowd. Soft jazz was playing.

Two well-dressed men entered the nightspot shortly after them and seated themselves at the next table. The dark-haired one with the small goatee appeared to be in his fifties. The other with graying reddish hair looked to be at least in his midsixties. His French had a weird accent with a Scottish burr. The pitch of their animated voices seemed to cut through the chatter of the others in the room. Maggie tried to pick up snippets of conversations, but only the two men could be heard. It reminded her of trying to tune her grandfather's shortwave radio; it always seemed that the most powerful station would win out over the one you really wanted to hear. She heard them say, "He's an old fool, but Alain will know what to do." Where had she heard the name Alain? It seemed oddly familiar, but her mind couldn't make a logical connection. Maggie ordered an espresso and a brandy, although she knew that now she might suffer a sleepless night. What did that matter in Paris?

Her eyes traveled around the room. At the far end, Maggie spotted Israel Hawkins looking bored and disdainful. With him was the stylish younger woman whom they'd met at La Coupole. The woman's mouth seemed to be in constant motion. Maggie wondered what kind of a relationship this was. Was this more than casual?

When Maggie looked up from her brandy, she saw Israel Hawkins's eyes focused intently on her. He waved. Although Nick was talking to her about their day together and some of the special things they had shared, she didn't hear him. She felt alone in Israel's gaze—warm and flushed—as if held motionless in a golden world. She waved back.

Nick cleared his throat very loudly. "Ahem!" he said several times. He reached over and clinked her glass. This brought her back. Maggie looked at him.

"I'm boring you, obviously. Where did you go?" Nick asked.

Maggie shook her head. "I'm sorry. I just saw Israel and his date." She pointed. As she did so, she saw the couple rise and walk toward them. In a few seconds, Israel Hawkins was beaming down at her.

"Here you are. And Mademoiselle, you look spectacular!" Hawkins said.

The dress was obviously doing its work, Maggie thought, but she couldn't seem to make her usually loquacious tongue do so. "Hi," was all she could get out.

"I'm so pleased you came," Israel said. "Both of you," he added.

Nick stood up and motioned to the two unoccupied chairs at their table.

Israel held out his hand to Nick and then to Maggie. Deferring to Sandy, he said, "You both met Sandy Winters yesterday. Are you Sandy today or Mélisande?" He asked.

"S-ah-ndy," she said, drawing out the broad "a." Then she laughed at her attempt to sound sophisticated.

After they'd gone through the pleasantries of introductions, Maggie said to Israel Hawkins. "It's funny. Sometimes being on a plane is kind of like being in an elevator. You see people. You notice things about them, but you hardly ever speak to them. It's like they're not really there. But it wasn't that way with you."

"No, it wasn't that way with you either," Israel responded, smiling.

"But there is often distancing on a plane. People seem to stay in their own worlds," Maggie commented.

"I was definitely in mine for much of the flight," Israel said. "It wouldn't be exactly macho to let on that flying frightens me."

Nick interrupted. "So we're into *old* times here—remembering Friday's plane ride?" He sounded testy.

Maggie looked at Nick in surprise, but decided not to comment. Nick didn't usually say things in that tone.

Nick saw her questioning look. His eyes direct on Israel Hawkins, in a less strident tone, he asked: "What brings you to Paris?" Maggie could tell Nick was sizing Israel up.

"I'm a historian," Israel answered. "European history is my field. I was lucky enough to win an award for my last book, and I came here to accept the prize. But for the plane ride, I can tell you, I don't mind coming to Paris at all." He smiled at Sandy, and she beamed back.

"Don't like to fly?" Nick asked.

"Leave it, Nick," Maggie murmured. "We've already discussed that."

"Nobody's discussed it with me," Nick said. "You two had your own *tête à tête.*"

Why was Nick acting so petulant? Maggie decided to ignore his behavior.

Sandy, who had been ogling the other patrons, said, "Usually this place is crowded with artists and French film aficionados, but they're not here tonight. I'll bet they're all at the Cannes Film Festival this week. It's always around this time in May. Just our luck." She got no response. She nudged Israel. "Are you listening to me?"

"Hmm? Oh, yes—the Cannes Festival. Did you want to go there?" he said absentmindedly.

"Go there. What? No. I just said I bet that's where everyone is tonight. Usually this place is jumping with celebs, and, obviously, it isn't tonight, now that *we're* here to people watch."

Maggie interrupted her, "I'm going to the ladies'. How about you, Sandy?"

In the elegant ladies' room, Maggie tried to engage the younger woman in small talk about her visit to Paris. With no encouragement, Sandy told Maggie that she had met Israel Hawkins two days before. She talked enthusiastically about how much she was enjoying having a companion and guide to escort her to places in Paris she might not otherwise have seen on her own. "He's a cool guy. Old, but cool," she concluded.

"I guess it's all in your perspective," Maggie said. Her comment appeared lost on Sandy, who turned and swished dramatically out into the main room, trying to attract any attention she could.

As she crossed the room back to their table, Maggie again felt Israel's eyes following her. She could see that he was paying no attention at all to Sandy's maneuvers. Back at the table, Nick had turned away from them to watch Sandy's extravagant waltz past every table, her fingers lightly touching the men's chairs as she passed, occasionally stopping to chat.

"Where are you staying?" Israel asked.

Maggie looked directly into his gray-blue eyes. There was something tired there, something restless. Could she trust this man? She definitely wanted to. The fluttering feeling within her that he seemed to cause excited her. "At the Chevreuse . . . it's a little place near La Coupole." she said quietly. She wrote the name of her hotel and her cell number on a napkin and handed it to him. Israel took her hand in his. They talked quietly for a few minutes.

Sandy returned to the table. Noticing the exclusivity of Israel and Maggie's discussion, she asked Nick, "What's going on here? Did we just disappear?"

"It appears we did," Nick said grudgingly. He caught Israel's eye and asked in a casual tone, "What's with you two?"

"I was thanking Maggie for her concern about a problem I experienced on the plane. I'd like to hear about the project you're working on here in Paris."

"Smooth," Maggie thought. But she was sorry when Israel dropped her hand. So much energy emanated from him. And he'd been sweet to remember how she'd put her hand on his arm to calm him on the plane.

Nick discussed his Paris project with Israel for some time. Sandy chatted on about her Paris plans, but Maggie soon tired of the conversation. Looking around the café again, Maggie noted that most of the people she'd initially noticed had now left. The place was almost empty except for the two men to whom she'd listened briefly when they first arrived. She nudged Nick. When she'd gotten his attention, she said, "Those two must be really enjoying themselves to stay so late."

"You're right. It is getting late." Nick stood up. "We'd better go, Maggie. We have to check on our baby."

"Baby?" Both Israel and Sandy spoke as one voice and in great surprise.

"He's joking!" Maggie gave Nick a kick on his shin. "There is no baby."

Israel stood and took Maggie's hand again. "I'd like to see you again," he said. Then he reached out to shake Nick's hand. "I hope we can get together soon. I enjoyed our conversation about your project. Here's my number." He pulled a card from his pocket, wrote quickly on the back of it, and handed it to Nick.

Maggie shook Sandy's hand. "I hope you'll enjoy your stay in Paris."

Maggie had a hard time keeping up with Nick as he pushed open Café Marly's door. "Nice guy," he commented brusquely.

CHAPTER SIXTEEN

Reflections on the Loss of Self

WHEN MAGGIE WAS back in her hotel, a feeling of buoyancy welled up within her. "What is this?" she asked under her breath. Inexplicably, a name came to her: Israel Hawkins. I like being around him. I don't really know him, and I may never see him again, but I know I'd like to. Maggie had lived her life matter-of-factly with little grandiose drama. But this . . . this felt like she was in one of those Technicolor time-lapse films showing a rapidly growing plant. She felt that something—a flower perhaps—might burst out of her belly at any moment. Maggie laughed to herself, "I'm blooming—or a blooming idiot—one or the other!"

Why haven't I felt this before? She thought. Maybe there's a part of me that's been missing. Did I give it away? Her mind raced back. Of course I did! Her fears of intimacy had continually threatened her romantic life. Of course she'd had dates—many of them, but they hadn't led anywhere. When attraction oozed up into her psyche, her fears fought within her to squash it.

Maggie wondered if there was something in this new man—Israel (odd name, really)—that subconsciously made her remember a dormant part of herself. Could that be part of the unexplainable magnetic attraction she felt? "Is this romantic love?" she asked aloud.

Maggie's thoughts moved to Nick. Dear, dear Nick. I am so happy he is in my life. Nick had a freeing effect on her. He encouraged her to be herself and to let her emotions out. His penchant for humor and his lack of concern for others' opinions had a strong influence on her, she realized. Those were voids in her that *he* had matched and filled.

She wondered about Nick's behavior tonight. He wasn't exactly rude, but there was something uncharacteristic in his tone with Israel and with her. Was he jealous? Perhaps his feelings for her were different than she'd thought. This confused her more. She loved Nick, but the fire that Israel Hawkins kindled within her felt so different, so much stronger, so . . . she didn't dare express it to herself. But the notion persisted that this man who kept showing up here in Paris—must be in her life to show her something about herself that was missing.

I hate not feeling whole, Maggie thought. I have to let go of my fears. Life is here. I want to move on. Maggie decided to record this in her journal, "Maggie's Musings." When she had finished, Maggie opened the journal and randomly selected a passage to read:

> December 1. Will I be free? From me? From the past? From what I think? From the depths? From despair? Ever? Grateful dead is an oxymoron. I am both, but not grateful for the dead part of me. Can I be a phoenix? Feathers are sprouting from little goose bumps on my hands and neck and now from my back. I picture myself as the bird rising so slowly . . . so slowly. Oh! When will the wings come? Why can't I feel the fire? How can I feel the fire if it is not inside me? But where does the fire need to start within me? Do I have to keep burning my fingers and toes? Can I burn away the dross of my life? Will anyone see the fire? No. Do I care? No. Can I become my own alchemist and turn my base metal into gold?

She didn't feel despondent tonight. Not a bit. But the passage reminded her that she was sometimes susceptible to that downward spiral.

That night Maggie dreamt: *not* of burning pyres, ascending birds, or the mystical chemistry in her journal, but, instead, of strange but pleasant images. A cool sonorous voice beckoned to her from an otherworldly place. "See the picture," the voice instructed. "If it is not clear, shake the picture. It will emerge true and then you will know that it is *your* picture . . . it is *your* story."

"See a forest now. Hear the forest sounds . . . the rushing rill . . . the birds trill . . . the soft crunch of the animals on the twigs. In the midst of the forest is a golden haired baby. It stands surrounded by light. As the baby toddles through the forest touching whatever attracts it, the trees lean away and a lush green meadow spreads out before it. The meadow is always before it. A clearing of the path is occurring."

"I see it. Is it me?" It was her voice, yet it sounded different.

The voice continued, "The singing birds bring gifts from the trees and the skies . . . many skies. The sun warms the baby. The animals protect the baby with their warm, friendly, furry bodies."

The pastoral scene welcomed Maggie.

"She is always safe . . . always free to explore. Forget the past. This baby has no past. Can you see there is no past?" The voice asked.

"Yes. I see that." Again, her voice sounded disembodied.

"She is only there as you see her . . . in her bower . . . in the world. The baby is moving forward. And it is being watched. And the light surrounds it." The voice stopped. The picture vanished.

What's wrong? Maggie wondered. Where is the picture? She tried to shake it to bring it back. The forest. The baby. The meadow. Where were they? The stress of the sudden loss brought a new awareness—she was waking. Oh no, she thought, I don't want to leave this beautiful place.

The neon red of her digital alarm clock read 3:00 AM. Maggie sat up and punched the square pillow up against the ornate headboard and leaned back to ponder the dream. She sighed. "What does the dream mean? Does this mean my life was finally going to get better? And what would have inspired this dream about a baby? Nick had made that joke about getting home to the baby—meaning the chalice. Could that be it? Or was she the baby?"

She dozed in and out of sleep until the light from a pale mauve sky woke her.

Across the Seine, after dropping Mélisande at her hotel, Israel Hawkins stopped for a nightcap at the lobby bar of his hotel. He swirled the tepid single-malt scotch around the glass and looked into it. Just what had happened tonight? Earlier that night in the Café Marly from across the room, he could swear he'd seen a faint golden aura reverberating around the woman with the burnished hair who'd sat next to him on the plane—he'd hardly considered her then, but now . . . she was all he could think about. But she'd mentioned the St. Clairs on the plane. He really shouldn't get involved with her. He knew too much.

Despite the moment of caution, a smile crossed Israel's face as he drained most of his glass. He wondered if he had ever really been in control of his life. He realized that along the way, he had compromised pieces of himself—to Emily, to his academic career, to financial survival at all costs, to his unhappiness and guilt. But now he felt freer and more alive than he had felt in months—as if he had been reborn—as if some missing links within his soul were reawakening.

Maggie Forsythe. He'd written her name and number on the back of his card. Could this woman with the distinct azure eyes—startling in their color, but surprisingly soft in their gaze—fill his emptiness? What was it about her that made him feel this way? Maggie's companion came into Israel's mind. He wondered how important this man—this Nick—was to her.

Then, as if on cue, his rational mind created a diversion. His sleeve knocked his glass over onto the counter with a clash of glass against polished wood. The barman headed over to clean up his mess. The questions went unanswered as he backed away from the shattered glass and flowing liquid. As he walked to his room, Israel sensed that this new feeling was one he had been searching for unconsciously for a long time.

CHAPTER SEVENTEEN

Marcel Devereaux

NICK RUFFLED THROUGH the tenants' mailbox. He found two letters addressed to M. Marcel Devereaux forwarded from a previous address in Colmar, but nothing for himself. *Hmm? I wonder if that could be one of the guys who moved into the apartment directly below mine.*

Usually, he stopped to pet the building's gray tabby who greeted him here, brushing back and forth through his legs. He realized he hadn't seen the cat for the last two days. Nick called, "Here kitty, kitty, kitty," hoping these words were universal enough that even French cats would understand. No cat appeared. *Funny.* He stopped at the concierge's door to ask about the disappearance. She only shook her head and said, "*Je ne sais pas, M. Nick. Les chats sont toujours indépendants. N'est-ce-pas?*"

Yeah, he thought, cats *are* always independent. Still . . . the cat's disappearance bothered him because it coincided with the arrival of the new residents on the first floor.

Wasn't there a play with a character named Maggie the Cat? His thoughts so often went to Maggie: *How lucky I am that Maggie is in my* life. She mirrors my good qualities back to me. She makes me feel gallant and worthy. Besides, she laughs at my jokes!

Thinking of Maggie reminded him of the chalice hidden in the small safe in his Paris *pied à terre*. When he returned to the apartment, Nick assured himself that all was well with their hidden treasure. Then he strolled over to an open window to enjoy the sunset, the Seine beyond, and the Tour Eiffel in the distance.

Voices drifted up from the terrace below. At first, Nick didn't pay any attention to the words. It was just background noise that blended with the sound of traffic from the street. Then the voices penetrated his thoughts. "The black market." "Sotheby's." "Monaco." "That dratted nosy cat breaking my things." "Mme. de l'Arbeau." "Wrinkled skin." "Damned selfish fool!" "What an idiot he is!"

Why was he listening to this jumble? Nick tried to ignore the conversation and concentrate on the view. Then he heard something he couldn't ignore—"St. Clair."

Could they really be talking about the same family— the same man? They'd said *calise*. Could that be? Well, what else would they be referring to, if they were talking about St. Clair? My god!

Spurred by intense curiosity, Nick walked casually out onto his small balcony. On the wider terrace below, he saw two men in lively conversation: A tall, large-boned man with a broad forehead, bald with a fringe of gray-blond hair, dressed stylishly in tailored slacks, shirt and cravat; and a handsome shorter man. The mellow gold light from the low sun gave the shorter man's tanned skin an iridescent glow, contrasted by the tight white shirt that showed his muscular physique.

The tall man looked up and spotted Nick.

"*Ciao!*" He waved to Nick. "The neighbor," he said to the other man.

Nick smiled, returned the greeting, and then turned away to reenter the flat.

"*Monsieur!*" A voice called to him.

Nick swiveled and focused again on the two below.

"Would you like to join us for an *apéritif*?" the taller man asked.

"Well, I . . ." Nick hesitated. "Sure. *Merci beaucoup.* I'll be right down. What's the number?"

"*Un-Zero-Un.*"

"*Merci,*" Nick responded. *St. Clair* still rang in his head. He wondered if the new neighbors suspected that he had been listening to their conversation. Well, why would they? He was probably being paranoid.

The tanned younger man answered the door. "M. Devereaux would like you to join us on the terrace, *s'il vous plaît.*" He flicked his head slightly.

As they walked through the apartment, Nick noted that number 101 was a much larger apartment than his one-plus-room affair. This apartment encompassed an entire side of the building length to length. The foyer led to a small kitchen on the left. They passed through a large salon in the center. An interior hall led off to other rooms on the right.

Massive furniture, unlike any Nick had seen, gave the salon a stark, but overpowering look. Austrian? He wondered. Or Swedish antiques, perhaps. The walls were painted a pale green that reminded Nick of pistachio ice cream. Paintings—mostly eighteenth century landscapes—were hung in disturbing regularity around the room. Surfaces were empty. No mementos or family photos, or even a pencil, could be seen anywhere.

"Marcel Devereaux." The tall balding man stood and held out his hand to greet Nick. Nick shook his hand. The man's handshake was firm, but his hands felt cold and clammy. "Guillaume Joinville," Devereaux said with a nod toward his companion. The younger man smiled and extended his hand. His handshake was limp.

"Nick Payne."

The shorter man said, "I know Guillaume is a difficult name for Americans, so feel free to call me Bill. That's how it translates."

"I'm okay with Guillaume," Nick responded.

"A drink for our guest," Devereaux said.

On command, Guillaume moved to the cart holding liquor and wine. He pointed to various bottles, and Nick nodded at the bianca vermouth. Guillaume poured a small glass and handed it to Nick.

The sweet vermouth lazed on Nick's tongue before it moved down his throat. He'd better be careful, Nick thought. Even though it was just vermouth, he sensed he shouldn't drink much tonight.

"So is that your flat?"

"Yes. I'm renting it for a month—subletting. I just came out on the balcony to stretch my legs a bit. I had been reading—studying, really. Did I interrupt anything?"

"Well, we were discussing my obsession. You see, I am a collector." Devereaux's English was perfect, but there was a slightly Germanic pronunciation of certain sounds. "I buy and sell antiques, and I collect *objets d'art*. I call them my treasures." Devereaux folded his hands in a prayerlike pose and raised them to his lips for a few seconds, then continued. "My particular passion is for Crusade artifacts that knights such as the Templars brought back from Palestine. Do you know the Templars with the large red cross on their white flags?"

"I have read about them." Of course he knew about the Templars. He knew they'd started a hospital for lepers, and he'd always wondered if that was the precedent for the insignia for the International Red Cross. Nick asked, "Is there really anything left from that ancient time? I'd imagine most anything from that long ago would be in shards under several layers of earth by now."

"Yes," said Devereaux. "Much of it is in the earth, but you may be surprised to know that I've found some very special relics from that era."

Very polished manner, Nick thought.

"You're obviously an American. Where do you live there? If I may ask," Devereaux queried.

"In the San Francisco area," Nick replied.

"Such a charming city in some ways, but I found it to be a bit tacky. Not up to its reputation for finery. The weather was gloomy. Very depressing for what you Americans call 'sunny California.'"

"Well . . . ," Nick began. He didn't want to sound defensive. "It has its flaws, like any place, but the city's setting between the bay and the ocean makes it unique."

Devereaux rested his chin on his folded hands as Nick spoke. Devereaux clucked his tongue ever so slightly and looked around the room. Nick thought: Can I have bored him already? He's a bit insulting.

The man, who had been introduced as Guillaume, smiled at Devereaux in a knowing way, as though he shared and understood his boredom, and then stared at Nick as though Nick had just disappeared.

Nick felt increasingly uncomfortable. He suspected the genial *politesse* Devereaux exhibited earlier was for show, and that here was an extraordinarily arrogant man who felt superior to most other humans. Two of a kind, in fact, Nick thought.

Devereaux changed the subject. "Do you, per chance, collect anything? I am always fascinated by people's need to show their individuality through their collecting impulses. Perhaps I should call them vices. Do you have any?" He chuckled.

"I have vices aplenty." Nick laughed. "The biggest one is procrastination. If I can put something off, I will. I read a lot. I like to escape through books. I don't know if that qualifies as a vice. But I don't collect anything of note—the only thing I collect is parking tickets." Nick laughed, but he got no response from his listeners.

He said, "But I'm fascinated with how a collector gets started."

"Ha! You have happened onto my favorite topic. How clever of you." Devereaux's faint smile did not match the enthusiasm in his voice, yet Nick saw a glint in Devereaux's eyes that he didn't understand. Were they mocking him? He shivered, feeling nervous. Yet he wanted to know how these two could be connected to the St. Clairs. He had to stay and listen.

"If you are not a collector and you do not read the journals on the collecting of antiques, then you may not have heard of me. I am quite well known in that sphere. I have one of the world's finest private collections of twelfth—and thirteenth-century religious artifacts, and my special enthusiasm is chalices."

"Really!" Nick did not have to feign interest now.

"The majority of my collection is at my home near Colmar in Alsace-Lorraine. I was born in Freiburg, across the river in Germany at the southern tip of the Black Forest. Have you been there?"

Nick shook his head no.

"You would like to know more about me, wouldn't you?" Devereaux asked.

Nick nodded. Was Devereaux insinuating something here? Nick didn't get it.

Devereaux smiled. "I thought you might," he said. "Freiburg is quite a prosperous city now. We moved to Colmar in France from Freiburg during the Second World War. My father, who was injured in the war, had been sent home." Devereaux crossed his arms and hugged them close. "He was not a happy man. It's hard to be a cripple. My father blamed everyone and everything—the world—for his war injuries and his unhappy fate. And my mother died when I was ten. In some ways, I hated my angry father, yet I guess I retain some of his Prussian discipline." He looked fondly and apologetically at Guillaume, who did not react. Devereaux sighed and said, "So some of my collection is in Alsace-Lorraine, and some, of course, is in safekeeping."

Nick said, "I thought I detected a German accent." He wanted information on these guys, but he hadn't expected this kind of personal detail.

"I spoke German at home and French at school after we moved to Colmar," Devereaux explained.

"That part of the world has gone back and forth between France and Germany several times, hasn't it?" Nick asked.

"Yes, indeed. Too many times—the Maginot Line, which the French built to repel the Germans in that war, is not far. It runs near Thionville and Metz. Metz, as you may know, was the capital for the Carolingian kings of France."

Carolingians. This guy did know his history. Nick said, "Boy that goes way back to the twelfth century." He was guessing.

"The eighth," Devereaux said abruptly.

"Of course," Nick said, giving credit to Devereaux's superior history knowledge. But he persisted, "I would very much like to see something from your collection."

"I do have a few pieces with me. I cannot bear to be apart from them. They are my family. They are my loved ones. They are my dears."

Guillaume gave Nick a quizzical look.

Nick wondered if the drink was affecting Devereaux. His dears, indeed! Devereaux was obviously pleased to be telling his story, and Nick wanted to know more. "So what inspired your collecting urge?" Nick asked.

Devereaux reached over and patted Nick's hand. "Ah," Devereaux said, "Thank you for asking. That is an interesting tale."

"I have something to attend to in the kitchen," Guillaume's voice had a sarcastic tone to it as he excused himself. "I enjoyed meeting you, M. Payne. I hope we'll have a chance to talk again." Nick saw Guillaume wink. Guillaume had obviously heard the upcoming story before.

"My parents were very religious. From the time when I was a toddler, my father told me stories of the grail from which Jesus sipped wine at the last supper. And somehow, intertwined with that are images of the leather-booted German soldiers who goose-stepped through our French village. For fear that the soldiers might harm me, my parents hid me in the dank wine cellar under our house. The soldiers, knowing that most of the houses in this wine-growing region had wine cellars, stomped down the stairs and broke into our stored wine. They drank and became raucously loud in their drunkenness, singing bawdy songs in croaking disharmony. I heard the violent sound of shattering glass as the soldiers hurled the bottles onto the floor as they finished each. The soldiers were too busy enjoying themselves to notice me hidden behind a barrel in a corner, but I'll never forget them. I was only three, and I've never been so frightened since. I still shiver when I hear the sounds of crashing glass. Still! Even in the daylight. It's in my dreams often. I hated those soldiers! Ironically, perhaps inspired by the sounds of the glass, I now value fine crystal. Later, my interest expanded to other beautiful and historic objects."

Why would this guy tell so intimate a tale from his past to a virtual stranger? Could this be his way of coming on to me? Nick wondered, feeling a bit squeamish at the thought of having to fend off a gay advance. Or was showing his vulnerability Devereaux's way of bringing me into his confidence? Maybe my first impression of the guy was wrong. Maybe Devereaux isn't as stiff and arrogant as I thought. But I'm certainly not interested in anything that he has to offer—other than information about how he's connected to the St. Clairs. Of course, he couldn't ask about that.

"Guillaume!" Devereaux's commanding voice brought Guillaume back into the room. "Bring me the Genoa box. S'il te plaît."

Nick asked the location of the bathroom. Devereaux directed him down the hall. On his return, he ran into Guillaume in the hallway carrying a small box. "He's a beast," Guillaume whispered. He shook his head in what Nick could now see was a haughty manner. "To treat me this way. It is an insult. I am not his servant. I am his friend." Guillaume's confidence surprised Nick, and he was even more startled to feel Guillaume's hand on his sleeve detaining him. Nick didn't know what to say. What have I walked into here? He wondered. Were these quarreling gay lovers or was this just a demanding employer—employee relationship?

Guillaume whispered in Nick's ear. "Don't let him get too close. He has a way of reeling you into his spell and that could be disastrous for you. Believe me, I know."

"Guillaume!" Devereaux called.

Guillaume let go of Nick's sleeve, and they walked together into the salon. Nick wondered, Why is he telling me this? Is he jealous of all the attention Devereaux is paying me?

Guillaume carried an ornate enameled box about five inches square with pearls surrounding its lid and base. He handed the box to Devereaux, who opened it, displaying a brilliant hammered gold interior. He watched Nick's response closely.

"It's lovely. It looks expensive. I know very little about antiques or their value, but I can appreciate beauty."

"I like you." Devereaux smiled benignly at Nick. Turning the box back to Guillaume, Devereaux added. "I like those who appreciate beauty. Now others envy me. My father wished for me to have success. I wish he could see me now."

Devereaux paused and looked at Nick—almost cunningly—then he continued. "My personal collection has grown substantially over the years. It is only missing one greatly desired object—a grail—like the one in my father's stories. I told you my parents were religious—Catholics—though I am no longer one. My father was fascinated with the Holy Grail because in the early years of Hitler's power, he, as a German soldier, was sent to southern France in Languedoc to find the grail. His army company searched for months around a small village called Rennes-le-Château, but they never found the grail that was rumored to be there. It was one of the Fuehrer's idle, perhaps silly, ideas of solidifying his supremacy. Who could argue with someone who possessed the Holy Grail?" He raised his eyebrows as he looked to Nick for his reaction.

"They say Hitler was an egotist," Nick said. "I've never believed that such a thing could really still exist."

"*Peut-être oui, peut-être non.* We can't know for sure. Whether the grail in Languedoc was the one from which Jesus Christ sipped wine or the vessel that collected Christ's blood when they took him down from the cross or whether it was a treasured religious object from another time—in any case, I believe one still exists right here in France. I will do anything to get it."

This was too close for comfort. Nick felt suddenly very anxious to get back to his flat. He hadn't heard from Maggie all day and that worried him. He chatted for a few more minutes so as not to show his distress, then thanked Devereaux and Guillaume and left.

Devereaux's statement, "I will do anything to get it," kept repeating in Nick's head.

CHAPTER EIGHTEEN

Thérèse

T HE NEXT MORNING, Maggie decided to take the St. Clair chalice back to the shop. The burden of the responsibility of keeping it hidden at Nick's flat was weighing on her. She hoped whatever crisis M. Hércule had referred to had passed and that she could return the chalice to him.

When she entered the shop, she was shocked to find another man there in M. St. Clair's stead. The man was considerably younger and quite tall in contrast to Hércule.

"Oh, hello," Maggie said, hesitating. "I, uh, was looking for M. Hércule St. Clair. Is he not here?"

"No," the man said, eyeing her keenly.

"Will he be back soon?" she asked.

"That I cannot say," the man responded. His manner seemed circumspect. Maggie wished he would say more about Hércule's whereabouts, but she didn't dare ask. She couldn't tell anyone her real purpose in coming to the shop.

"Oh," she said, afraid that her disappointment showed. "Please tell him that Maggie Forsythe was here to see him. He knows how to contact me."

"I will surely do that," the man said noting her name on a pad.

Maggie left quickly, clutching the bag with the chalice to her side. What should she do now? God! This was so scary. She decided to return the chalice to Nick's flat. She quickly replaced the grail in its hiding place. She was about to head out to do some shopping when her cell phone buzzed in her pocket. A woman's voice introduced herself as Thérèse de Beaufort. "Who?" Maggie asked. "How did you get my number?" She was about to hang up when the speaker mentioned Hércule St. Clair. "Yes," Maggie said. "I know him. Did he ask you to call me?"

The woman said she could not talk longer on the phone, but she would like to meet Maggie in an hour near Les Invalides. Maggie hesitated, but she agreed. She had to see what this was about. Again, she took the chalice with her, hoping that this might be a way to get it back to Hércule. Maggie left a message on Nick's cell saying that she might be late.

Arriving at 3:45 according to the instructions, Maggie waited for close to half an hour on a bench outside the dome over Napoleon's tomb. The garden was in bloom. Normally, she would have enjoyed this, but today she was too nervous waiting for she knew not what. At 4:30, a slim woman with curly dark hair swept back from her face with a tortoise shell band walked casually toward her and seated herself at the other end of the bench. The woman looked to be in her thirties. She fumbled in her bag, searching among its contents. She turned to Maggie. "*Je cherche une cigarette. Avez-vous en?*" She asked.

Maggie shook her head and shrugged apologetically. "*Non. Je ne fume pas.*"

"*Ah. C'est la guerre!* They say it is better for one's health not to smoke, but it relaxes me." Then she asked, "Are you waiting for someone?"

Maggie nodded. "*Oui.*"

"*Est-ce* Thérèse de Beaufort?"

Maggie wondered if she should respond. She had no clue as to who this woman was. She waited, saying nothing.

"*C'est moi.* I am Thérèse de Beaufort." The woman held out her hand. She looked intently at Maggie through cool brown eyes. Her expression was calm and serious. Still, Maggie hesitated.

"You do not trust me? This is not surprising. However, we hope to be able to reconnect you with Hércule St. Clair very soon. Someone has demanded to see the chalice and now it is missing. We must be very careful."

Maggie asked, "Who do you mean when you say *we*?"

The woman slipped back into French. "*Je me suis une membre du Prieuré de Sion. La coupe est très importante à notre organization.*"

What was that? Maggie hadn't caught the name. Puzzled, she asked, "A member of what organization?"

"*Le Prieuré de Sion.* The Priory of Sion." Thérèse hurried on. "The details are not important for you to know. We need to find the Sion Grail. You were recently in the shop of St. Clair et fils. Do you know anything about its whereabouts?"

"*Moi?*" Maggie shivered and shook her head, "No. I only came to M. St. Clair's shop to investigate whether my mother was related to the Paris St. Clairs."

"Hmm," Thérèse muttered. "I thought perhaps Hércule may have talked with you about it. You have a record of my cell phone number from my previous call. If you hear anything from Hércule, please call me. Meanwhile, we will keep our eyes out for your safety. I must go." She rose from the bench, gave Maggie a slow, formal nod, turned, and walked quickly away. Only her scent remained, hanging in the humid air. L'Air du Temps.

Where had she smelled it before? Maggie wondered. But she was so relieved that this woman had not questioned the contents of her bag, she didn't pursue the memory. Oh, God! Why was she carrying this valuable thing around in broad daylight? And why hadn't she asked the woman about Hércule? And why did this woman say "they" would be keeping an eye out for her safety? This was getting scarier by the minute.

The Priory of Sion. What in the world was that? Had Hércule mentioned that? Maggie wasn't even sure what a priory was, but it sounded religious. She hoped Nick would know. She had to talk with Nick. She pulled out her cell phone and dialed his. No answer. Darn! Typical Nick. She decided to go back to his apartment. If he wasn't there, at least she could do some research on his computer.

Maggie let herself in with the key Nick had given her. She shrugged off her jacket and dropped it on the one straight-backed chair. What a stressful afternoon! Maggie sighed. She replaced the chalice in the safe, locking it again with the key they had hidden in the medicine cabinet. Tired from the stress of the day, she wandered into Nick's tiny kitchen where she found an open bottle of Chablis in his refrigerator. She didn't really like Chablis, but she needed to relax. She poured the wine in a water glass before opening his computer to research the Priory of Sion.

In Google, she read, "The Priory of Sion, a secret society begun in 1188, was formed to promote and protect a royal family line that claims to be descended from the first Frankish kings—the Merovingians, a dynasty founded in 417 CE, not long after the gospels of the Bible were written. The family ruled parts of France and Germany from the fifth to the mid-eighth century."

Maggie remembered her father's caution before she left. He'd said something about a line of kings. Could this be what he meant? That sounds pretty far-fetched.

She read, fascinated. "According to legend, the Merovingians were occult adepts who were capable of some of the same feats as Merlin. Coincidentally, they held sway in France at approximately the same time as another legend—when King Arthur and his Court were ruling England and Arthur's knights were off on jaunts seeking the Holy Grail."

Maggie puzzled over this. She said aloud, "But Merlin and King Arthur weren't real, they were just stories, weren't they?"

She wondered if there could have been an ancient British king who was a model for those legends. She thought, well, when it's that far back, maybe the legend lives on without the proof of actual history.

Maggie read on. "The Merovingian kings each had an unusual birthmark—a red cross over the heart or between the shoulder blades." Maggie pulled out her T-shirt and checked her left breast. Surprised, she saw a light trace of red there that she'd never noticed before. Then she remembered the red *X* Nick pointed out on the medieval tapestries at the Musée Cluny.

CHAPTER NINETEEN

Triste Tryst

"HI, MAGGS." NICK'S warm friendly voice broke through her concentration. "What's up?"

Startled, Maggie jumped and turned. "I didn't hear you come in. You scared me. I hate that!" She rose and punched Nick in the arm. "Don't do that to me!"

Nick laughed. "I didn't know you'd be here. I worried when I didn't hear from you."

"I left a message on your cell. Oh, Nick. What a day!"

"Me too. You tell first." Nick offered.

Maggie began, "This afternoon I met a woman who is connected with M. St. Clair. She said she was a member of the *Prieuré de Sion*." Maggie pronounced the name slowly in French, and then added in English, "The Priory of Sion. Have you heard of it? I was researching it on your computer. Apparently it's an ancient secret organization descended from a line of French kings who were eventually deposed by the Avignon pope."

Nick commented. "You know back then there were Popes in Rome and in Avignon, France vying to control the Catholic Church. Obviously, the Romans won."

"The Priory of Sion," Nick repeated the name several times. "I know that from somewhere." A few moments later, he said, "I've got it. I read a book about it years back. It's starting to come back to me—something to do with a really wild theory about Christ and Mary Magdalene being married." Nick paused. "And then, of course, it was in *The Da Vinci Code*. Why?"

"Oh, of course, I should have remembered that."

"Are you okay?" Nick asked.

"Yes, I'm fine. But it was kind of frightening."

"I'll be the gallant host and make cocktails. My afternoon was weird too."

Maggie stood. Nick kissed her on each cheek and pulled back slightly to look at her. "You're glowing."

Maggie smiled. "It must be because I find this information so fascinating." She went back to the computer, and Nick looked over her shoulder. "A familiar name at last! Charlemagne, the Holy Roman Emperor. The kings that followed the Merovingians were named after him. They were called Carolingians. All those *Ingians* will get to you after a while," Maggie said laughing.

"French *Injuns*!" Nick laughed. "Is there any more?"

"A bit," Maggie continued reading from the computer screen. "While the descendants of Merovée no longer held the governmental reins, throughout the centuries that followed, the Priory of Sion continued to have power, money, and influence. Wow! I guess! Leonardo da Vinci, Victor Hugo, Claude Debussy, and Jean Cocteau are said to have headed the secret society. Though the original purpose of the Priory was to return descendants of the Merovingians to the French throne, they were never successful."

Nick stepped into the kitchen and came back with two water glasses. He tapped Maggie on the shoulder. "Ready for a little relief, *Mademoiselle de Research*?"

"Well, what has my gallant host prepared?" Maggie asked as she rose from the computer.

Nick moved to the sofa covered in faded floral tapestry. He smoothed the covering. "Please do sit down, Mademoiselle. I have made you a very un-French cocktail, and I have much to tell you." He handed one glass to Maggie and settled on the sofa next to her.

Maggie took a sip. "Hey, this isn't water."

"No, it's a regular old US of A martini. I didn't have the *correct* glasses. Nor did I have any olives."

Maggie gave Nick a mock grimace as she clinked his glass. She listened to Nick's story of his day and then, as she relaxed with her drink, she shared her story of the meeting with the woman named Thérèse de Beaufort.

"Nick, remember the red *X*s you pointed out on the medieval tapestries at the Cluny?" Maggie asked. "Do you think there could be a connection between the Merovingians, the Cathars, and Mary Magdalene? I wondered about the Christ and Mary Magdalene connection to the tapestries when we were there, but it wasn't clear enough in my head to speak of it."

"It's hard to know," Nick said, "because the Cathars existed about five hundred years after the Merovingians."

Maggie mused, "I wonder what the Priory does currently. Obviously, there isn't any French throne to recapture now."

"Well," Nick commented, "if the members have wealth and influence, I'll bet they have other political agendas. Those people always do."

"Isn't this exciting, Nick? I'm so glad you're here with me on this trip. I don't know what I'd do without you—un-French as you are." Maggie reached over and hugged Nick.

"I wouldn't want to be here without you, either. In fact, my other vacations seem pretty boring compared to this," Nick laughed.

"Thérèse said the Priory is concerned about our chalice," Maggie said. "I took it with me to St. Clair et fils today and then again when I went to meet Thérèse in hopes that I could find Hércule and return it to him. But once there, I didn't dare give it to the person at the shop or to Thérèse. I didn't trust them."

"You are one nervy woman! I wouldn't have removed it from the safe."

"I know. But it doesn't sound as if they know that I have it. How would she know? Yet why would she contact me if she didn't? Maybe they've been following me because someone saw me at the shop?" She looked to Nick, worried. "It's all a bit strange. The organization that Dan Brown wrote about in *The Da Vinci Code* seemed carnally evil. I can't imagine M. St. Clair being involved in something like that. Of course, as fiction, he could have made the Priory into anything he wanted."

Nick said, "An evil organization does make a more interesting story. But for now, should we check and see how our chalice is? Oh, that's right, you had it out already today."

"I never opened the covering. I can hardly wait to hold it again. There's something so phenomenal about it." They took the chalice from its hiding place.

"Here," Nick said as he carefully unwrapped the golden object and handed it to Maggie. He watched her lift it close to her face. He said, "You know, it's as if it should belong to you, Maggie. It fits with you. You're even more radiant when that chalice is in your hands."

"Do you think so? Thanks, Nick." Touching the chalice again gave Maggie a special sensation. All her fears disappeared, replaced by a feeling of sublime happiness. She didn't understand how an object could bring such a feeling, but for now she just wanted to revel in it.

"Shall we christen it?" Nick moved to his improvised wine rack and pulled out his oldest and most expensive red.

Excited, Maggie nodded her agreement. She set the chalice down. When the cork popped, she fell back in a dramatic swoon. Nick rinsed the chalice and wiped it clean. He filled it to its golden rim. "You first, Madame." He thrust the chalice into Maggie's hands. She breathed in the fragrance of the wine, took a large gulp, swirled it around her mouth, and let it gently slide into her throat. She thought of orange blossoms, cinnamon, and deep dark caverns. She handed it to Nick, and he took a sip from edge where her lips had been.

"Wait," he said. "I think we need to do a little service now, a little incantation—something to show our sincerity in our role as the new stewards of this honored vessel." Nick grabbed four individual candles from his stash in the small kitchenette and stationed them in the four corners of the room, lighting each as he went. Maggie, now seated cradling the grail, watched Nick's movements with quiet amusement.

Nick lit the three-armed candelabra that sat on his dining table and placed it firmly in front of Maggie. "Seven," he said. "That's a very holy number." He moved to the couch and, with a flourish, pulled off the paisley shawl that was draped over the back. "Rise, ye inheritor—if temporary—of the St. Clair grail." Nick intoned in a deep serious voice.

Maggie doubled over in controlled silent giggles that occasionally burst out in little coughs and squeaks through her nose.

"Rise, I say!"

Maggie stood. Nick pulled the paisley shawl over both their heads, making a tent. He pointed to her right hand. "You have to be a tent pole." She moved the chalice to her left hand, and Nick's right hand circled hers over the stem. Maggie raised her right arm to lift a corner of the shawl.

Nick's voice was intimate as he said, "This is *our* treasure, Maggs." Then he stood slightly apart from her and continued in a solemn voice, "Repeat after me. Under the powers vested in us as the caretakers of this valued object, we vow to protect it from evil influences and cursed hands and to serve it only with noble deeds."

Maggie repeated Nick's words.

"In partnership in this worthy cause, I, Nicholas Payne, swear my allegiance to Mary Magdalena Forsythe and her welfare."

Maggie bowed to Nick. "And I, Mary Magdalena Forsythe, swear my allegiance to Nicholas Payne and his welfare and the welfare of this holy object."

Nick bowed to Maggie.

"Now, we drink together." Nick lifted the vessel to each of their lips in turn. Eyes meeting, they drank until the cup was empty. Nick took the chalice from Maggie, set it down, and pulled Maggie into an embrace. He kissed her gently on the lips and then deeply and passionately. "This is a moment we'll remember," he whispered. The tent-shawl crumpled to the floor.

Maggie had always felt close to Nick, and she'd valued their intimate friendship since it began two years ago. But tonight being here with Nick felt more special than she could have imagined. Knowing she could always trust and rely on him—sharing this secret—being here in Paris together with him . . . all felt right. She returned Nick's kiss joyfully. In her head, she began to hear ethereal and haunting music. Nick lifted her up in the air, and they danced around the room, wafted along by buoyancy that seemed within and yet outside of them.

Nick was different tonight—the most free she had ever seen him—ready to *fly to the moon*, like the song playing in her head. As Nick whirled her around, she asked, "Do you have gossamer wings?"

"What?" Nick stopped in midair and almost dropped her. "Gossamer wings? What are you saying?"

Maggie laughed. "Nothing. Words just came into my head from an old song my parents used to sing. I love this. Don't stop."

When they finally stopped, Nick said, "Stay with me tonight. Please. You can keep watch over the chalice, and I'll keep watch over you." He held both her hands in his.

The wine and the twirling had made her dizzy. Maggie hesitated. Should she stay? She wanted to stay. She was having such fun. The chalice's bitter metallic aftertaste lingered in her mouth. Maggie began to wonder if it were folly to drink from this valuable family treasure. Had they honored or desecrated the chalice by drinking from it?

She enjoyed Nick's warmth and strength so close to her. Then suddenly it was more than just dancing to music playing in their heads. She was on the sofa. Nick was kissing her, and she felt passion that she hadn't felt before. It felt wonderful and natural. Maggie thought about resisting for a second or two, but she wanted this. She wanted it now. There was no question.

Their bodies gyrated to the tunes that played in their heads: fast, furious, hungry. For her it was a tango, the languid steps, the swaying and connecting, legs curved around each other, with no missed beats. Maggie wondered how it was for Nick. What song was he listening to? Whatever it was, she loved moving to his music.

In her ecstasy of shuddering release, Maggie instinctively knew she had come. Closely after, as she felt goose bumps on Nick's back and then felt him sigh, relax, and lean back, she looked down and saw that some of the wetness running down her thighs was red. Blood! Then it dawned on her that her hymen must have broken when she felt that sharp pain. At last! Her celibacy was over! With Nick. And she hadn't hesitated or even considered for a moment keeping herself for that mythical special someone as she'd always done before. Had the wine dulled her senses? They hadn't drunk much, but it was from the St. Clair chalice—the holy, the ancient, and the beautiful. Did this mean she was bound to Nick through this act? As lovely as their joining had been, she also felt confused.

Nick roused himself and moved his fingers down her body. "You are fantastic!" He grabbed a handkerchief and wiped her gently. "Here, let me . . . Hey, you're bleeding. God, I'm so sorry. I didn't mean to hurt you. I must've gotten too carried away."

Maggie grabbed his hand and took the handkerchief. "No, it's okay. I'm fine." I'm just embarrassed to tell you that this is my first time." She put her face in her hands, and she could smell the slightly sweet odor of their lovemaking on her hands.

Nick said, "Wow! And you chose me? That's wonderful news. You were great—you *are* great. I can't tell you how much this means to me." He pulled her face up to his and kissed it.

She let him kiss away her tears, but her earlier uncertainty nagged her. She'd waited all these years for just the right man, and it turned out to be Nick. She loved Nick. He was, in some ways, the ideal man—gentle, sensitive, caring. She knew instinctively that he loved her, without his ever having told her. It had been a spectacular experience that she could relish for some time, but she couldn't convince herself that this was to be her only love. Something felt missing. A voice within her argued: "You selfish child. You rotten spoiled infant. This is a wonderful man!" Maggie knew the voice spoke truth, but she wasn't sure it was her truth. It was just too soon to know if Nick would be her great love. These thoughts were making her feel guilty. Now, she just wanted to sleep and not think anymore.

They awoke to a rumbling sound that came from below. The floor and the bed began to shake.

"What's that?" Frightened, Maggie sat up and looked at Nick.

Nick rubbed his eyes. "Don't know. New tenants moved in downstairs—a couple of guys. I met them yesterday. I wanted to tell you about them last night, but somehow I got distracted." Nick smiled at Maggie.

Maggie's frown made Nick laugh again. "Are you worried that they heard us? Don't worry. This is Paris," he whispered.

As she glanced around the room, Maggie spotted the chalice sitting right in the open on Nick's desk where they had abandoned it the night before as desire overwhelmed them. Maggie leaped from the bed and ran to it. She held it tightly between both hands. "Oh, Nick, I can't believe we left this out!"

Nick took the vessel from her, rinsed and dried it, and began wrapping it carefully. Maggie picked up her discarded clothing and began dressing. When Nick had finished, they placed their treasure back in its hiding spot.

"How do you feel? Great, wasn't it? It was for me." He looked at her, unsure.

Maggie looked down at her bare feet. "Yes. It was great. But I felt possessed—swept up into something that maybe shouldn't have happened. I mean," she paused. "You're my friend, but . . . I haven't thought about you exactly that way." She stopped. She didn't want to say anything that might hurt Nick's feelings. He would be vulnerable now.

"I know. Everything feels different in Paris. Maybe it's Paris working her magic on us. Or maybe it's the grail. Whatever. I'm grateful." He moved toward Maggie to kiss her and reassure her.

"It was very special, Nick. You were so funny during that ceremony."

"You made a vow. We both did."

Maggie put the back of her hand to her forehead. "I remember. That was a crazy thing to do."

Vows. She needed time to process this. Maggie reached for her shoes and slipped them on. "I've got to run, Nick." She put her arms around Nick's neck and kissed him. She whispered in his ear, "Thanks, Nick. You're so . . . so special to me."

"Can't you stay? What's the rush? We could just relax for a while, cuddle, you know, nothing—ah—intense." Nick looked confused.

Maggie moved to the door. "I'm sorry, Nick. That sounds nice, but the chalice has to be my first concern. I need to find Hércule and find out what to do with this awesome thing," she said.

"Got it," Nick said. "But tonight . . . I'll see you tonight, won't I?" He pleaded. "We'll just pick up from here." She heard the false brightness in his voice. Maggie waved good-bye. She wanted to cry.

CHAPTER TWENTY

An Unexpected Trip

THE HOTEL PHONE rang. Maggie hoped it would be Nick. She owed him an explanation for her abrupt departure that morning. To her surprise, it was Henri Diamond. "Oh, Henri," she said, stalling as her mind searched, then remembered, that they'd exchanged phone numbers the day they'd met at Chartres.

After the usual opening pleasantries, Henri said, "I am driving south to visit a relative near Aix-en-Provence tomorrow morning. If you don't have other plans, I wonder if you and your friend Nick would like to accompany me. Driving alone for such a distance is boring for me, and I'd like to show you the cave we discussed—the one where, according to legend, Mary Magdalene lived for thirty years and where she died. Do you remember?"

Maggie's heart pounded. She struggled for breath, and then blurted out "Yes!"

"Did I hear a yes? Would you join me?"

"I'm so excited; I couldn't get the word out. Yes! I would love to go. I'm pleased that you remember me from Chartres. What time do you plan to leave?"

"As early as we can arrange."

Nick, she thought. She needed to push her mind away from last night. "Yes. I'll see if Nick can go. He's working on a big project that has rather strict deadlines. Could we put the trip off for a couple days?" Maggie asked.

"Unfortunately, I can't do that. I have to return to Paris for business in three or four days, but you may stay on longer. I plan a short visit *avec ma cousine* in Aix. I have not seen her for quite some time. It will take us more than a day to get there by auto. There is room for four if you have others you might wish to invite."

Maggie smiled. What luck it was having met this friendly man. Henri offered to pick her up at 9:00 AM the following morning.

Maggie placed the phone down. She wondered if Nick would be able to come. He was so busy with his project. She hoped he could, because although she enjoyed Henri, she wasn't sure she wanted to travel all that way alone with him.

She dialed. "Nick. Something extraordinary has happened."

"Yeah, I know—last night."

"Right. It was a great evening—very special." She paused to let that sink in. "But I want to talk about something else. You remember Henri Diamond? He's invited us to drive with him down to Provence tomorrow. He's going to show me the cave where Mary Magdalene is said to have lived in the first century. Isn't that marvelous?"

"Well, yeah. I guess so. It's interesting that the little guy came through right away with his offer. But, Maggie, I can't go tomorrow. I made these appointments before I left the States, and these people are very difficult to get to see. And by the end of the week, I have to get my first draft off to California. I can't make that deadline and go with you."

"Can't you get that postponed? This is such a great opportunity."

"Maggie, I want to come with you. I can't think of anything I'd rather do with my time. You know that. And yes, it's a great opportunity for you to go with Henri, since he appears to have a lot of historical expertise, but I just can't do it this week. If you can get Henri to postpone it a week or even for three or four days, I could do it."

"He can't, Nick. I asked him if the trip could be postponed, and he said no. I want to share this with you."

"Well, I don't think you should go alone with that funny old buzzard, but I just don't see how I can go," Nick sighed.

Maggie laughed. "Henri is just a sweet older man. He's got to be in his fifties or maybe even his sixties. God, Nick, I am a grown woman. I'm capable of handling myself."

Nick sounded a bit sheepish. "Yeah, I know, but if I were there . . . I just don't like you being alone with him. Guys in their fifties still have blood running through their veins, and you're a very attractive woman."

"I don't believe this!"

"I . . . ah . . . I really don't think you should go alone with the medieval munchkin."

"He's harmless. I like him. Well, if you think I shouldn't be alone with him, who else could I invite?"

Nick was silent for a few moments. "I don't know," he said.

"I could ask Israel Hawkins. He'd be a real asset to the trip with his knowledge of French history."

"No, I don't like that idea either. I could tell he liked you when we had drinks together the other night."

"Oh, come on Nick! You can't be against everyone that's pleasant to me."

"Okay," Nick finally said, "I'm not nuts about the idea of you going with him either, but he strikes me as the more respectable of the two, and he did mention to me that he was familiar with the French Black Madonnas."

"Black Madonnas—gosh! They are one of my main reasons for coming here. I've never asked Israel if he knows anything about them. If he does, it would be ideal. Maybe we could stop and see some on our way. What a great idea, Nick. And because we're going to an ancient historical place, it just might interest him. If you're worried about Henri, Israel can be my chaperone." Maggie smiled to herself. Nick was brilliant.

Nick asked, "What about the chalice? Have you thought about that? What if Hércule or that Thérèse person tries to contact you? They don't even know I exist, do they?"

"Oh, shoot! I didn't even think about that. I'll try again to reach Hércule to tell him about the trip and that the chalice is safe, but he wasn't there yesterday." Maggie shook her head. "What if I can't get hold of him? Nick, what do you think I should do? Should I go? Should I stay here and wait?"

"This is a real opportunity, Maggie. You should go. I'll watch over the chalice. You know I'll do anything for you," Nick said. "We made a vow to each other and to the chalice last night, remember? I consider it partly mine now."

Maggie sighed in relief. "Thanks, Nick. I know you can't risk sacrificing your new position to satisfy my obsession about Mary Magdalene. I couldn't possibly do this without your help. I need someone I can trust to take care of our treasure."

"Yeah, I know, but you be careful." His voice sounded stern.

Maggie grimaced. Nick had never been stern with her before. His attitude was probably a downside of their having made love. Even though it had been a lovely moment between them, she knew that after sex, men often got possessive. She understood Nick's disappointment, but resented his wanting to control.

"Uh huh," Maggie said. "Don't worry. Everything will be okay. I promise."

CHAPTER TWENTY-ONE

Raining Women

I SRAEL FELT AT loose ends. He had a disturbing feeling that he was waiting for something to happen. He had not been writing, other than notes he had taken on the individuals he watched from his viewing spot at various Paris cafés. He couldn't quite get into anything constructive. He'd convinced himself that he was taking some time to just *be* here. But a part of him felt he needed to accomplish something—the production command had been with him since childhood. Sometimes he wondered if he'd ever be free of it.

Lately all he could think of was the radiant redhead he'd met. She had a certain "*Je ne sais quoi*" that baffled and intrigued him. She had spirit and pluck. Yet there was also the tenderness she'd shown him on the plane.

The phone interrupted his thoughts. "Hawkins," he said into the receiver.

"Hi, Hawkins! What are you up to? Want to tramp over to les Halles for some lunch and people watching? I saw the most fantastic artist over there yesterday. He does colored chalk drawings on the sidewalk that you'd swear are as good as Chagall's. And then there's the fire-eater. We could bring hotdogs and cook on his breath."

Israel sighed. Sandy was indefatigable. Her onslaught of calls made even the sound of her voice fatiguing. "I'm sorry, Sandy. I'm not up for it today. Not feeling too great."

"Maybe I should just come over there and pick up your spirits," she hinted in a sultry voice.

Israel laughed. "Hmmm. That's a tough one, Sandy. I appreciate the offer, but not today."

"I'm going to call you every couple hours until you say yes," Sandy warned.

He knew she was as good as her word. This was her third call today, and yesterday she had called five times, until he'd finally weakened. They'd had lunch together followed by a walk along the Champs-Élysées. What had he started? "Ciao, Sandy," he said hoping he was through with her for the day.

"*À bientôt!*" she said cheerily.

He hung up the phone, pulled a beer out of his little refrigerator, and sprawled on the bed.

Sandy exhausted him—but not Maggie. Not with the emotional connection that he felt when he was with her. She was as old a soul as he. He could feel that. Perhaps they had shared a previous life? There must be something that was creating this link. Was it her kindness? Or her stunning looks? She wasn't beautiful in a traditional sense, but her coloring was striking, and there was a kind of effervescence about her that brightened her surroundings. In the short moments they'd been together, his life had felt brighter.

Women. He ought to be a connoisseur by now. In his maudlin mood, Israel pondered his past. He'd had other relationships after the eclipse of his marriage. The sky had darkened for about three years after the divorce, but Israel found that with virtually no effort on his part, women seemed to come to him—wherever he was—in his classes, or even in the supermarket. If he stopped for a drink at a bar, he was never the lonely patron for long.

One night, when he was surrounded by a group of attractive women, he thought of the little black-and-white Scottie magnets his father had given him as a child. The magnets could pick up a whole slew of his mother's sewing pins from the floor. He laughed, remembering.

Israel sometimes wondered if this would continue as he aged. His men friends thought he was incredibly lucky, but lately he felt he didn't want to attract just any woman who came his way. He'd begun to see a pattern in his life that was leading him to experience exactly the opposite of what he really desired. It happened slowly, a little at a time. But he began to realize that the things he held most dear had quietly slipped away.

His flirtations had been only one of the reasons his marriage failed, but they surely hadn't helped it survive. Then his illness came, after the divorce, after he left Michigan, after he'd struggled to write his first book. Why did his body have to give him trouble when he was embarking on a new venture? It wasn't fair. But thankfully, in the end, the illness didn't take his life. However, it was frightening, painful, and threatening, especially for someone who had never been ill, except in childhood when he'd had the chicken pox. The cancer had not spread. But the disease had been there in his body. It was telling him to beware—to pay attention to his life—to look beyond, to see what he had neglected.

As he mused, a vision appeared. Israel saw a furrowed field before him. Somehow he knew it was unseeded and, at the same time, that new seeds would not be necessary, because despite his failures, the original seed within him held the memory of who he was, his relationship with the creative forces in the world, and his role in it. He *could* change the patterns of his past.

The phone rang, interrupting his thoughts. Had it been two hours already? How long could he keep holding Sandy off? He picked up the phone. Without listening, he snapped, "No, I told you I couldn't. I need to rest." He hung up.

A few minutes later, the phone rang again. "What now?" Israel said harshly. Then he heard Maggie's voice cautiously inquiring as to what he meant. "Oh, God! I'm sorry. I was rude. Please accept my apologies. I thought it was someone else—someone who's been bugging me all day. I'm in a foul mood."

Three minutes later, Israel hung up the phone, leaned back, and thought: "What luck!" The tempting Maggie of the rust tresses, the aquamarine eyes, and the elusive spirit was offering him the opportunity to drive south to Provence. This would give him a respite from Sandy. Maggie said that she thought he'd be interested in the historical aspects of the trip. Did he want to go? Of course he did. Amazing how things happened.

The threesome left early the next morning. When they picked Israel up, he smiled broadly at Maggie, assuring her that he was delighted to be invited on this trip. In fact, he could hardly stop smiling about this bit of luck that had occurred.

CHAPTER TWENTY-TWO

Another Black Madonna

MAGGIE HAD TRIED to get in touch with Hércule, but she was told that it might be a day or two before he could return her call.

Henri Diamond was full of interesting historical tidbits about the areas they passed through. They stopped for lunch at Dijon, and he led them past the Grey Poupon, the famous mustard shop, its windows and shelves filled with antique crockery and glass mustard pots, all labeled with the Grey Poupon name. They visited the *vielle ville* briefly. There, they walked to the Palace of the Dukes of Burgundy, who reigned for over one hundred years until the late 1400s. The palace, designed in a similar semi-circular fashion by the same architect who planned Louis XIV's auspicious Palace of Versailles, disappointed Maggie, because its courtyard was now a busy street filled with intruding tourist buses. "Here we have beauty ruined by progress," she complained.

They stopped for the night in Lyon, finding an inexpensive pension in a residential area with three available rooms. "Lyon is sometimes known as 'the Chicago of France' because it is the second largest city in France," Henri told them over dinner. He said Lyon reminded him of World War II because the city was the center of the French resistance to Hitler's invasion. Then, tears welling in his eyes, Henri told them how, as an infant, he was taken from his Jewish parents' home in Lyon to a rural village where he was hidden, schooled, and sheltered by Protestant Huguenot families. "Without them, I wouldn't be here with you now," he murmured.

The power of Henri's childhood memories had not been lost on Maggie. She was moved by the older man's emotional story, and she wondered if that had been the beginning of his interest in early Christian history.

The following day, after their *petit dejeuner*, Henri Diamond insisted that they stop for a few minutes at a cathedral on their way out of town. "I have a surprise for you Mlle. Mary Magdalena" was all that he would say. A raft of gargoyles watched from above as they entered the church. Once inside, it took only a few minutes for Maggie to spot the surprise. In its own area, set apart from the nave of the church was a small Madonna carved from dark wood. The Black Madonna was dressed in an elaborate golden-filigreed gown, much like the Chartres Madonna. However, this Black Madonna was smaller in size and less prominently placed.

Henri watched Maggie's reaction. He was beaming when Maggie looked back at him. "I knew you would like to see this," he said. "Remember, that is where I saw you first—in front of the Chartres Black Madonna."

Maggie put her arm around his waist and hugged him. "I love it! You must be a mind reader. I haven't even told you that part of the reason I'm here in France is to research the Black Madonnas. How did you know?"

Henri said, "Henri Diamond did not know that. He just made the connection with your name. As I mentioned at Chartres, the Black Madonnas have evolved into Christianity from the ancient goddess worship of Isis by the Egyptians. There are some who believe that before Mary Magdalene came to France, she went to Alexandria with Joseph of Arimathea. Perhaps that is where they picked up the Egyptian serving girl called Sarah who came with them to the Marseille area. Many of your Christian practices originated in earlier pagan ceremonies. The church was afraid to change people's beliefs for fear that they might lose their new followers."

Israel chimed in, "Some considered Isis a fertility goddess. Perhaps that interpretation extended to the Black Madonna. Both represent the sacred feminine spirit."

"Really," Maggie commented. The word "fertility" set her mind to worrying about her love session with Nick, but she didn't let it show. "Does this tie back to the Cathars?" she calmly asked Henri.

"*Oui, bien sûr,*" added Henri. "The Cathars believed that Christ and Mary Magdalene were married partners, and the Black Madonna came to symbolize Mary Magdalene with Christ's child. Many still believe that. Of course, the church did not interpret the statues that way."

"It's a little like the Cinderella story," Israel said. "The besmirched maiden (Mary Magdalene) is loved by the prince (Jesus, the Christ), despite the evil stepmother's efforts."

"Then who is the evil stepmother?" Maggie asked.

Israel laughed, "The Catholic clerics — the men in skirts."

CHAPTER TWENTY-THREE

The Magdalen Cave

TALL, SMOOTH-BARKED, PLANE trees lined the boulevards in Aix-en-Provence. After stopping for lunch, they drove east via a freeway until they came to St. Maximime. They turned off and entered a small village with narrow streets and a circular center in the main village square. The change from the freeway to the ancient village was dramatic.

Henri led Maggie and Israel first to the eleventh-century church dedicated to Ste. Mary Magdalene. The exterior of the drab gray church was not impressive. Inside, however, Maggie found a magnificent carved wooden pulpit, called "*La chaire,*" and a large wooden plaque which stated as its title, "*Brève histoire et traditions Provençals,*" which told the legend of Mary Magdalene's arrival and stay in Provence. The man named Maximime, who eventually became the Saint Maximime of the town's name, had, according to the legend, come to France with her. He had preached in the village. Perhaps they both had preached here. But when Mary Magdalene was ready to die, she found her way down the mountain to his side in this village and died in his arms.

A reliquary in the church claimed to hold Mary Madeleine's bones. "Look," Maggie said to Israel. "They call her Mary Madeleine. That's

French for Magdalene. My parents certainly could have done better by me in the names department. Madeleine sounds much more sophisticated."

"Do you want us to start calling you Madeleine now?" Israel teased.

Maggie laughed. Israel was definitely fun.

In a nook carved out alongside the stairs leading to the crypt was a reclining statue of Mary Magdalene. A bouquet of fresh flowers had been placed in her arms. Maggie leaned over and sniffed their fragrance, but Henri motioned her back up into the center of the church. "*Voilà la Gloire,*" he said, pointing to the area behind the high altar and in front of the windows in the nave. High above the earthly functions of the church was the *Gloire*, a carved golden sculpture of multiple angels welcoming Mary Magdalene through the sun's rays into heaven.

Maggie held her breath. "Oh my god! What a wonderful word—*gloire*. Her rapture must have been glorious—truly glorious. And you know, that was my mother's name—Glory. Maybe she has a connection here, too."

Israel came up behind her and put his arms gently around her shoulders. They stood looking at the *Gloire* together saying nothing. A blindly happy feeling swept over Maggie. There was something here that she knew and yet didn't know. Was Israel a part of this? It didn't matter. The moment was perfect.

Henri broke the silence, saying, "*Alors, mes enfants,* this is just your appetizer. The *pièce de résistance* lies yet ahead."

They headed south into the country and, after a fifteen-minute drive, parked at the foot of a stone-faced mountain. A winding path led up the hill from the parking lot where a half-dozen cars were parked.

Henri announced, "*Maintenant, nous sommes dans la Ste. Baume.*" Israel asked what he meant. "The Sainte Baume Massif is the southernmost mountain range of the Haute Provence. This is where Mary Magdalene came as a refugee from her tormentors in Palestine, where anyone connected to the man some considered to be the Messiah was in great danger. Now you will see the cave where Mary Magdalene is said to have made her home for thirty years before she died."

Maggie felt her anticipation rise. Her veins felt full of tiny bubbles of energy ready to be released.

"Henri Diamond will remain here. He is not up to that steep a climb today," Henri announced. Maggie tried to cajole him into joining them, but he was resolute in his intent to relax after his drive and leave the ascent to Maggie and Israel. Maggie nudged Israel as they started off. She asked slyly, "Is Israel Hawkins up to this climb?"

Israel looked at her curiously. "I don't get it."

"Henri Diamond is not climbing today," she repeated.

Israel laughed, "Yes, Israel Hawkins is ready for the challenge. And is Mary *Madeleine* Forsythe up to the climb?"

Maggie nodded happily.

The steepness of the ascent and their need to pay attention to their new surroundings quickly ended their third-person chat. The trail wound through ancient primeval woods. "I wouldn't expect forests here to differ much from those in the US," Maggie commented to Israel, panting slightly from the climb. "But the plants in this wood are very different." Israel agreed.

White and yellow bells of paper-narcissus and fragrant purple flowering grape hyacinths vied for space among the fern-laced depths of the lush wooded floor. In every sunny space, a yellow dwarf iris appeared. Vines lazily, but possessively, invaded the branches of tall, gnarled trees.

The steep climb flattened at intervals. Maggie and Israel stopped to catch their breath when they came upon each coved wooden prayer vigil. Here, apparently, pilgrims often stopped to rest and ask for holy assistance or perhaps to give thanks that they'd made it this far.

After climbing the first sixty feet, Maggie thought she saw a huge cross carved into the massif's stone face, but as she drew closer, she could see it was a dark stain and not a carving; still, it seemed symbolic. A wooden building hung onto the side of the cliff as though glued there. A monk in a long brown robe strolled on a path near it. "That must be the Dominican monastery Henri mentioned." Israel said, pointing.

"Look. It's Christ and the others who were crucified." Maggie exclaimed. High above them to the left of the monastery, they could now see statuary that seemed to float away from the cliff face. The figures grew more distinct as they climbed, until, after the last row of steps to the entrance gate, directly over their heads, Christ and his fellow sufferers on crosses loomed larger than life.

They passed the crucifixion scene and followed the path to the cave. The front of it had been walled-in with bricks. Small stained glass windows and a heavy oak door had been added to enclose the chapel inside. A gardener busied himself in the small garden outside the entrance.

Once her eyes adjusted to the darkness in the cave, Maggie could see that it was a large, roughly semi-circular expanse of perhaps sixty or seventy feet with an uneven earthen floor. The fungal dampness that permeated the cave was muted by the smell of burning wax from the dozens of candles burning at makeshift altars throughout the room. Two thousand years of burning candles had left waves of soot on the ceiling and walls of the cave.

A veil of sadness descended on Maggie when she entered the cave. Tears came unbidden, without being prompted by any particular thought. Maggie felt as though she had no control over her movements. She was guided first to the ancient fragile looking bones housed in a two-foot-long glass box—perhaps pieces of an arm or a leg—rested on white satin in the gold-rimmed glass reliquary. Could these really be Mary Magdalene's?

Lying on a stone sarcophagus in an excavated lower portion of the cave, Maggie found a stone statue now too broken and chipped to be recognizable. Maggie touched the stones and felt a rush of sympathy for the sculptor. Was this a memorial to the spirit he had felt in the cave?

Toward the center of the cave, a simple white wooden altar had been constructed for the daily services the monks conducted for visitors and penitents. Wooden folding chairs were placed in neat rows in front of the altar. Maggie sat on one of the chairs for several minutes trying to calm her emotions. But she couldn't shake the sadness—it was there upon her—its torpor weighing her down. "Holy Mary, Mother of God, what am I doing here? Why do I feel like this? Why is this so sad? Tell me what this means."

After some contemplative moments, Maggie moved to the other end of the cave. She stood in front of a beautiful sculptured *pietà* of Christ's dead body draped lovingly in Mary Magdalene's arms—the heavenward look on her face of sorrow and disbelief. Nearby, impromptu cardboard altars covered with white cloths and topped with brass candlesticks and bouquets of flowers attested to pilgrims' worship.

Maggie stood at that spot for a long time, tears streaming down her cheeks. She wondered why someone as dedicated as Mary Magdalene was to furthering Christ's teachings would have ended her life alone in a cave. It seemed so ignominious, so self-sacrificing. Even though some say this kind of contemplative life is satisfying, Maggie couldn't quite imagine it being so.

Maggie knew this place was holier than any other she'd ever encountered. She wondered at the power in this cave. She couldn't remember ever feeling so happy, sad, and totally unglued at the same time. Were these strange unstoppable tears grief for the Magdalene's lonely last years? Or were they for the difficult journey in life this woman had chosen? "I wonder if Mary Magdalene had the same feelings about this place two thousand years ago." Maggie mused.

Maggie also wondered if the overwhelming force she felt at this moment was evidence that some time, somewhere, she had known Mary Magdalene and had been a part of her struggle. Could she have lived in those important times? Could she have lived in France before? Perhaps that was the tie to her loving the French language and all things French.

A large white statue of an ecstatic looking Mary Magdalene being hoisted high into the air by two powerful angels drew her. As she moved toward the statue, a high-pitched female voice at her side said, "They say every day the angels lifted her to the top of the mountain so that she could hear the celestial music. Isn't that just lovely?"

Maggie peered through wet eyes at a small, wiry brown-skinned woman of indeterminate age. By the look on her face, the woman seemed to be as enthralled with the cave and its stories as Maggie. Maggie held out a shaky hand. "Yes," Maggie said, "I'm sure she heard celestial music."

The act of speaking brought Maggie a sense of reality. She remembered Israel. She looked around for him, but did not see him. She hadn't meant to ignore him, but her experience in the cave had consumed her. She'd had no sense of time passing. She began to wonder how long she had been there. Though she hated to leave, she felt she could no longer bear the emotional distress of the cave.

Outside, when she was surrounded by the sunshine, the sadness lifted. It left more slowly than it had come, but the memory of it would never leave her. Maggie knew from past experience that tears bring an emotional tension that flirts with the edge of stability and eventually feeds other sadness within. After several seconds of adjusting to the outside light, Maggie noticed Israel sitting on a ledge nearby. He came to her side. She turned to the magnificent view before her. In the valley below she could see miles of farms and varied land in a 180-degree arc, all glistening from the mist that had just lifted. Maggie felt the same way. The sun was erasing the intense and heavy emotion she had felt in the cave. Her voice took on a more secure timbre than she imagined possible when she spoke to Israel, who stood close to her. "Isn't this breathtaking? Anyone could feel at peace here." With the sunshine and the fresh air,

Maggie felt her strength returning. But she wondered if she would ever be exactly the same person again.

"Were you there all the while I was in the cave? I just ignored you, didn't I? Sorry." She put her left hand over her eyes to shield them from the sun. "I must have been really out-of-it."

"I was there—the whole time. But I didn't want to intrude on your experience. It was powerful just watching you. Actually, the cave felt mysteriously, vaguely familiar to me, but I didn't have the same gut reaction to it that you obviously did. In fact, I marveled at your sensitivity. I know there are spirits in this place, but they didn't affect me in the same way." Israel smiled at her sudden happiness. He held his hands out to her. She took them.

Maggie looked up at him and smiled wanly. "Thanks for being here with me. When I was in the cave, I felt this extraordinary sadness, like I had died there, too. And a pulsating energy ran through my body several times. I couldn't shake it off. I don't know why I was so sad. I'm still not quite in control." Maggie dabbed at the corners of her eyes. "The place felt extremely holy to me. I was honored to be here. I can't explain why, but this experience feels like it's a life-changing moment for me—a kind of rapture, even. What do they call that?"

"An epiphany?"

"Yes, an epiphany. It felt like an illuminating discovery that hasn't totally revealed itself to me yet. It sounds strange I know, but I need time to think it through."

They slowly retraced their steps down the steep winding incline. Lost in thought, Maggie had trouble staying on the path. Israel put his arm around her, concerned that she might make a misstep, especially after the intensity of emotion he had witnessed in the cave. Maggie stopped. "I wish I could be alone . . . somewhere . . . on a mountaintop or in a grotto . . . where I could commune with the spirits who guided me here."

Israel moved his hand slowly away from her shoulders. "You only need speak to me when it feels right to do so. If you like, I can move on ahead and leave you to your thoughts." Maggie nodded. She didn't want Israel to feel she was putting him off, but she needed to be alone to process her experience. They would be with Henri Diamond soon enough. "Thanks," she said simply as she watched Israel jog down the trail. He was soon out of sight.

Her head was still full of Mary Magdalene: the presence she had felt; the holiness; the rapture of the *gloire* at the church; imagining the bell-like celestial music; her own rapture—she could still hardly breathe from the sad joy. The memory of the sight of the beautiful *pietà* with the Magdalene cradling Christ's body at the foot of the cross returned to Maggie. Maybe the sadness she felt was Mary Magdalene's sadness at losing Christ. Maybe Mary Magdalene's sadness was so great it had remained in the cave all these years after she died. Or perhaps her spirit returns from time to time to be present again in this place where she suffered? Pilgrims had come here for close to two thousand years to pray and pay homage to this exceptional woman. Could their conjoined energies have made the place as evocative and spiritual as it felt now?

Absorbed in her thoughts, she asked: Could I feel this intensely spiritual if Mary Magdalene had not really been present in this cave? I believe the Provençal legend. It doesn't matter that some may not believe it. In my heart I know that Mary Magdalene was here. Surely, others must have felt that too.

As Maggie rounded the last turn, she could see the parking lot ahead of her. Israel and Henri leaned against the Peugeot, chatting. She was so grateful to Henri for this experience. She ran down the last hundred yards. As she neared, Henri spread his arms out to her.

"Well? What did you think, Mlle. Maggie?"

"Thank you. Thank you so much for bringing me here." Her body was shaking, and her voice wavered for the first time since she left the cave.

"It was a fantastic experience. I have never been in a holier place. I am so grateful that I met you and that you brought me here. I don't know how I can thank you enough. There is something of me here." The tears started again.

Israel handed her his handkerchief. Maggie blew her nose noisily.

Henri said, "I thought you would like this place. It impressed me when I came here six years ago. It is not in most of the guidebooks. It is a wonderful secret, is it not?"

Maggie nodded, wiping her nose and trying to get herself back under control so that she could speak.

"Well," Henri continued. "Shall we be on our way? Perhaps we should think of getting something to eat. That climb does make the stomach desirous, doesn't it?"

CHAPTER TWENTY-FOUR

An Alabaster Jar

TO NICK'S SURPRISE, the day after he visited his new neighbors, Guillaume knocked at his door. "*Bonjour,*" he said, "M. Devereaux enjoyed your company the evening past, and would like you to visit us again. He has something else he would like to show you from his collection."

The invitation was unexpected. Nick had found their rather quick invitation the other night a bit curious too, and he had no sense that either Devereaux or Guillaume had found anything interesting about him, so why this invitation? "Well, when would this be?" He asked.

"Tonight, if your schedule allows—about seven or seven thirty? Is that agreeable?"

Nick paused trying to think of any reason he could not be there. He could think of none. His afternoon meetings would be finished by then. "Yes, I believe I could make that."

"*Bon.*" Guillaume turned, about to leave, and then turned back. "Yes. I want you also to know that I really appreciated you being there last night. At least now someone else can see the way he treats me. He treats me like dirt. I'm his whipping boy, just as I was for my parents." He paused. "We are too close," he said. "We are too much together with no one else to play off of. It can get stifling." Guillaume looked pleadingly at Nick and then went on. "It was like that at home, too." His voice took on a petulant tone. "My parents didn't understand me either!"

Nick knew his mouth was agape. He didn't know what to say to this outburst. "I . . . uh."

Guillaume spat out, "He thinks you're cute, you know. You better watch out. Pretty soon he'll have *you* running errands." He stomped the heel of his boot on the floor, turned, and sped down the stairs.

Strange guy, Nick thought. Why is he confiding in me? It must be a lonely relationship. And why am I suddenly so popular with Devereaux? Is he really interested in me? Can't he tell I'm not gay? No one else has ever thought I was. Nick sighed. He wondered if Guillaume were jealous. Perhaps he shouldn't have accepted so readily. Though confused by the innuendos, for whatever reason, Nick sensed he was supposed to get to know these two.

Nick arrived at seven thirty as directed. Devereaux was in a genial mood. Drinks were offered and accepted, and when they had exchanged the usual pleasantries and Nick had listened to a treatise from Devereaux on the abominable traffic he'd faced that afternoon, Devereaux suggested that Nick might wish to see another of his treasures. Already forewarned via Guillaume's invitation, Nick was enthusiastic about seeing the item. Devereaux instructed Guillaume to bring "the alabaster jar."

Guillaume returned with his hands curved gently around a small object. As he drew near, Nick could see that it was a jar about three inches high and made of the most translucent alabaster he'd ever seen. Guillaume handed the object to Devereaux as though it was a treasured feather from a rare tropical bird. Devereaux held it close enough to Nick so that he could inspect it. He gently grasped Nick's hand with his other hand. In surprise and revulsion, Nick pulled his hand away quickly. "I wouldn't dare touch that," he said, to cover his possible faux pas.

"This," Devereaux said, "is my most prized possession. We think it could be first or second century. I'm sorry I can't let you touch it. Only Guillaume and I have that honor—for its safety, of course."

Nick, recovering from his surprise at Devereaux's hand-holding, didn't want to chance touching the jar, but he peered into it as Devereaux held it out toward him. Nick detected an ever-so-faint fragrance. The small, smooth, rounded jar was completely plain, but faint markings on its bottom might have once carried a message. Nick said, "This is amazing! How could something so delicate have survived all these years? It is unimaginable." He was afraid that if he coughed or sneezed it might dislodge the jar from Devereaux's fingers. He said as much to the two doting onlookers, "I wouldn't want to spend the rest of my life working off that kind of a mishap," he joked. Excluding the chalice upstairs, he'd never seen anything as valuable as this before.

"Do you suppose it originally had a cover or some kind of stopper?" Nick asked.

"Yes, I imagine it did," Devereaux replied. "I agree that it is surprising that such a piece could have survived all these years. We were amazed as well. Some young farm girls found it in a box buried in a clump of clay under six feet of sandy soil in northern Provence in the 1920s. I feel very fortunate to have this beautiful and ancient object in my collection." Devereaux turned to Guillaume with a questioning look. In a patronizing tone, he asked, "Shall we tell this nice young man how we got this?" The piece demanded a story.

"Well," Devereaux began. "I have several pickers who are always on the lookout for me. They frequent the antique stores and the *brocanteurs* on my behalf, knowing the kinds of items I will buy. I assume they have other clients as well. I am sure some of them do. When they make a find for me, I pay them well."

As Nick listened, he wondered if Devereaux had sent a picker to St. Clair's shop, or if Devereaux had gone there himself. Perhaps both. How strange it was that Devereaux was here, directly under the chalice for which he probably would have bartered one of his ears.

Devereaux continued. "Many of my favorite treasures are really the finds of my scouts—my pickers, but *not* this one."

Nick could see Guillaume shift in his chair and put his hand over his mouth. Guillaume looked beyond Devereaux into the distance. Devereaux caught the action. "Let's not have another *ennui* exhibit, my dear. I am speaking. You know this is an important story. Remember what happened last time? Yes?"

He turned back to Nick. "Excuse the slight interruption. It was a spring holiday. A friend and I were in Provence looking for wild asparagus and champignons. We hoped to buy some of the famous truffles. We stopped to enquire of a local farmer as to possible truffle sellers, and there the jar sat on a shelf over the stove. Over the stove, mind you!" Devereaux's voice was now a pitch higher—he was almost shouting.

"I offered the farmer's wife a very generous amount for it, but she refused to part with the jar. She and her sisters had found it while playing in a newly plowed field. Other things had turned up in their fields before—pieces of pottery and metal utensils—that sort of thing. But this they found completely intact in its box. Never thinking it something of value, they kept kitchen matches in it. But with the uncanny perception of children, she and her sisters sensed that the jar was special. Each fought to possess it, so the parents eventually moved the alabaster jar to a high place where children could not reach."

Devereaux said, "I could not understand that woman's attachment to this simple jar. Yes, it was very old. But she knew nothing of its value and yet, she wouldn't hear of giving it to us at any price. I kept asking her what it would take to buy the jar from her. The woman thought for some time. Finally, she looked up and in a very alert manner said, 'My eldest son is about to start his medical education. His studies have drained us financially. If you would support him during his future years through his examinations and during his residency, I will let you have the jar—but only when he has completed all of his degrees and certificates.'"

Devereaux looked at his guest and asked in amusement, "Well, what do you think was my response?"

"Obviously, you paid the ransom."

Devereaux looked confused. "Ransom?"

"Never mind. It's what a kidnapper asks for," Nick said quietly. He told himself, don't try to be clever with this guy or you'll get in trouble. Smiling, Nick said, "You now have a *médicin* of your very own. Right?"

"Yes," responded Devereaux, "Now I have free medical care of the very best sort, and I have a son. It is unlikely I would have a son any other way." Devereaux seemed in his element. Nick had the sense that he was greatly enjoying impressing his audience.

"I won't ask you what it cost you in dollars, but how long did you have to wait for the jar?"

"Ten years—a small price to pay for this."

"Did it just sit on the farmer's kitchen shelf then until the boy finished his schooling?"

"Oh my, no! The jar was placed in a bank vault under both our names until my commitment to Georges was complete."

"That's quite a story. You could build a novel around it." His gut was telling him that this was a pile of bullshit. Devereaux just didn't seem like the kind of guy who would do something like that. Nick had looked at Guillaume several times during Devereaux's presentation. Guillaume subtly rolled his eyes and shook his head a time or two, but never said a word. Nick wasn't quite sure how to interpret Guillaume. He was a strange one.

"Aren't there quality antique shops here where you could buy something like that?" Nick asked.

"Certainly, but objects as old and as valuable as this usually are traded on the black market by dealers from the Middle-East—Egyptians, Iraqis, Iranians. I was very lucky to find this piece on my own."

I'll bet you know a few of those, Nick thought.

"Did you know that Mary Magdalene is said to have come to Provence after Christ died?" Devereaux asked.

Nick nodded, thinking bitterly of his lost opportunity to join Maggie, Henri Diamond, and Israel Hawkins. They were undoubtedly there now. He wondered why Devereaux was bringing the subject up. But he only said, "I've heard the legend. I don't know that I believe it."

"This could have been the jar she used to anoint Christ's feet."

This new turn shocked Nick. Mary Magdalene? A hushed "What?" emerged from his mouth. "It's such a simple jar. It could be from anywhere."

Devereaux seemed irritated at Nick's remark. He said, "Of course. One can never know for sure, and it certainly didn't occur to me at first. However, the more I held the jar and spent time with it, the more I started wondering about the possibility. When I held this jar, I could see a woman with long hair and I could smell a fragrance I didn't recognize. It made me curious about what fragrance it could be. I don't often have those kinds of sensations. This was different. I suppose you could call it experiencing a certain *je ne sais quoi.*" Devereaux looked lost in thought for a moment. Then he continued, "But this would have been the type of jar Mary Magdalene used. It is of the era, and it was found in that area of the Haute Provence."

Nick said, "You know, I smelled something too—just the faintest. I wonder if it could be spikenard. That's the oil they say the Magdalene used. It was supposed to enhance fertility."

"Fertility? Perhaps I should order some and see how it compares," Devereaux joked with a wink at Guillaume.

Nick thought, If Maggie could have heard this! He said, "I have a friend who would very much like to see this. She is out of town just now, but, when she returns, could I bring her down for a look?"

"I do not show this often or to just anyone. You are very fortunate, my friend, that I am in a hospitable mood this evening. But let me know when your friend returns, and we will see."

Devereaux gently placed the ancient cruet on the glass table. Guillaume, about whom Nick had forgotten, rushed over to cover it in layers of wool and then cradle it into a wooden box that he then locked with a tiny key he kept on a chain at his waist. He left the room with the box.

Nick rose to leave. Devereaux held up his hand. "Wait. Sit a moment longer. I'm having another *apéritif.* Won't you join me? After you've viewed a treasure like this, you need to savor the experience."

Nick sat back calmly and accepted Devereaux's offer. "Guillaume!" Devereaux called. In a few moments, Guillaume appeared in the doorway. Devereaux pointed to the liquor cart. "Excuse me a moment," he said and left.

Guillaume poured three drinks of varying contents and handed a bianca vermouth to Nick. "What do you think?" he asked. "The old cow has some stories, no?" He swaggered around the cart. "I don't believe him," he whispered conspiratorially to Nick. "You can't trust him. Believe me, I know."

Whew! Nick thought. This guy is too much. He seems angry with me and yet he's warning me about Devereaux. Is he jealous or just ornery? Nick felt extremely uncomfortable with Guillaume and his confidences. He didn't want to share in this guy's troubles. Well, at least he didn't come on to me like Devereaux did.

Devereaux returned. He looked suspiciously at Guillaume. "What have you been saying to our friend?" he asked.

"I told him I'd met your son."

Devereaux nodded, and they both sat. Devereaux began. "I have had a great interest in religious artifacts from the time I was a boy. I have been obsessed with the idea of owning the Holy Grail ever since."

Nick wondered if Devereaux was hinting that he knew about their chalice. But then, how could he?

Changing the subject, Devereaux said, "I was thinking about the friend you mentioned. Is this a man or a woman? Is this a European or an American like you? I would like to know more about this friend."

"I was thinking of my friend Maggie Forsythe. She's American—here vacationing for a few weeks."

"And what does she look like?"

Nick wondered why Devereaux would care about what Maggie looked like. He could understand Devereaux might need some background before showing the alabaster jar—but her looks? "She's a redhead—quite beautiful actually. You'd remember her if you saw her."

"Hmmm. She sounds lovely. Does she have an interest in antiques and art?"

"Well, I guess as much as anybody." Puzzled, Nick asked, "You mean would she want to see the jar you showed me tonight and others from your collection? I'm sure she would."

"Um, yes, that of course. I wondered if she would go looking for such treasures on her own."

Nick didn't like this. Why was he zeroing in on Maggie's shopping habits? "Who knows what a woman's going to like or dislike, especially when it comes to shopping?" Nick laughed. "I know I can never find the right gift for her."

Devereaux did not look amused.

Nick rose. Devereaux was a pompous ass, but Nick couldn't deny that he'd enjoyed this evening. He thanked Devereaux. "This has been an amazing and a very entertaining evening." Nick sensed that Devereaux was the kind of person who appreciated the pleasantries of genteel behavior, so he acted accordingly. Devereaux put his hand on Nick's shoulder and looked into his eyes as they shook hands. Guillaume winked almost maliciously when his turn at hand shaking came.

I don't want to mess up with either of these guys, Nick thought as he negotiated the stairs. There's something creepy about both of them. And the idea that Devereaux thinks I'm cute is disgusting. Devereaux's touching me made me want to say "Hands off," but I thought that might be impolite. I don't want to do anything that would threaten my relationship with these two. I need to get all the information I can.

Elated to be back in his own small flat, Nick checked on the grail. Relieved to see it safely in its current home, Nick's nervous energy began to dissipate. He laughed as he held up the grail and said to it, "You wouldn't want to be anywhere near those two strange ones down there. But you are safe with me—just remember that."

CHAPTER TWENTY-FIVE

St. Maximime

THEY DECIDED ON the mustard yellow restaurant with emerald green shutters across from the St. Maximime village fountain called *Du Côté de Chez Nous*. The waiter's surliness at serving anyone past the normal lunch hour didn't bother Maggie, because she was solely intent on exploring Henri and Israel's knowledge of Jesus and Mary Magdalene.

Looking from one to the other, she asked, "What kind of woman do you think Mary Magdalene was?"

Henri answered first. "As you know from our discussion at Chartres, I see Mary of Magdala as a powerful woman."

"Henri, why do you call her Mary of *Magdala*?" Israel asked.

Henri responded. "Some say the name 'Magdalene' comes from Magdala, a quiet fishing village in northern Palestine. For a woman to be called Mary of Magdala, she must have had some importance and, I would guess, money. For her to have left a prominent, perhaps affluent life, to join the entourage of an itinerant preacher with uncommon ideas makes her a radical. She did not fit the pattern of women in that era who knew their place as the property of their husbands. In Jesus's time, women were chattel—property—valued not much higher than a donkey."

"A donkey?" Maggie said, appalled.

"Yes," Henri added, "Christ's open attitude toward women was culturally unacceptable at that time."

Henri continued, "Others believe that Magdala is her title based on prophetic scripture in the book of Micah about a strong woman. Mary Magdalene fits the prophecy. Yet the church essentially eliminated Mary Magdalene's true importance from the gospels. They didn't want their subjects to worship the sacred feminine or have a symbol of it like Mary Magdalene."

Israel interjected. "There are many famous paintings of Mary Magdalene as the fallen woman who was saved from her sins. For me, she has always been the symbol of desirability—the forbidden woman. In most of those paintings, she's portrayed with red hair, like yours Maggie."

Maggie knew Israel was flirting with her. She looked up from her soup. Pleased with the attention from Israel and that he was connecting her with her beloved namesake even in this joking, negative way, she laughed and said, "I'm not exactly a fallen woman . . . not yet!"

Henri spoke. "The reason you think of her as a temptress, Israel, is because in the sixth century, the pope at that time, Pope Gregory, decided to change Mary Magdalene's image. He combined two other women described in the New Testament with her. One was the woman from whom Christ cast out seven devils—in other words, a mad or melancholy woman, possibly mentally ill. Some understood the 'seven devils' language to mean that the woman was a prostitute, but that was not the meaning of those words in that time. However, with the church's encouragement, by Victorian times, prostitutes in England came to be called 'Magdalens.' That popular image has lasted for one thousand four hundred years."

"The other woman was Mary of Bethany, the sister of Martha and Lazarus, who reportedly anointed Christ's feet with oil and dried them with her hair. I believe this is the true Mary Magdalene."

Maggie couldn't stand it. "Why? Why take the woman who was known to be Christ's closest associate and make her into something she was not? It's so unfair. What purpose did it serve?"

"I can guess why the church did that," Israel answered. "Women were a threat to male celibacy. They've always been considered to be corrupters and temptresses. So if you take a well-known biblical figure and turn her into a fallen woman who can be redeemed, you have set up an example for uneducated people who only knew what the church told them."

"You're right," Henri acknowledged Israel's deduction. "Also, Mary Magdalene was the 'apostle to the apostles.' Even St. Augustine called her that. And most importantly, she was the apostle to whom Christ chose to appear after he arose from the tomb."

"Aha!" said Israel. "In the church's terms, she had the initial moment of Christianity, didn't she?"

"Right." Henri nodded in deference to Israel. "Interestingly enough, the Gospel of Mary, which records some of the philosophies of Mary Magdalene, the apostle, exists today and documents her role as an apostle."

"I've never heard that." Maggie interrupted. "Did she write it?"

Henri answered, "I can show you a copy when we get back to Paris. But no, she would not have been the author. We don't know who wrote the Gospel of Mary or many of the other gospels for that matter. According to the authorities, the Gospel of Mary was probably written in the late first or early second century. Only portions of it have been recovered. A Greek version was published in the late 1930s, and the Coptic version came to our attention in the fifties. According to the Gospel of Mary, Mary Magdalene took over Christ's role after he died. She comforted the other disciples, kept them focused on Christ's words, and gave them special teachings to help them live at a level beyond the world's temptations. She understood Christ's visionary revelations, and her spiritual understanding was clearly higher than some of the other disciples'. Peter had difficulty understanding

Christ's true teachings, and he refused to accept Mary Magdalene's status or her teachings, creating a rift among the disciples."

Henri paused to clear his throat and take a sip of his coffee. "The Catholic Church changed its position on Mary Magdalene in the late 1960s, stating that she was not the prostitute whom Christ redeemed. But unfortunately, that's what people remember—that and the Mary with the flowing hair and the alabaster jar."

Israel said, "I prefer Pope Gregory's version to yours—the harlot who becomes a saint. It's a lot sexier material. Those early popes knew how to please an audience." He paused. "And I guess you couldn't please the pope unless you could get an audience."

Maggie laughed. "Stop it!" Henri shook his head and continued to sip his coffee.

In a quieter, more serious voice, Maggie spoke. "Mary Magdalene must have been an extraordinary woman. Strong. Complex. Courageous. Loyal. She, of all women, was singled out to spread Christ's message. What an assignment! And yet, because of that, the other disciples formed the early church without her ideas. Maybe that's why she came here."

Henri took Maggie's arm, as Israel settled the bill. "Well, my dear, we know that the early Christians were persecuted by the Romans and perhaps by other religious sects. Many of the threatened early Christians escaped to other territories besides France. It's possible that Jesus is the 'Teacher of Righteousness' described in the Dead Sea Scrolls. Some believe he is the descendant of the House of David who actively struggled against the Roman oppressors during the lost years not recorded in gospels."

Maggie shivered. For a few seconds, as though in a vision, she saw Roman soldiers surrounding people gathered to hear Mary Magdalene speak Christ's message. Some in the group jeered at her. Then, as quickly, she was back at the table with Henri and Israel. She wondered, Did I just imagine that or did I live a life during those times?

CHAPTER TWENTY-SIX

Road Trip

IN AIX, MAGGIE, Israel and Henri stopped for an afternoon break at a sidewalk café called Les Deux Garçons where Cézanne was said to have taken his afternoon absinthe. City folk and students sat at tables nearby sipping coffee or swigging *pastis*.

"From here I suggest that you two go to Languedoc to see the ruins of the twelfth-century Cathar castles. The Cathars were an unorthodox and wealthy religious sect that developed in southern France near the Pyrenees during the Middle Ages, only to be annihilated later by the Roman church and a politically motivated king. There are those who believe that Mary Magdalene inspired this group." Henri smiled at Maggie, amused by the look that came over her face whenever Mary Magdalene's name came up. "You'll find it fascinating."

"I'm already fascinated with the Cathars. I've read a lot about them. We discussed them on the plane. Remember, Maggie?" Israel glanced at Maggie to catch her reaction.

Maggie asked, "What do you mean 'you two,' Henri? Won't you be with us? This is your trip."

"Well, my dear, I have responsibilities back in Paris, and they can't wait. My employer has called me from Paris, and I am expected to perform certain duties for him *toute suite*." He sighed. "But don't let my plans stop you. You two must go on, and I want you to take my rental car. You can return it in Toulouse."

"Oh, no, Henri. That's too much," said Maggie, astounded by his offer.

"No, I definitely want you to see the Cathar area," Henri insisted. "You can't see it by train or bus. You must have an auto. If you drop me at my cousin's place here, I can spend the rest of the afternoon with her, and she will take me to the train. When you're down in that Cathar area, you must stop at a little town called Rennes-le-Château. You'll find that very interesting as well. It's a tiny peasant village, but there are fascinating stories surrounding it."

Israel laughed. "What a small world! I've just been reading about that place. Remember the book I had on the plane, Maggie? *Holy Blood Holy Grail.* That was the town!"

Maggie leaned over to Henri and held his hands. "Henri, I'm disappointed you're leaving us. You've been a marvelous guide—all the amazing information that's in your head. Now what will we do?" Turning to Israel, she said, "What do you think, Israel? Should we venture forth on our own without our trusty history-savant?"

"I'm game, but I can't compete with Henri," Israel said smiling. "You'll have to accept a truncated version with me as the historian. But I am dying to see that area."

Henri's cell phone jangled. Maggie had been unaware of its presence in his pocket. He lifted it to his ear. "Yes. I understand. I'll be there late this evening. Of course." He grimaced as he placed the phone back in his pocket and nodded at Maggie and Israel. "He called earlier. He's a very impatient man. I must get back. I'll forego seeing my cousin. You can drop me at the train station. Hopefully, I'll see you when you get back to Paris."

Maggie hugged Henri and thanked him.

Maggie and Israel spoke only sporadically on the drive from Aix toward Rennes-le-Château. Maggie was thankful for the time to ponder her dilemma. Was she committed to Nick through their spontaneous lovemaking? It had been so exciting at the time, but now she could only remember their dancing and drinking from the chalice. Was there something about drinking from the St. Clair chalice that had influenced her? Nick had said something about the vows they'd made. She tried to remember. Yes. They'd vowed to protect the chalice from evil influences and to serve it with only noble deeds. But what kind of a vow had she made to Nick? She didn't remember the exact words, but vows or no, she had to be responsible for her actions. Nick was so sweet and trusting—she couldn't bear hurting him. Despite her boozy memory, the scene was still vivid, except for the actual act. Was it just two nights ago? God, it seemed like last year.

It frightened her that the remembrance of something she had wanted so badly was now eluding her. Why couldn't she see this? It was so damned important and yet, she couldn't get her mind around it. Was it hidden in the catacombs of her brain? Sarcastically she thought, Maybe my brain tilted in the Magdalen cave and now tiny sandlike particles are slipping out into the atmosphere from the base of my skull—leaving me brainless.

Every time Israel spoke to her or she looked at him, she saw the chalice. It unsettled her. Why did she see blood pouring over the edges of it? She and Nick had drunk red wine, but this was too thick for wine. Was this about her sexual release with Nick—that she had bled a little? Was this a symbol? Red. What does red mean? Heat. Fire. Death. Life. Sperm. Babies. They hadn't used any contraception, had they? "Stop!" she yelled.

Israel pulled to the roadside. "Okay? Did I do something? Was it that truck back there? It came so close. It scared me too. I hate trucks on roundabouts. As you probably noticed, I got off on the wrong exit and had to circle back. I feel like a real dope."

"What truck?" Embarrassed, Maggie shook her head. "I'm sorry. I was just obsessing in my head about something that happened recently. I'm the problem, not you. I'm usually quite sane—at least saner than now. I need to use your mobile. Mine hasn't been working. I need to call Nick."

Israel handed her the phone. Maggie got out of the car and dialed Nick's number. It rang for a long time with no answer. "Damn! Why didn't his message come on? Damn!" I've got to know that the chalice is safe. Where the hell is he? She knew Nick would always do his best to protect it, but why was she seeing all this blood? If only she could talk with him and feel assured of its safety. She opened the door, handed the phone to Israel, and sat down.

"Look at that field of yellow rapeseed over there," Israel pointed. "We could walk over to it. I've always wondered what the plants look like up close. Maybe you'd feel better after a walk?"

"Rapeseed?" Why did that have to come up now? Ironic, Maggie thought. Maggie focused on the vivid yellow field in the distance. She imagined women from another time in long homespun skirts with kerchief-covered hair reaping the crop in the blond canola fields. Her mind swayed between the disturbing reality of her current situation and a past time she couldn't quite remember. She tried to clear her head and stop worrying about Nick and the chalice.

"It's beautiful, but we've a long way to go, and it's getting late. No, just go on. I'll open my window. I'm fine now."

It was almost an hour before they came to a hotel. Large and imposing, it stood high above a wide gorge. Israel followed behind as Maggie entered the hotel to check on rooms. The outer door opened onto a spacious lobby highlighted by a large expanse of polished marble floor. Heavy moss-green velvet drapes partially cloaked floor-to-ceiling windows. The furniture around the edge of the lobby was ornate in design and gleamed with a luster from years of faithful hand polishing. Quality was everywhere.

Israel stood back with his hands in his pockets, watching as Maggie moved to the male concierge who was seated at an antique secretary to the left of the entrance. "*Bonjour*," she began. "*Avez-vous des chambres pour ce soir?*"

Perhaps he suspected that she was an American, because he responded in English. "Good day, Madame. You are enquiring about a room for this evening?" His falsely cheery tone made her think that he might just as well have said, No matter who you are, I am better than you.

Maggie grimaced. She hated his tone. He had understood her perfectly. It was insulting that he would not speak French with her. "*Oui. C'est ce que j'ai dit.*"

"Was this room for you, Madame?"

Tired of the game, Maggie gave up on the French. "Yes. Two single rooms. One is for me."

"We do not have single rooms at La Belle Vista. We do, however, have a lovely three-room suite available this evening."

"What is the cost?"

"Three hundred euros, Madame. Shall I call for assistance with your bags?"

"Hold on. I didn't say I'd take the room."

The concierge looked as though someone had just slapped him. "So sorry, Madame." He spoke quickly and turned away abruptly, busying himself with papers on the desk.

"Don't you have something less costly?"

He turned back to Maggie, gave her a sympathetic look, and, in a "poor baby" tone, he said, "Of course, we do have rooms on the lower level that aren't often used. There is a toilet on the landing that serves four rooms and a public shower on the top floor. Every room has a sink and a bidet for your convenience. I can give you one of these rooms for only one hundred euros."

Maggie seethed. This affected beast was trying to get her into his most expensive room by humiliating her. They did need to find a place soon, but she didn't need this guy jerking her around.

"*C'est de la merde, ça!*" she burst out angrily. "*Je chercherai un autre hotel où le concierge ne fait pas le connard et qui est honête.*"

Maggie turned and marched out the door, her teeth clamped tightly, her breath pushing out from her nostrils in irregular puffs. "*Quel grand con! Merde!*" She said it loud enough for all his fancy guests to hear. She addressed those sitting in the lobby, pointing at the arrogant concierge. "*Oh, qu'il est chiant, ce concierge!*" She wanted to ruin his image of refinement.

"Wow," Israel said, as he followed Maggie out. "You were spectacular in there! I've never seen that spirited side of you. The guy was a real jerk, and you told him all right!"

Maggie glowered back. "Just drive! I'm afraid I've already lost my ladylike image, if I ever had one!" After a few miles, she said, "I don't usually say those kinds of things. I'm surprised I know how to say them, but obviously I picked up that street language someplace."

Israel turned to Maggie. Her color had returned to normal. "I'm glad to see you've relaxed. A purple face doesn't really complement red hair."

Maggie started to laugh. "I guess it doesn't." But the angry charge she'd felt held so much emotion it brought her close to tears. "God! I hate self-importance and pomposity."

Israel's free arm squeezed the back of her neck. "I do too," he said quietly.

About twenty kilometers further on, they stopped at a medieval-looking hotel with two round towers whose sign read "Château des Ducs Joyeux" in a town called Couiza.

"At least this sounds like a happy place," Israel joked as they got out of the car.

A woman and a man greeted them at the entrance desk.

"*Bonne nuit,*" Maggie began, hesitant to use her French after her previous angry encounter.

"*Bon soir.*" The woman's voice was gracious.

"*Avez-vous des chambres pour ce soir?*"

"*Oui, certainement.*" She looked from Maggie to Israel. "*Une chambre?*"

"*Non!*" It came out wrong. Maggie's response was more vehement than she had intended. "*Non, deux lits, s'il vous plaît.*" She held up two fingers, as a child would, then felt embarrassed that she'd done so.

"*Une chambre, deux lits?*"

"*Non, non!* Not two beds. Two rooms. Adjoining. *Deux chambres adjacentes.*" As she said *adjacentes*, Maggie put her hands together in a clap that resounded through the room, embarrassing her even more.

"*Ah, deux chambres adjacentes. Bien!*" The woman smiled at Maggie and began pulling out the registration forms; the man began to chuckle to himself. He laughed and wagged his finger at Maggie and Israel as he turned and left.

Maggie turned to Israel, chagrinned. "It seems my hotel registration abilities are a continuing problem," she whispered. "And I didn't even ask the cost!"

Israel put his arm around her shoulders as she turned back to fill in the form. He whispered in her ear, "I think the lady had it right. I would have said, '*Une chambre est parfaite.*' That would have been the end of it." Maggie shook her head, but smiled to herself. She knew he was teasing. He hadn't shown any signs of coming on to her before.

CHAPTER TWENTY-SEVEN

A Diamond in the Rough

NICK WONDERED IF Maggie had told Hércule St. Clair that she had given the chalice to him. She didn't mention it before she left. Though Nick knew it might not be wise, he decided to contact M. St. Clair to ask whether anyone resembling Devereaux had been to his shop. Nick was suspicious of the two downstairs, and he wanted to know if they were involved with this in any way. That was all there was to it.

He cancelled his appointments and headed out. The dampness from the spring rain the night before was dissipating as he neared the shop on rue des Saints-Pères. The sun, already high in the sky, had not yet erased the chill in the air. A neighboring church bell tolled eleven times as he neared the shop.

The tall thin man with an aquiline nose who greeted him when he entered the shop did not look as he had imagined M. St. Clair. This man was much taller and younger than the man Maggie had described.

"*Bonjour, Monsieur. Puis-je vous aider?*" the proprietor said. His face had a calm nobility that made Nick feel immediately comfortable.

"*Je cherche des coupes anciennes pour une collection.*"

"Ah," the man said, curious about the strange usage of *coupes*. "Old cups? Old awards?" he asked in an unbelieving tone. A laugh he obviously couldn't prevent followed. "We don't have anything like that here, Monsieur. *Seulement les meubles anciennes*—only the antique furniture. No cups. No small items, Monsieur."

"Well, I guess I misspoke. I didn't mean cups. I meant like chalices—like you'd use in a church, you know . . . not exactly cups." Shoot! Nick thought. I ought to glue my tongue to the top of my mouth! He wanted to ask who this man was and why he was here. Where was older M. St. Clair whom Maggie had described? He moved toward the shopkeeper, who was looking at him curiously.

"Can you tell me, is M. St. Clair here? I usually deal with him."

"M. St. Clair was called away unexpectedly," the man responded. "*Je m'appelle Alain.* Is there something else that interests you besides chalices?"

Nick spotted a lamp in a corner. "That lamp," he pointed. "It's an odd style. Is it valuable?"

"No, not truly valuable, but it goes well with the pieces we sell. You know, more modern styles do not go well with antiques, so the lamp is here as a possible accompaniment."

"I see." Nick wanted to ask more questions, but he was afraid that anything he might say would let this man know he had a connection with Maggie or the grail. "*Merci.* I'll just look around a bit." The tall man nodded and retired to the desk at the side of the shop. Nick inspected several pieces for a few minutes and then left.

He began walking toward the Seine. He hadn't gone far when he noticed a man approaching in the direction of the shop on the opposite side of the street. Wait a minute, Nick thought. I know him. It's Diamond. The guy we met at Chartres. Nick considered waving, then changed his mind and moved into the shadow of a building until Diamond had passed. What's he doing here? I don't understand. Damn! Diamond's supposed to be down in southern France with Maggie and Israel.

He had to know what had happened. He crossed the street and began walking in the same direction as Diamond, who was now half a city block ahead of him. Nick saw him stop and gaze into the window of St. Clair's. Strange! Had Maggie told Diamond about the chalice? He couldn't believe she would be that foolish. Nick knew there was nothing interesting in the display—only two similar sixteenth-century landscapes with heavy gold frames sitting on a narrow ledge with azure blue taffeta scrunched beneath the paintings to give the space a refined look. Behind the window facing toward the street was a large marquetry chest with tiny decorated drawers, one of which was slightly open. The window's contents would not hold someone's attention for more than a few seconds.

Nick hung back until Diamond entered the shop, then Nick crossed the street to a garden surrounded by shrubbery where he had a clear view of the shop without being exposed. Within ten minutes, Diamond again emerged and headed off in the direction from which they had both come.

Nick followed, trying to stay a block behind Diamond on the other side of the street. He lost Diamond once when a traffic light changed and delayed him, but within two blocks, he saw Diamond seated on a bench near the fountain at St. Sulpice. Nick tried to look casual as he sauntered up and greeted him. "Diamond! How nice to see you. *Comment ça va?*" Nick held out his hand.

Henri rose from the bench, smiled and doffed his newsboy cap in a salutary greeting. "*M. Nick. Quelle surprise. Je vais bien, merci.*"

Nick sat down next to Henri. "I'm surprised to see you here. I thought you were in southern France with Hawkins and my friend Maggie. I expected you would all return together."

Nick tried to sound upbeat, but he didn't feel that way, knowing that Maggie and Israel were probably together somewhere. He had hoped that they would return by this afternoon. He missed that interplay, that deference, that joy that Maggie brought to him. Nick felt he was growing stale and lifeless without it. He wanted to let her know that she'd lit a fire in him that couldn't be put out. And he really didn't like her traveling alone with that damn Hawkins.

"Oh," Diamond smiled ingratiatingly. "I sent them off to explore Cathar castles in Languedoc and a curious old village called Rennes-le-Château. I left them in Provence and returned. I could not stay, though I would have liked to."

"I wonder when they'll return." Nick said quietly.

"Oh, I would imagine that they should be back within a day or two—if they are only exploring the areas I suggested, that is. If they went on into other territory . . . well, who knows? And how have you kept yourself busy while your friends are away?" Diamond asked.

Nick wanted to ask Diamond about his visit to the St. Clair shop, but he had to be cautious. "Oh, just a bit of sightseeing here and there—the usual," he said vaguely.

"The usual—is there such a thing in Paris?" Diamond's look was amused and teasing.

Nick didn't answer. "If you don't mind my asking, what do you do for a living, Henri? You have a lot of historical knowledge. I know that from our meeting at Chartres. Can you use this erudition in your profession?"

Henri laughed. "A Frenchman would not ask me that, but you Americans get right to the point, don't you? Yes, you could say that, in a way, I do use my historical expertise in my *métier*—if you can call it that. I am what they call a 'picker.' I search for valuable antiques for my collector clients. My livelihood allows me to pursue my interests in medieval history and art. My heart's desire is within my grasp every day that I enter a museum or an antique shop. It's like living history over and over again."

"That's a curious profession. Your clients? Do they come to you or are you on their payroll?" Nick asked.

"Either way. It's an interesting job. Collectors are unique people—some honest, some not. I try to do my job without judgments. In fact, I have to report to one of my clients fairly shortly. I just stopped here to catch my breath and enjoy the sunshine for a few minutes. It was pleasant running into you. I must say I find your friend Maggie very charming and your friend Israel very astute—a delightful couple. They liked Henri's stories. That pleased me. I hope they'll contact me when they return. I'd like to hear about their escapades."

Nick winced internally at the "your 'friend' Israel" comment. Did Henri have to tell him what a wonderful couple they made? Escapades? He could imagine! Diamond stood to leave. Nick gave Diamond's hand a hearty shake along with his casual "*Au revoir.*"

Nick wanted to see where Diamond was going, but he had to let Diamond get enough of a lead so that he wouldn't see or suspect Nick was following. That certainly wouldn't do. He'd probably goofed up enough already today by going to the shop and asking about M. St. Clair.

Why the hell hadn't Maggie and Israel returned with Diamond? What were they up to? Were they sleeping together? She'd only just left his bed the night before they took off with Diamond, and it had been so tender, so special. Could she do that to him? That would be insulting. Nick couldn't get it out of his mind. He strolled off alone. Preoccupied, he paid little attention to what else was going on around him. His safety certainly didn't cross his mind, although he knew one could find pickpockets, toughs, and other slugs of society almost anywhere in Paris. He heard a noise. He looked around to see where it was coming from just as the blow struck his head and everything went black.

CHAPTER TWENTY-EIGHT

Turn-of-the-Century Mystery

ISRAEL PUZZLED OVER Maggie's odd behavior. He didn't want to pry into her personal life. Well, no, that wasn't exactly true. He did want to pry into her personal life, but he was afraid to do so. He was afraid the answer to his unasked question would be that Maggie was in a committed relationship with Nick.

He was pleased when Diamond left, although he did find the strange fellow charming, and he appreciated Henri's considerable knowledge. Now, perhaps he could find out whether this emotional attraction to Maggie was anything more than his libido and his imagination running wild. The problem was that he found it almost impossible to be close to her without reacting; he desperately wanted to touch her and tell her how he felt. Yet Israel knew that for now he had to be a gentleman. He didn't want to blow it.

After they'd settled in their rooms, Israel went down to the desk and asked the woman where he could buy a bottle of the local wine. She suggested the Minervois red or the Côtes du Rousillion white and pointed him down the street to a small local market. When Israel returned, he knocked on the door between the rooms. When Maggie opened it, nodding toward his room, he said, "Come-on-a-my-house. I've something to show you." Maggie followed him through the room and out onto a small balcony that overlooked the river Aude and a portion of the town. Two bottles of wine, two glasses, a small box of crackers, a round of cheese, a bottle opener, and a knife sat on the small table. "Your pleasure, Madame," he said, motioning to one of the chairs. Maybe she'd warm up tonight with a little wine. He wished he knew what was holding her back.

"Oh, lucky you," Maggie said, "You've got a balcony. Why did they give me the room without one?"

"Ahem. They must have guessed which of us the romantic one is. Let's just consider it 'our' balcony. Your preference, Madame?"

Maggie pointed to the white. Israel filled their glasses and offered a toast. "Here's to a splendid day tomorrow and to solving the mystery." He clinked Maggie's glass, noticing how her eyes sparkled when she was relaxed.

"I'm for that. Cheers! Wait a minute—what mystery?" she asked.

"As you know, I've been reading the book I showed you about Rennes-le-Château, and it's been very enlightening. You better put on your sleuth shoes tomorrow.

"Sleuth shoes!" Maggie laughed. "Then you'll have to get one of those Sherlock Holmes hats, and it's too warm for earflaps here in the south of France."

He was pleased to see her smiling and joking. He said, "It's a mystery on several different levels. First, there's the village priest who comes to Rennes-le-Château utterly impoverished and then suddenly becomes wealthier than Rockefeller, or so it appears to people in these parts. Nobody can figure out how this guy could suddenly build churches, towers, mansions, the village water supply, roads, etc. on his priest's salary. Then he's hobnobbing with elegant types in Paris, like Claude Debussy and the internationally known opera star, Emma Calvé, and even some of the Austrian Hapsburgs, who aren't exactly shabby types either. The guy builds a bizarre church dedicated to Mary Magdalene that's full of eschatological symbols—demons, zodiac signs, crazy stuff—mixed in with the usual Christian themes; and the word is, he held equally bizarre services in it. Some say he held rituals to Venus that had sexual overtones."

Israel paused to admire his companion. God, she was beautiful. He took another sip from his glass. Maggie had been listening in rapt attention, which pleased him. "Then," he continued, "the priest built a watchtower dedicated to Mary Magdalene and it's an absolute stone fortress with automatic steel doors to protect his 'papers.' From whom? The Vatican perhaps—who knows?"

Maggie said, "When you said the word 'watchtower,' something I read came into my head. The Hebrew word for watchtower is 'magdal-eder.' That's pretty close to Magdala or Magdalen. Henri mentioned that one of the Old Testament prophets . . . Micah, I think . . . predicted that a woman (a daughter of Zion) will be the watchtower of the flock (Jews or early Christians). Maybe Saunière was honoring Mary Magdalene for the role she played in leading the disciples after Christ's death."

"That's very insightful, Maggie."

"I wish I could remember more about it. It's fun to think about because it's my name, too. Well, back to Fr. Saunière. I guess the mystery is, where did he get the money?"

"Yes, and how did the money bring him the kind of influence it apparently did?" Israel added.

"And why, even if he had the money, would he build a fortress? What was he afraid of?" Maggie mused.

"It's pretty strange," Israel commented. "Although unusual, the story would probably have remained only a local legend, but for the fact that around 1970, two British researchers discovered that, around 1895, this local priest, Fr. Saunière, had become suddenly wealthy and had lived quite ostentatiously until his death in 1917. The priest had found mysterious parchments hidden in the church's altar pillar. Coded messages in the parchments led the researchers to theorize about the mystery of the priest. Several books, including the one I'm reading now, and BBC television productions on Rennes-le-Château resulted."

He added, "That's just one aspect of the place. I can see why Henri encouraged us to come here. In geography, geology, and topography, the town and its landmarks are said to be laid out on some kind of a mysterious geometric grid of pentacles and triangles that line it up with other important historical religious sites in other parts of Europe. It's on a ley line to Paris called the Paris meridian. The line goes straight through St. Sulpice." Israel's mouth was dry. He gulped his wine.

"Really? Isn't that interesting that all the lines lead through Rennes-le-Château and one goes straight to St. Sulpice? I was there just a couple days ago. It felt odd to me. I don't know why." Maggie remembered she sensed someone watching her there.

"Should we open the red?" Israel asked.

Maggie nodded. "The white was lovely. Its taste reminded me of apricots and a hint of almonds—so I'm looking forward to trying the red."

As Israel filled their glasses, he said, "I haven't been in St. Sulpice for years. Anyway, as you can imagine, the Catholic Church had major problems with Fr. Bérenger Saunière—that was the priest's name. There were several trials. The church wanted to find out the source of his wealth, but he steadfastly refused to tell them. They took his parish away from him, but he refused to leave. He just set up an altar in his home, the Villa Bethania, and had services there. Strangely enough, at his death, the church absolved his transgressions. I guess no matter how bizarre a priest's behavior is, it doesn't matter to the church. We've seen a lot of that in the US in the last few years."

Maggie nodded, "Sadly true. But you seem excited about the mystery surrounding Rennes-le-Château. You must be a really curious person to be this interested in religious history."

Israel laughed—if she only knew—it was more than the mystery or the history. He clinked Maggie's glass again and said, "I am excited. I love history. Rennes-le-Château was a strategic Visigoth outpost in the early fifth century when they were conquering this part of Europe. Two other Visigoth outposts in the area make an exact isosceles triangle with Rennes-le-Château. Of course, you have to imagine that there are lines under the ground out there, as if you were a surveyor with your own mental instrument."

"Could they really measure that accurately back then?" Maggie asked.

"I don't know how they did it, but now, with GPS, most of the earlier pentagonal and triangular lines have been corroborated," Israel added, clearing his throat.

"That's fascinating—that all the lines would connect to Rennes-le-Château. I'm impressed that you learned so much about this place in such a short time." Maggie complimented him. She realized Israel's intellect was part of his attraction.

"I just devour this stuff. It's my *métier*—my calling." He really didn't want to talk about himself. "Should I go on?" Israel asked. He was feeling uncomfortable in the small patio chair. He stood and stretched to his full six-foot height for a moment.

"Yes. It's fascinating. And this wine is wonderful too. It makes me think of raspberries or cherries—something tart, yet sweet. Was it expensive?"

"No—three euros a bottle. Can you believe it? I was a little afraid to buy it at that price. They don't export this wine to the US because it is all consumed here."

"We were lucky to find this lovely spot right on the river Aude. The hotel could use a little sprucing up, but look at the view—the town, the old chateau, and the river. That jerk at La Belle Vista can keep his place."

"You were magnificent there—you gave that jerk his due," Israel said admiringly.

Maggie smiled. "Thanks. Go on with the history—if there's more."

Israel said, "I feel like I've been talking too much already, but there is more. Indeed. The Merovingians followed the Visigoths. One of their kings—Dagobert or something like that—held court around here. Then, in the Middle Ages, along came the Knights Templar. Despite their vows of poverty, they accumulated great wealth and reportedly brought back much treasure from their crusades to the Holy Land, including possibly valuable religious articles from Solomon's Temple such as the Holy Grail. The ruin of a Templar chateau is nearby, east of Rennes-le-Château. I've always been fascinated by the Templars."

"Is that why you came on this trip?" Maggie asked.

Israel looked at Maggie, amused. Was she playing with him? That would be a good sign. He casually ran his hand through his resilient curly hair. "One of the reasons."

"Other reasons?"

"You."

Maggie smiled at the sparkle in his gray eyes, but she didn't want to react in a way that might cause him to end his story. "So there was some kind of treasure hidden here?"

"Yup. Apparently."

"Maybe this priest found the treasure and sold it. Maybe that's where he got his money."

"Could be. That would be the most obvious answer." Damn, he hoped he hadn't just insulted her. There was nothing to do but to go on. "Fr. Saunière definitely found something of great value. The church's lenience with him may have been the result of his blackmailing them regarding the information he had, but nobody knows. He died without telling his secret."

Maggie quaffed the last of her wine and rose. "This has been so nice, and I'm impressed with how much you know about this area's history. I needed to relax. I don't know who I was this afternoon."

"You did seem distracted."

"I apologize. I wasn't very good company on the trip."

"You're very good company tonight."

"Thanks. So are you. The cheese and crackers helped, but now I'm absolutely starving. Do you think they'll still serve us downstairs?"

Though it was late, the owner insisted that there was plenty of food left to serve them. The hearty *cassoulet* seasoned with garlic and sweet onions, which they washed down with a local red, proved just the thing. As they said goodnight, Israel could swear he saw something welcoming in Maggie's eyes. "I'd like to . . . ," he began.

"No," Maggie said quickly. "It's been a very special evening. I'm excited about tomorrow. 'Til then." She kissed him on the cheek and closed her door.

Damn! I'm falling in love with this woman. Maybe all I have left to look forward to is her rejection. Should I give it up? But he knew he couldn't. Something was drawing him deeper regardless of his self-protective nature. He had to see this out. The image of his head only one wall away from Maggie's kept him awake for some time that night.

CHAPTER TWENTY-NINE

Employee

AS HENRI DIAMOND walked away from St. Sulpice, he thought with amusement of the triangle of Nick, Israel, and Maggie. He'd sensed Nick's disappointment at learning that Maggie and Israel were off alone together without Henri as chaperone. Henri chuckled to himself, "Ah, the treachery of love." He'd enjoyed the visit to Provence. He knew that he'd played a role in their quest—a role he found satisfying. And he'd drawn a vibrant energy from them that he hadn't felt in a long time.

Diamond put his hand to his head and realized he'd left his cap on the bench near St. Sulpice. He ran back to the spot where he and Nick had been chatting a few moments earlier.

He was just in time to see someone dragging a collapsed Nick into a car. He tried to catch the car's license number, but it sped away too fast. My god! What happened here? Was Nick being kidnapped? Who would have done that? Henri hated violence, and it was especially upsetting when it happened to someone he knew. Some days, Paris seemed to be full of *miscréants*. Henri considered alerting the police, but he really had no solid information to give them.

Sighing, Henri picked up his cap and turned back to his original route. His thoughts turned to the meeting ahead. Devereaux would not be pleased with the news that he had not been able to get any information out of Alain DuClos. Today Alain had been a brick wall.

Henri had, for some time, been a scout for Devereaux. He'd learned to survive many difficulties, but he hadn't learned to deal with his extreme dislike for his employer.

Yet as far as his livelihood, Henri Diamond knew he had to accommodate Devereaux. Although some of Devereaux's acquisitions had come under questionable circumstances, that didn't bother Henri because he had learned much from Devereaux's expertise. He told himself: Devereaux is an egotist, to be sure, but, despite my dislike for him, he lets me do the exploration. So if I make money finding Devereaux his precious objects, so what? That is the way of the world. Perhaps I would do the same, given the right opportunity. So I do as I am bidden. It's a living. And I love the old shops with their musty smell and their strange and exotic treasures. To me this is not work; it's fun.

Henri mused philosophically: No one should capitulate to their government or their church or any leader or, in some cases, even to their mother or father in adulthood. Yet at times, it was necessary to salute and say, "I do" or "I will."

Henri still didn't understand, however, why Devereaux was so emphatic about this particular chalice. Devereaux had told him, "I *must* have it! It is a feeling deep within me . . . almost as if it were once mine and was taken from me. This desire is powerful beyond reasoning." Diamond knew he would have felt that way about the menorah his family used at Hanukkah or the samovar his grandmother had so valiantly brought with her from Russia. But those items he had seen from childhood and knew to be from his family. This chalice was not the same. He knew of no connection between Devereaux's family and the chalice.

Diamond remembered having seen Maggie come out of the St. Clair shop a few days before they headed off to Provence. He hadn't told Devereaux. Henri laughed to himself at the irony of it. If Devereaux knew that he'd once seen Mlle. Forsythe at the St. Clair shop, their trip to Provence would have taken on a much different context. Perhaps Diamond had unwittingly kept a suspect under close observation for three days without realizing he should have been doing so. Then today, he'd glimpsed Nick coming out of the shop, plus he had a vague feeling that Nick had followed him to St. Sulpice. This was getting increasingly suspicious. What was their connection to St. Clair and that shop?

He hoped it had no relationship to the object Devereaux so badly wanted—the Sion Grail. That would not bode well for them. Though he hadn't been personally involved, he knew that Devereaux could definitely be dangerous to anyone who got in his way. Perhaps he should alert the police to Nick's abduction after all. But if Devereaux were involved, there would be hell to pay if he knew Diamond had called the police in. He just couldn't risk it.

At Diamond's arrival, Devereaux immediately said, "Report on what you've accomplished today, Henri. Did you find the chalice as I requested?"

"I found nothing new today on the chalice. DuClos's mouth is zippered, but he must be worried about St. Clair, who hasn't been around for several days. He didn't explain why he wasn't there as usual. Perhaps St. Clair is just away for a few days."

Devereaux's eyebrows twitched. "How dare you give me such a lame report? What's the point of hiring someone like you—an imbecile who can't squeeze a worm from the soil? I must know if the chalice is still at the shop, or if not, where they've hidden it. I'll let Heinrich and Sid work on St. Clair. They'll get him to talk."

Diamond hesitated, wondering why Devereaux said that. Why send me out to the shop if he knew how to find St. Clair? But Henri knew he had to redeem himself. Henri said, "I saw someone in the neighborhood near St. Clair's today. It probably doesn't mean anything," Henri added. "I ran into him near St. Sulpice. I couldn't say for sure, but I had a feeling he'd followed me there. We chatted briefly."

"Aha! Tell me more. So you know him?"

"Yes, his name's Nick Payne."

Devereaux put his hand to his mouth. "Really? The American who lives above us. Amazing."

"I met him a week ago at Chartres. He was with a young woman, Maggie Forsythe. I especially liked her, but I've had a curious interest in the two of them. I've been sort of off-handedly keeping track of them."

"Excellent!" Devereaux clapped him on the back.

Devereaux's compliments were rare. It appeared it had been worth it to tell Devereaux about his encounter. Henri continued, "Anyway, today, after chatting with Nick, I started to leave, then I turned back because I'd forgotten my cap, and I saw someone dragging poor Nick into a car. He was all wobbly like he'd been coshed. I was too late to do anything. What a shame! He seems like such a nice fellow."

"Hmm," Devereaux commented, "Very interesting. Did you get the license number of the car? I'd like to know who is involved in his rescue."

Rescue? A strange word for Devereaux to use. Puzzled, Diamond shook his head and said, "No."

Now he was beginning to feel sorry that he'd brought Nick to Devereaux's attention. You could never trust him. Did Devereaux already know about Nick? Could he or his thugs have been involved in Nick's abduction?

CHAPTER THIRTY

Rennes-le-Château

RENNES-LE-CHÂTEAU LIES IN the area that separates the eastern Pyrenees from France's central massif, about five kilometers south of Couiza. Maggie and Israel took a tarred road out of Couiza that wound uphill through fields guarded by substantial oaks and heavily covered with yellow broom. The town of Rennes-le-Château came into view as a sprinkling of houses at the top of a rounded hill. A crenulated tower and a church spire stood out above the houses.

"It's so bleak," Maggie commented. "I was expecting something considerably more charming." They passed three streets of houses.

"Me too—this looks pretty uninteresting."

They passed the church and came to the Magdala Tower. They parked near four tethered horses. Two couples dressed in riding gear approached and rode away.

"That's odd," said Maggie. "This *is* the twenty-first century, isn't it?"

"This must be horsy territory. Let's go in and nose around."

From the lower level of the Magdala Tower they could see four slightly higher peaks at various points in a radial circle from the tower.

A young French woman greeted them and offered herself as their guide. "Do you know the history of Rennes-le-Château?" she asked. Israel said, "I'm in the process of reading one of the books on it—*Holy Blood, Holy Grail.*"

"Then you know about the parchments?" the guide asked.

"I don't," Maggie said.

The guide began, "The researchers translated the Latin on the parchments into French and then used a complex code to decipher possible hidden messages. The first parchment's Latin message was the story of Mary Magdalene washing Christ's feet with oil from her alabaster jar."

Israel heard Maggie's little gasp and felt her hand touching his. As he clasped it, he turned to look at her and saw that she was very pale. The guide went on, "This led them to a painting by Nicolas Poussin. That's a copy over there. The painting is titled *The Shepherds of Arcadia*, and it depicts a large stone sarcophagus on a hilltop with three shepherds and a shepherdess near the tomb. Some think it symbolizes Mary Magdalene, John, and Peter, with the risen Christ on Easter morning. It was painted in the early seventeenth century, and at one time, it hung in the private apartments of Louis XIV at Versailles. The original is now in the Louvre. Many believe that neighboring hill was the model for this painting." She pointed. "A stone tomb very much like the one in the painting once stood on that hill, but it was removed in the 1980s by the owner because treasure hunters kept digging there."

Israel pulled Maggie over to the framed print on the wall. "Look, Maggie. I read about this painting. See, something's written on the tomb."

Peering closely at it, Maggie read, "*Et in Arcadia ego.*" Maggie sucked in her breath. "I don't believe it!"

"What do you mean you don't believe it? It's right there."

"That's my family's motto—and Hércule St. Clair's."

"Hércule St. Clair? So you know him?" Israel looked curiously at Maggie.

"I'll explain later." She turned to the guide, "Does the inscription on the tomb have meaning?"

"Very definitely. One translation is 'Even in Arcadia, the land of perfect happiness, I, death, am present.' It's connected to the Priory of Sion—a secret organization. They were the inner sanctum group of the Knights Templar. Have you heard of the organization?"

Maggie nodded.

"The phrase is also on several other tombstones here and on the parchments that Fr. Saunière found."

"What about the other parchment?" Israel asked.

"The second parchment's Latin message is a story of Christ and his disciples walking through wheat fields on the Sabbath. The researchers found another hidden message in that parchment that, roughly translated, says, 'This treasure belongs to Dagobert II, King, and to Sion, and it is the death.'"

"It is the death! That sounds ominous," said Israel.

Maggie shivered. "Sion? Does it mean the Priory of Sion?" she asked.

"Sion could refer to the Priory of Sion or to Zion, the name the crusaders gave to Palestine. The members of the Priory of Sion are said to be descendants of Dagobert II, who was the best known of the Merovingian kings. People have believed for many years that there is treasure here. Near the tomb pictured in Poussin's painting lies another grave of a descendant of one of the grand masters of the Knights Templar. On the headstone is a message that refers to 'the gold at Rennes.'"

"So," Israel began, "the treasure that is or was here probably came from the Knights Templar?"

The guide responded, "There are several possible other sources of the treasure rumored to be in or near this village. After the Palestinians revolted against Roman rulers in 66 CE, the emperor's legions sacked and razed the temple in Jerusalem and carried back to Rome some of the Holy of Holies, including, they say—and it's only a perhaps—the Holy Grail, the Ark of the Covenant, and other Christian and Judaic treasures. Then, three hundred fifty years later, historians say, the Visigoths, who were headquartered in this area of southern France, sacked Rome and took the treasure away from the Romans. Also, during Dagobert's reign, he reportedly amassed great wealth through military conquest of the neighboring Visigoths. In those times, the king's treasure was buried with him. Whatever the treasure here is or was, it likely traveled through many hands to get here."

"Sixty-six CE," Maggie murmured as she leaned against the wall. "Mary Magdalene would have left Palestine for Provence long before that."

Israel turned back to the guide. "Guess we should have brought shovels," he said, joking.

"Many others tried their luck and failed." The guide smiled at Israel's suggestion. She explained that no one other than, perhaps, Fr. Saunière had ever found the treasure, although many had sought it. "Richard Wagner, the German composer, made a pilgrimage to Rennes-le-Château while composing his opera, *Parzifal,* which was based on the medieval grail legend. And Hitler's troops, who occupied the area from 1940 to 1945, also dug for the treasure."

After leaving the Magdala Tower, Maggie and Israel stopped briefly at Fr. Saunière's three-story stone house called Villa Bethania—for Mary of Bethany, Maggie guessed. As they walked the path from the house around the grounds, past Fr. Saunière's garden, and through the church graveyard to his grave, Maggie said, "Do you mind if we sit down for a minute. This place exhausts me. I have such a strong connection to Mary Magdalene. I feel woozy. I didn't sleep well last night. I tossed and turned all night."

The loose lid of the raised tomb wobbled as they sat down. "Oops," Israel sat down hesitantly. "I had a rough night, too. I kept thinking of you on the other side of that wall. Or maybe I just had a presentiment about this place . . . Hey, this lid is loose. Shall we look inside?"

"No! I don't want to know what's inside. Yuck."

Israel laughed. "Chicken!"

"It's strange," Maggie mused, "that he built a tower and a church dedicated to Mary Magdalene and named his house after Mary of Bethany. Do you think that Fr. Saunière believed that Mary Magdalene and Mary of Bethany were one and the same?"

"Probably. He wouldn't be the only one who thought that," Israel commented.

Buried next to the priest was his faithful housekeeper, lifelong companion and confidante, Marie Denaraud. Her headstone announced that at her death in 1953, she had outlived her employer by thirty-six years.

"They say she died without ever divulging the secret of Rennes-le-Château to anyone," Israel commented. "That's real loyalty. I know something about that, but I ultimately failed the test."

"What do you mean?" Maggie asked.

"I was thinking of my marriage. I haven't told you much about that. My wife became mentally ill. I stuck by her for several years, but eventually I had to let go. The craziness became too much for me. I had to survive." Israel looked down at the ground.

"I'm sorry," Maggie touched his sleeve. This man did have more vulnerability than she had seen so far. "I hope you'll tell me more about that someday," she said. They sat in silence for several minutes. Then Maggie decided to turn the conversation back to their current circumstances.

She said, "Can you imagine keeping a secret that hundreds of people would have paid handsomely to know for over fifty years? I doubt that I could have done that."

"Maybe she was too scared to tell," Israel commented. "Three bodies were found buried in this churchyard in 1956. They may have been murdered, and the reason for their deaths remains unsolved. One was a priest in a neighboring parish that knew Fr. Saunière well. Even Saunière's death is suspicious. Though reportedly he died of a sudden heart attack, his casket was ordered well in advance. And supposedly he was visited by a mysterious stranger the day of his death."

"This place gets creepier and creepier. Looks like whoever wrote the parchment was right in forewarning, 'It is the death.'" Maggie hesitated, wondering if she should tell Israel about the St. Clair chalice.

But he spoke first. "You know," he said, "This whole thing has really disturbed me."

"Yes, me too."

"So you're feeling it?" Israel asked.

"Um. Yeah. I think I . . . I hope I know what you mean. I feel something happening, and I really don't know what it means. Do you feel it too?" Maggie asked him.

"That's what I wanted to ask you. I didn't want this to be one-sided."

"Oh no. It might have something to do with the Magdalene. It's hard to explain. I've never experienced so much *déjà vu* before."

"I think you and I should be together tonight."

"What?"

Was she hearing him right? They were definitely not on the same track. Damn! She spoke from her irritation. "This isn't about sex. I'm trying to tell you about me and my life," she said, "about something very precious." Then she changed her mind. She couldn't tell Israel about the St. Clair chalice. After all, she didn't know enough about him to totally trust him, and the consequences could be devastating.

The expression on Israel's face was one of surprise and disbelief. "I guess my remarks were on a different track. I didn't mean to upset you."

"It's okay. Let's just move on," Maggie said thoughtfully. "I still want to see Montségur this afternoon, but after that, we'd better head back to Paris. I'm worried about Nick. And this place spooks me. I have this strange feeling that I've been here before, and yet I knew nothing about this place until Henri mentioned it."

"Do you want to call Nick again?"

"I don't know what to do," Maggie stubbed her shoe in the dirt.

"You can try him from a land phone when we get near Montségur. We're here now. Let's see the rest of the place," Israel said.

They headed around to the front of the village church that Saunière dedicated to Mary Magdalene. As they were about to enter, Israel noticed a Latin inscription over the door and stopped to read it. "Look here, Maggie. '*Terribilis est locus iste.*' 'This place is terrible.' A strange welcome, isn't it?"

As they entered, the first thing they saw was a grotesque crouching demon that looked ready to pounce on them. Maggie screamed, "Ahh!"

"It's just a statue," Israel assured her. "However, it is a bit odd to have a devil holding the holy water fount."

"How can the water be holy with that devil underneath it?" Maggie's voice trembled.

"The book said he's supposed to be Asmodeus, the mythical guardian of Solomon's treasure," Israel said.

"He's horrible and so are those ugly salamanders above him." Maggie pointed to the lizard symbols of the four elements (earth, air, fire, water). Four angels were stacked totem-pole-style above the lizards.

"Maybe the angels represent good winning over evil," said Israel.

"I don't feel much *good* here, and look," Maggie gestured, "the Stations of the Cross are all going the wrong way. Usually you follow them clockwise. That's not kosher for a Catholic Church." She shivered. "It's cold in here. Do you feel it? I'll bet that strange priest is still hanging around."

Israel stopped to admire a mural on one wall showing Christ preaching on a flower-covered hill. "Hmm," he said, "Roses are the symbol of the Rosicrucians—the Rosy Cross."

Maggie said, "I suppose you could find meaning in everything in here."

"Weird but interesting place," Israel said. "I can see why the Vatican didn't exactly approve of Fr. Saunière. But I'll bet he knew and could prove something that the Vatican didn't want known in the outside world. This gave him power. His secret must have been something very important or they would have destroyed this." He looked toward Maggie and saw that she wasn't listening to him.

She motioned to Israel. "Mary Magdalene is surrounding us here. There's that statue over there and the stained glass windows by the altar—one of Mary and Martha at Bethany and one of Mary Magdalene meeting Christ after the Crucifixion. It's like the Ste. Baum cave in a way, but this place doesn't feel holy like the cave did. This is the creepiest Catholic Church I've ever been in. When you walk in here, you feel like you're in a weird dream."

Israel smiled at her. "Come on. Let's get out of here." Israel grabbed Maggie's hand and pulled her out into the sunshine. Maggie blinked. Israel pulled her face up to look at him and put his arms around her. "Maggie, forget what I said earlier. I'm content to be here with you on your journey. In fact, here's what I'm wondering: Were we both together in another time? Are we now just remembering our ancient connection?"

CHAPTER THIRTY-ONE

Captive

NICK AWOKE IN a place he'd never seen before. He blinked, made the effort to prop himself up on his elbows, and looked around the room. It was night, and lights were on. He lay on a sofa covered in silky taupe damask. It appeared to be a sitting room or a library; there were books on shelves. This is too comfortable to be anything but someone's home, he thought.

A woman was watching him intently. He noticed that, as she moved, the tendrils of her dark, curly, shoulder-length hair caught at the expensive earrings dangling from her ear lobes. Hazel eyes that might indicate dark Moorish and lighter Frankish genes looked at him in intense interest and with some compassion. God! How his head hurt! What happened?

Nick's right hand moved to explore the pain. Just the slightest touch made him groan. He tried to say "*bonjour*," but no sound emerged. The woman smiled at him. "*Pas bonjour, maintenant, Monsieur. Bonsoir est plus opportune.*"

The woman, who was leaning against the rosewood library table opposite him said, "You are wondering why you're here?"

Nick's voice emerged in a gravelly slur. "Yes. Who hit me? How did I get here?" he asked, rubbing the new knob on his throbbing head.

"You are here for protection. Someone coshed you."

Nick reached in his pocket to see if his wallet with his passport and credit cards was still there. It was. He started to pull it out, but stopped because the action made the pain increase.

The woman continued. "I don't think they got anything from you. We prevented that. My friends were following you. Two shabbily dressed men raced away when we approached. We brought you here.'

"Why was anyone following *me*?" Nick's words came out in a shaky voice. He couldn't hide that he was worried about his present circumstances.

"You were at the St. Clair et fils shop inquiring about a chalice," the woman stated matter-of-factly.

Feeling a bit stronger and clearer-headed, Nick shoved his body against the arm of the sofa until he was almost sitting. The movement brought back the grogginess and the pain. The woman waited quietly, saying nothing.

After a few minutes, Nick replied, "Well, that chalice thing is no big deal. Every American who comes here probably wants to take home some kind of souvenir."

"Ah, Monsieur, but they do not all want to have an ancient treasure, do they?"

"I don't know about any treasure. I just like antiques." Nick was beginning to feel defensive. How did this woman know he'd been to St. Clair's shop? The pain in his head distracted him. He blurted out: "Who are you? You say you're protecting me. From what?"

The woman's nostrils flared slightly, but her voice remained calm. "*De vous,* Monsieur. Yourself, mostly. You have been seen with people who are suspects in a devious plot against our organization. A valuable item is missing from the shop of Hércule St. Clair. You were there today. If you know the whereabouts of the missing item, there are those who could harm you for that information." The woman spoke calmly, but patronizingly, like a nurse or an invalid's companion.

"This is confusing." Nick asked again, "Are you part of a group? Tell me your name."

The woman walked to the sofa and leaned down closer to Nick. "My name is Thérèse. We have our reasons to be interested in you. Do you have expertise in ancient religious items?"

"No. I know nothing about that. I'm in the social sciences," Nick said quickly. God! This seemed like dangerous territory. He must be cautious.

"Why do *you* think you are here?" she asked, giving him a knowing look.

Something in the woman's voice made Nick nervous. "I have no idea. None at all." Determined not to show his fear, Nick grinned and added nonchalantly, "Perhaps you are spider woman, and you thought I was a fly."

"*Mon dieu. Quelle image!* Me, the spider woman?" She laughed softly. "Well, my fly. You had better watch out!"

They both laughed, and the release dissolved a portion of the restraint between them.

"Come on," Nick said, "Let's get down to it. Why are you bagging flies like me and dragging them off to fancy lairs?"

Thérèse returned to the rosewood table, took a cigarette from a china box, lit it, and poured herself a sherry from a decanter with twining silver vines curving around it. "Would you like one?"

"Cigarette? No." Nick looked warily at the amber liquid circling in her glass. "Sherry? After you, my dear."

Thérèse took a sip from her glass. "Do you think I would poison you? I told you we want to *protect* you, not kill you. Now, would you like some sherry or not?" Her voice held a hint of irritation. "I don't like babysitting," she said abruptly.

Nick nodded. She poured a larger portion into a glass with the same design as the decanter and handed it to him.

They sipped the pungent Spanish sherry silently for several minutes. Nick emptied half of his glass. He could feel his headache blur a little. He was feeling better. "You haven't answered my question. Tell me what this is about."

"Ah," Thérèse sighed, smiled to herself and tapped her cigarette out on a flowered china dish. "It is a long story—one that goes back several centuries. You see, my grandfather was the Count of Monte Cristo." She paused.

Nick's laughter caused his head to hurt even more, but he raised his glass in salute. "*Touché*, your highness!"

Thérèse chuckled at Nick's gesture. She said in a more serious tone, "What do you know about the Holy Grail?"

"What I read in the Bible. And then, of course, there are the various legends of it being in all sorts of places around the world: King Arthur certainly went out of his way to find it; Joseph of Arimathea supposedly buried it under a well near Glastonbury in England. Others legends say it went to Turkey with the Mother Mary. I even know somebody that thinks it's in a little Wisconsin town called Galesville that's known as 'the Garden of Eden.'"

"How did you know there was an ancient chalice that belonged to Hércule St. Clair?"

"I didn't. Not until you just told me. I was just shopping for a friend who likes *objets d'art*. I thought I'd see what the shop had to offer. Anything that's old is valuable. Right?" God, he hoped this woman couldn't read minds. He could feel himself perspiring.

"I don't believe you, but you do amuse me. It feels good to laugh again." Her smile was genuine, if tenuous. She was reaching out to him. He could feel it, but he didn't know if he could trust the feeling.

Nick looked at her intently. "Can't you give me a clue as to what this is all about? What kind of organization would want to protect me?"

"You would not understand."

"Try me!"

"I really can't say." The coolness was returning to her voice.

The phone rang. Thérèse excused herself to answer it. While she was gone, Nick stood and tried to walk. He realized that, despite the slight dizziness, he could handle himself quite well; his strength was returning. He wondered if he could just overpower this woman and escape. But where was he? And where could he go?

Thérèse returned. "Oh, you're up. That's good. But you better sit back down. You don't want another fall." She looked disgusted, "I'm sorry I had to leave. *They* are always checking on me." When he heard her apologetic remark, Nick knew he had won some affinity from Thérèse.

"They're just like all males . . . always wanting to control!" Thérèse said in an irritated voice.

Nick grimaced, and his clownlike face brought on a bout of laughter in Thérèse. Breathless, she said, "You have to stop doing that." Thérèse hesitated for several moments. Then, looking almost brutal in her determination not to succumb to laughter again, but still smiling to herself, Thérèse began, "Well, I guess it would be all right to tell you something. It was a closely held secret for at least seven hundred years, maybe more. But now many know about us. They know, at least, that we exist."

"Does *us* have a name?"

"The Priory of Sion. Have you heard of it? Of us?"

"Yeah. But I don't know much about it."

"For me," she continued, "it is a family thing."

"Oh, the Monte Cristos again?"

Laughing, Thérèse wagged her finger at Nick and said, "Shush! Don't be so naughty! Of course they are *not* the Monte Cristos. But there are many famous people in our organization—Debussy, Cocteau, da Vinci, the St. Clairs, and many others. These are some of the luminary's who belonged to our *family* organization. We are interested in preserving the family Grail."

The family? Nick wondered if this was some kind of French mafia.

Thérèse continued. "We are, you see, the descendants of the House of David via Mary Magdalene. We have the *sang real*—the blood royal." Her face was expressionless. It did not appear that she was trying to shock him with this ridiculous statement. Nick wanted to bolt up from his semi-reclining position and yell "Preposterous!" but he waited for more.

Thérèse poured them each another sherry and then sank into a mauve velvet overstuffed chair. A few slightly embarrassed coughs preceded her next words: "Most traditional Christians would think me mad." She waited for Nick's reaction.

He didn't speak. He was not going to mess this up now that she was talking.

"Do I look Jewish?" she asked.

"No," he said quietly.

"Of course, I don't." Her voice was defiant. "But if I take my family back far enough, I am. Those of us in the Priory who can trace our heritage were Jewish when the seed was sown nearly two thousand years ago. But now we've become a polyglot, mostly European, spread throughout the world. The organization hasn't spread, but the *line* is now diverse and, perhaps, even common."

"The House of David? I don't remember that Mary Magdalene was related to David. Some say she had a connection to Joseph of Arimathea, and was of a Jewish sect, but I don't remember reading that she was a descendant of King David."

Thérèse shook her head. "No, but her husband was."

The wheels in Nick's mind were turning ever so creakily. It was as if he understood what Thérèse was implying, but he couldn't put it into words.

Thérèse continued, "You see. There is so little left that is truly symbolic of that ancient time. That's why the St. Clair Grail is so important to us. We can't let it be sold or held by those who do not value it as we do. That's it . . . what is it you Americans say—in the nutshell?"

Sound from a doorbell came through the open door to the entrance. No modern melody here. Nick could picture a hand turning the metal crosslike knob on the door. His parents' house in Poughkeepsie had such a bell. The sound stopped Thérèse's story. She put her finger to her lips and then moved toward the door.

She came back shortly, followed by the tall man he had seen in St. Clair's. Gaunt and angular, in another era, he'd have worn a black cape. He reminded Nick of De Gaulle. There was a haughty lift to his chin, but his eyes were serious and surprisingly soft, and his large, bony nose overpowered everything else on his narrow face. There was strength here. Nick could feel it.

"Alain DuClos." Thérèse introduced the tall man whose hand extended toward Nick.

Nick clasped the outstretched hand. "We've met before. Nick Payne."

"Well, Mr. Payne. We are sorry about your mishap this afternoon. Are you feeling better?"

Nick nodded.

"You are quite a curiosity, Monsieur. You came to St. Clair's *magasin d'antiquités* this morning looking for antique chalices, did you not? Cups, you called them," DuClos said with a slight grimace.

"Yeah, I was there. You saw me. I didn't say *antique*."

"You could see that the shop is filled with furniture and paintings, not chalices, not bric-a-brac. So why would you ask for items that are obviously not being sold there?"

"I just happened to be passing, and I asked because . . . because my fiancée collects these in every country she visits. I thought I might be able to pick one up for her."

The tall man cut him off. "Do not insult me with this story. You were also seen talking with a man called Henri Diamond. We brought you here to protect you. We believe you may be in danger."

Nick's right hand touched his head. He winced again and looked back and forth between the two. In danger? From whom? Not that pipsqueak Diamond? This didn't make sense, but Nick knew he was in serious trouble. Even though these two were telling him they were protecting him, one of them could have been the person who hit him.

CHAPTER THIRTY-TWO

Montségur

THE ROAD EXTENDED on with no visible ending. They'd been driving through intricately curving valleys surrounded by mountains for almost an hour since leaving Rennes-le-Château. Maggie was impatient to see Montségur, the mountain castle where, in March 1244, between two and four hundred Cathars were burned to death as religious heretics by the Pope's army of ten thousand. Purple-gray clouds pregnant with rain hung over the stony mountain peaks. On those occasions when the sun shone, emerald green burst from the mountainsides. It reminded Maggie of photos she had seen of Ireland.

"If we climbed that peak, I'll bet we could touch those clouds," Maggie said, pointing. "You know, this countryside looks familiar—the mountains, the clouds, the green-on-green. But that can't be. I've never been here before. I must be thinking of when my parents took us to the Canadian Rockies."

Israel said, "You wouldn't have this kind of green there. I've been there too. Those mountains are higher and more imposing, but Montségur is supposed to be about three thousand feet."

Maggie, who was driving, stopped quickly as a herd of twenty goats claimed the right-of-way. An old woman goatherd wearing an apron and knit cap showed no interest in hurrying her flock. Israel jumped out of the car and began snapping photos. He yelled to Maggie. "We're back in another time—this is absolutely wonderful!"

When Israel got back into the car, Maggie said, "Strange that you said that. That's exactly how I feel—like this can't be the twenty-first century. I don't know what it is, but it feels weird and scary."

"Why? Those goats weren't smart enough to even sense you were around."

"I know," Maggie said. "It doesn't make sense. But that old woman looked familiar—like someone I've known."

Israel shook his head and rolled his eyes.

They drove slowly up the incline, and they reached the parking lot near the path to ascend Montségur at about two in the afternoon.

"There it is! Oh my god! It looks like somebody sliced away the sides of the mountain."

"Are we really going to climb that?" Israel looked dubiously at the steep path.

They stopped at a stone stele at the beginning of the path.

"This is where the pyre was," Israel noted.

"Pyre?"

"Right. This was erected in memory of the people who died. That's how it ended. The Cathars all burned together in a huge pyre, probably inside a high-walled corral. Many jumped into the flames from the mountain above."

"That's awful! Come on. I need to get to the castle. I've got to see it." Maggie pointed to the high walls straddling the stony outcropping. "This is so disturbing. Miles back I started to get this strong feeling that I've been here before."

They began climbing. The cliff face was incredibly sheer—almost as steep as their climb to the Magdalen Cave in Provence. A strong circling wind snapped at their clothes, resisting them at every step.

Israel said, "I can see why they named this Montségur, the secure mountain. Of course, it proved *not* to be secure, despite the castle's formidable position and design. Did you get a chance to look at that book Henri gave us on this place?"

"No, I saw it in the car, but I've been absorbed with other things. You'll have to clue me in."

"Well, there was a seven-month siege by the Pope Innocent's forces. When that wasn't successful, the church hired Basques to scale the stone face of Montségur. They put together a makeshift catapult. Three months later, after constant pounding with stones like cannonballs, the Cathars gave up."

"Pope Innocent. That's irony!"

Maggie pointed to a neighboring peak. "Look. It's raining in sheets over there."

"Let's hope those clouds like that peak better than ours. I can give you a little more history of this place as we hike if you'd like. Okay?" Israel asked.

"Sure, I know something about them from our previous conversations, but I'm happy to listen to anything new. I do need to watch my feet. This could get slippery if it rains. Just fighting that wind takes all my concentration." Her whole body felt queer. Memories flashed into her mind at almost every step, but she didn't want to make a big deal out of it with Israel.

She asked, "Why do you suppose the Catholic leadership hated the Cathars so? The Cathars sound so harmless—the Good Men and the Good Women in the Church of Love. From what I know, women could play a role in the church. They let all their members have access to the Gospels in their own Occitan language, while the Catholic Church only allowed monks and priests to read the Bible. I know there were differences, like the Cathars' belief in reincarnation and the laying on of hands rather than baptism, but I just can't understand how the church could justify killing them all."

"It's hard to fathom, but the church was very corrupt at that time. The bishops had tremendous power over the people. They grew wealthy and lived ostentatiously despite the poverty around them. And according to the book Henri gave us, even the locals believed there was treasure hidden in this Cathar stronghold. Some local citizens became mercenaries for the church. It was a really good deal—all their debts and sins were forgiven, and there was the opportunity to plunder whatever the Cathars owned. But they didn't get the Montségur treasure. In January, two months before the extermination of the Cathars, two of the castle's inhabitants escaped through gaps in the enemy lines surrounding the mountain with all of the Montségur Cathars' treasure. Supposedly they hid it in nearby caves for later use."

"Are you sure that's where it was hidden?" Maggie stopped to catch her breath. "There used to be a tree there by the path," she said, pointing to a hump in the earth.

"What did you say? Something about a tree?"

"Nothing important. I wonder if the Montségur treasure could be buried near Rennes-le-Château."

"It's not that far away," Israel noted. "I'll bet the leaders of the Inquisition suspected that the Cathars had the grail."

"The Holy Grail?" Maggie could hardly believe this.

"Who knows? The Cathars believed that their church tenets came directly from Christ. They believed that he didn't die on the cross, but came to France with Mary Magdalene. If that turned out to be so, what more likely place would there be?" Israel paused and said thoughtfully, "Actually it's probably the same holy treasure that they told us about at

Rennes-le-Château. The rumor was that the Knights Templar had the grail, other religious treasures, and even the Jerusalem manuscripts. Suppose they left them here and not at Rennes-le-Château? The church wouldn't want those documents to circulate and ruin their version of the true way of Christianity."

Maggie, puffing from the stress of the climb and scarce oxygen, stopped again. "This just keeps getting worse."

"The climb?"

"No, the whole thing—the mass killing, the evil intent, the hiding of the truth."

"I know." Israel agreed. "And it wasn't just here at Montségur. The pope's Albigensian campaign cut a bloody swath through all of southwestern France. Starting in 1208, more than a hundred years of burning thousands of Cathars in cities like Béziers, Carcassonne, Albi, Minerve, Termes, and Lavaur had passed before it was over. It wasn't always burnings. Sometimes they just dismantled the water supply and let the villagers die of thirst—a really nasty business. The Inquisition paid handsomely for information on any living Cathar, and they finally found and burned to death the last Cathar in 1321."

"The pope's forces offered the Montségur Cathars an opportunity to leave their castle safely if they abjured their belief, confessed their sins to the Inquisition, and paid penance. The Cathars who lived at Montségur had two weeks to ponder these alternatives. But in the end, no one left the citadel. They chose fiery death over lying about their faith."

"I wonder how we'd have responded."

"I'm definitely a chicken," Israel said, laughing. "You already know that from the plane."

"I'd rather jump than be burned." Maggie asked, "Do you think the Inquisition found the grail?" The chalice hidden in Nick's apartment came to her mind. Her heart began palpitating, and she began to feel lightheaded.

"No, I doubt it. But they totally quashed the Cathar religion."

After twenty minutes, including a few rest stops, they were walking beside the thick thirty-foot-high twelfth-century stonewalls of the Montségur fortress castle. Both were panting from exertion when they reached the ruins at the top.

Israel looked at Maggie and said, laughing, "First one to collapse is a rotten egg." Then he dropped to the ground near one of the outer walls.

Maggie leaned against the wall. "You're the rotten egg," she said matter-of-factly. Suddenly nothing seemed funny to her.

After resting, they approached the main entrance to the inner ward of the castle, Maggie stopped. She couldn't breathe. "Wait! I can't go in there."

Israel turned to look at her. "But you're the one who wanted to come here."

"I know. I can't explain it. I'm frightened."

"There's nobody here—only old stone walls. But I can see why you're frightened. Look down, Maggie. Some of the Cathars probably threw themselves over the fortification walls here. It must be three thousand feet."

Unable to hold herself together any longer, Maggie began weeping. "How could they do this? How could they burn four hundred people in a stockade, like cattle? All that flesh burning. All those lives. How it must have hurt." She slumped to the earth in a corner of the castle's main hall.

"Yes, it is sad. But Maggie, that was so long ago." Israel shook his head in disbelief at her reaction.

"This is so painful. They're gone now. All my friends. My family. My child. I still miss them. It's the most extraordinary thing I've ever felt."

"What are you talking about? Your friends? Your child?" Israel gave her a curious look. "What's with you? You're taking this much too personally."

Israel turned away from her gruffly. "Do you want me to leave you alone for awhile? I'll take a walk around the place."

Why had she said that? The words just came out of her mouth. Maggie stood up. Just as she was getting herself back in control, a whoosh of energy descended through her, as if another kinesthetic being inhabited her. Woozy, Maggie sat down again. She looked over the edge of the steep mountain face to the tiny village of Montségur nestled into a crevasse below the mountain. Except for the path they'd followed up the mountain, even today, you could not climb this side without special equipment. The valley below gazed up at her threateningly, ready to receive anyone who jumped.

She leaned back. She thought she saw a woman walking on the path toward her. This was no modern woman; she was tall and wore a flowing cloak. Her long brown braids were tied with blue homespun woolen strips. Her cloak was a dull greenish-brown—the shade of the World War I army blankets Maggie had seen at her grandmother's summer cabin.

Maggie could see that the woman carried something in a bag on her left hip. It banged against her at each step. Sometimes she slipped on the wet mud between stone sections. She was obviously in a hurry. There was something else, besides the bag—there was a child slung across her chest—a baby.

The scene wavered as if seen through heat waves in the desert. There was a familiarity about the scene—a remembering. "Rachel!" Maggie heard her voice call out in apprehension. "Rachel! Rachel! Rachel!" Her voice reverberated between the remaining castle walls. As she yelled, she felt herself slipping over the edge, following the woman. As in a dream, she saw herself floating down through the soft air. She reached for something to hang onto and clutched a large boulder as her legs flailed in the air.

Hearing Maggie's calls, Israel returned and grabbed her quickly under her arms. "My god! You were almost over the edge!" Israel pulled her back from the ledge and held her tightly.

After a few minutes, he asked, "What were you trying to do? Where were you going? You look like you're somewhere else." He gently slapped her cheeks.

"Huh?" Maggie looked at Israel. She wondered how she could feel she was following Rachel down the mountain, and yet, at the same time, be here with Israel, in his arms.

"I heard you calling someone's name."

"I saw her. She was here—with the grail—and the baby."

"What? Who was here? We're alone. A baby?"

"I saw a woman. I don't know what thirteenth-century women dressed like, but she looked real. She had long braids and wore a woolen cloak. She only turned around once, but I saw her face. I knew her. I was afraid for her. She scrambled down a path and then it seemed as though she was floating free from the mountainside, yet close to it, as if someone from above had ropes around her and was lowering her down the cliff. She carried a bag and a baby in a sling. A boy."

"A boy? You know it was a boy?" Israel looked at Maggie incredulously. He laughed derisively. "And you knew the name of the woman you saw? Have you suddenly become Joan of the Vapors?"

Maggie paid no attention to Israel. "I know what I saw! You don't have to believe me. I don't understand how I knew her name. I've been experiencing déja vu since we left Rennes-le-Château. It may sound silly, but there's no question that I saw what I saw." Maggie shook her head, trying to bring back the vision. She wanted to dig into the sack under the woman's cloak. What was in there?

"Why did it have to end?" Maggie moaned. "I need to know if she had the grail."

"I want you to rest until you feel ready to tackle the climb back down. We've had enough excitement for one day. This is a queer place. It's certainly had a strange effect on you."

A brief shower erupted from the threatening clouds and drenched them as they huddled together. When it ended, they shook themselves off and began their descent to the car. Maggie's mind concentrated on her vision and not on the wet stone path, unkempt and worn after eight centuries of weathering. Her foot slipped. She tottered between the path and the steep rocks below. "Israel!"

Israel, who was directly behind her, reached out and grabbed one of Maggie's arms from behind and jammed his right foot against the rock wall along the path. He held both arms around her tightly. Maggie collapsed in his hold and turned her head sharply to look into his face. He smiled encouragingly, but there was a solemnity in his voice as he said, "You seem to have a thing about getting down this mountain the quickest way possible."

Maggie's voice trembled as she looked at the distance to the bottom. "Not really."

Israel held her tightly for several moments. "You know," Israel said, "this feels absolutely perfect. I can feel your heart beating against mine. We're in rhythm. I've been feeling that for days—in Provence, at Rennes-le-Château. Do you feel it?"

"Yes," Maggie nodded into his chest and then raised her eyes to meet his. "I feel it, too. They say that everyone that comes into your life comes in for a reason. It feels right for you to be with me on this quest."

"I wouldn't have missed this for anything. I feel ecstatic when you're in my arms. It's as if you've been missing and now you're home. Home! Here with me. Together."

"It felt the same for me at Rennes-le-Château, but I wasn't sure if I should say anything," Maggie confessed.

Israel kissed her, released his arms, and threw them up in the air. "What a glorious day this is!" he crowed.

Maggie relished the kiss. It had been a long time coming. Israel's exuberance was catching. She wished they could stay like this forever. But after several moments, she felt the need to speak.

"Thanks for rescuing me." Maggie tried to curtsy but lost her balance again. Israel reached to help her up, but instead, his movement sent her onto the ground near the steps.

Righting herself and brushing off her behind, Maggie yelled back at him. "Who's the biggest klutz here? You or me?"

They both laughed—a relief after the stress of the near-accidents and the tension of their physical closeness. Maggie pushed Israel ahead down the path. "I'm not playing the 'fallen woman' again. I'm giving up the lead. You can be the first to fall. And if I do fall, I'll have a big soft place to land."

"Big?" Israel turned around with a look of mock horror.

When they reached the red Peugeot, he asked, "How are you now? Recovered from your skydiving attempts?"

Maggie was trembling.

"Hey! You were a little goofy up there, and you still need a little calming." He reached for Maggie and pulled her to him. He held her. His lips brushed her hairline and pushed the damp strands back from her face.

CHAPTER THIRTY-THREE

Return to Paris

ISRAEL WANTED THEM to get a hotel for the night. Maggie was clearly tempted. Their hormones were raging. They could hardly keep their hands off each other. She wanted it, too. But she had to assure herself that everything was still okay with Nick and the St. Clair grail back in Paris. "I need to call Nick to check on something before we decide," Maggie said. "I may have to go back." She dialed.

Here she was, wanting Israel. What would she feel when she heard Nick's voice? She remembered that after she and Nick had drunk from the chalice, they'd made love. The remembering felt strange and removed now. Her feelings were just too complicated. Suddenly she knew that she would have to go back either way. Nick didn't answer.

The drive to Toulouse took several hours. Maggie slept fretfully most of the way. They dropped the car at the rental agency there and boarded the fast train to Paris.

They ordered dinner on the train, but Maggie couldn't eat. She listlessly played with her food. She kept seeing piles of bodies at the foot of the mountain and burned carcasses hanging from spikes. And the smell—she could never go to a pig roast again. Maggie excused herself, ran to the bathroom, and vomited. She wiped away the disgusting regurgitated remains of her lunch, her mind reeling. She had almost died today! What was it about Montségur? She could see the castle rooms and the cottages outside as they had once been. She felt the menacing icicles of fear that rose from the hearts of everyone there. That's why she couldn't catch her breath this afternoon. The contagious all-consuming fear must live on in the ground at Montségur and in the castle walls. But she could feel the determination of the Cathars too. Tears welled in her eyes as she hurried back to her seat.

"Hey. Are you sick?" Israel asked. "You've hardly eaten a thing."

"I'm sorry. I know I'm not good company. I am feeling ill. I just can't get over what I experienced today. I don't know if you can understand how connected I felt at Montségur, and then . . . then almost slipping over the cliff. I could have died!"

Israel tried to comfort her. "I know. It's okay. You're with me now," he said.

During her vision, Maggie could swear she saw someone in the castle carrying a chalice. It looked just like hers and that had to be what was in Rachel's bag.

Israel reached over and grabbed her hand. He held it fondly in his.

Maggie smiled at him. She wished she could tell him about the St. Clair chalice, but something always stopped her. Why did she have to be so attracted to Israel? How could she explain her situation to him? Just saying, 'I can't do this right now' wouldn't help him understand. But she had to get back to Nick and the chalice to see if both were safe. People had died trying to keep it safe, and she didn't want that to happen.

"Can't you tell me what you're thinking about?" Israel pleaded.

"I can't. You'll think I'm bonkers."

"I already do."

"More bonkers than I want you to know about," she said, trying to avoid Israel's concerned look. The two of them sitting solemnly across from each other were reflected in the window now shrouded by night. "I'm sorry for all this," Maggie said to the man in the reflection. He nodded.

It was almost ten when Israel dropped Maggie at her hotel.

"I don't want to leave you—you haven't recovered from Montségur, have you?"

Maggie shook her head and sighed. "I'm exhausted. It's physical, but somehow more than that—hard to explain."

Israel pulled her into his arms, "Shall I see you to your room?" he asked. The press of his body against hers emphasized the question's ramifications. He wasn't giving up easily.

Maggie's eyes sought his. She hoped they were saying, "I know it would be wonderful." Then, almost against her will, but knowing she spoke the truth, she said, "I can't. It's the wrong time."

Israel looked at her curiously.

"I'm sorry. It was a great trip, but there's something I need to do yet tonight. I wish . . ." Her voice trailed off.

"It's okay. You can reach me tomorrow if you need me," Israel said quietly. He turned and headed out into the street.

Maggie wearily climbed the garish red-carpeted stairs to her room. She wondered briefly if she'd made a mistake in not letting Israel come up. But tonight she didn't really have the strength, and she knew she had to find out what had happened in her absence.

Once in the room, Maggie kicked her shoes into the corner and sat on the bed. She undid her belt and threw it toward the shoes. She picked up the phone and rang Nick's apartment. Then she tried his cell. No answer again. Where could he be? Had something happened to Nick? Suddenly she felt panic. Maybe she was just being silly, but the feeling wouldn't go away. Maggie retrieved the shoes and belt, walked downstairs, and asked the night concierge to call her a cab.

It took forever for the cab to come. Maggie's stomach felt queasy during the ride across the Seine. It had been a long day, and her only food had been a quick lunch at the outdoor café at Rennes-le-Château, which she'd subsequently lost on the train.

Nick had given her the code to his building and had copied his apartment key for her. The key turned, but the door to Nick's apartment stubbornly refused its command. The sound of laughing male voices floated up the stairwell from the downstairs flat as she struggled to open the door. She put her hip to it and shoved the way she had seen Nick do. It groaned open.

"Nick? Nick?" She called, "Are you here? It's Maggie. Hey!"

She heard footsteps on the stairs, and she turned around to face the open door behind her. A tall balding man with exceptional eyebrows and imperious questioning green eyes stood in the doorway.

"*Puis-je vous aider, Madame?*" the man asked.

Startled, Maggie responded, "Oh! *Non, merci. Je vais bien.*"

"I live in the apartment downstairs. Let me introduce myself. Marcel Devereaux." He extended his hand to Maggie as he approached.

She took his hand. Moist, cold, and large-boned, his handgrip was overpowering. Maggie involuntarily shuddered when he released her hand. She couldn't clarify her feelings logically. The man's touch and his presence repelled her, but she didn't want to be impolite. Her voice was low. "Maggie Forsythe. I'm looking for Nick Payne, a friend of mine. We're both from the States."

Marcel Devereaux watched her keenly. "I have not heard Mr. Payne coming or going at all today. But then, I am often out and about myself."

"You know him, then? He didn't mention you to me." Then she remembered that Nick had mentioned there were new neighbors below him. He hadn't said he'd met them.

Devereaux nodded. "We have become acquainted. You are worried about him?"

"Well, no—I have been away for a few days, and I just wanted to . . ." She didn't finish her answer. Why should she tell this man anything? Abruptly, she said, "Thank you for offering to help. There's no need to concern yourself. I'll just wait here for Nick. He must be out on the town." Maggie moved to shut the door. Devereaux made a courteous, if overdone, bow. As he turned on his heel to leave, he smiled at her in a curious way. Malevolent, she thought, but why?

She shut and locked the door as soon as he passed through it. As the lock clicked, Maggie raced to the bathroom and kicked open the cupboard with its small safe. Quickly unlocking it, she pulled out the softly wrapped chalice. "Grail," she said. "I'm going to call you Grail from now on. You really are something special." She caressed the worn chalice with her hands. The familiarity of it struck her. I wonder if you've ever been in that cave in Provence."

Assured that all was safe, she replaced the chalice. Then she dug into the linen chest at the foot of Nick's bed and pulled out a quilt, wrapped herself in it, and curled up in a cocoon on the bed.

The man who had appeared at the door minutes before again came into her mind. Maggie knew immediately that she didn't like this man. His manner was Prussian. It would not have surprised her if he had clicked his heels. Was it that Prussian manner? Was it the sound of his voice? She wasn't sure what distressed her, but an ominous feeling persisted. Yet Marcel Devereaux hadn't said anything that should have made her feel that way. Maggie decided to put the downstairs neighbor out of her mind.

CHAPTER THIRTY-FOUR

Breakfast at Devereaux's

THE ATTEMPTED MUGGING and his subsequent sojourn and conversation with Thérèse left Nick exhausted. But along with some residual pain, his head was now full of surprising and confusing information about the infamous Priory of Sion and their bloodline. Nick wondered if Thérèse was wise to tell him as much as she had. Secret societies were probably never pleased when any of their secrets were revealed. He hoped, for her sake, that this situation would be different.

Alain DuClos had been very intent on learning about Nick's connection to the chalice. Nick didn't tell them that he had it. Although DuClos said he didn't believe Nick's tale of innocence, there had been no direct physical attempts to make him say otherwise. Maybe they really were protecting him—but he still didn't know from what.

Everything seemed so complicated now. As Alain DuClos drove him back to his flat, Nick wondered if it might be better if he just turned the chalice over to them. Then they'd be done with this whole blasted business! Hiding the old chalice had become a huge pain in Maggie's and his life. Still, it was not really his to give away or give back. Hell, he thought, at this point, I don't care who has the damn thing! I just want to be in my bed.

It was close to two in the morning when Nick returned to his apartment. Things were slightly out of place from the way he'd left them. Who could have been here? He looked over to the bed. Maggie's here. Why isn't she at her hotel? She must have come in to check on the chalice. Or was she here just to greet him after being away for several days? He hoped that was it. At any rate, he was pleased to see her lovely face in repose and her glorious copper hair spilling over the bed cover.

Nick couldn't wait to tell her about his adventure. He sat on the edge of the bed and shook Maggie lightly.

She squinted up at him. "Huh?"

"Hi, beautiful."

"Umm," she moaned and twisted in the quilt, but didn't speak again.

Nick undressed and slipped quietly under the covers on the other side from where Maggie lay scrunched on top. He moved cautiously close to her. He blew on the back of her neck. Nothing. Maggie's arm flipped back over him. Her breathing was heavy. She must have had as hard a day as mine—if that's possible, Nick thought just as he fell into sleep.

A loud rapping at the door at eight thirty the next morning awakened them both. Maggie roused herself enough to look around. Nick was sleeping next to her. He started to get out of bed, groaning sleepily.

"Nick!" she squealed in relief. She grabbed him about the neck in a strong hug. "I'm so happy to see you." The knocking continued.

"Hold on!" Nick yelled. Maggie and Nick looked at each other and began laughing.

"Stop that infernal noise!" Maggie commanded at the top of her voice.

They couldn't stop laughing.

"Who can it be?" Maggie asked. She thought of Israel. Was he coming to claim her? Then, she remembered that he didn't know Nick's address.

"*Bonjour mes amis!*" The deep voice came through the door in friendly greeting.

"Damn!" Nick unwound himself from their embrace and headed to the door.

"Pants, Nick. Pants!" Maggie yelled, as she jumped out of bed and began smoothing the wrinkles out of her rumpled slacks before stepping into them.

Nick looked down. He strode to the pants he'd shed the night before and quickly stepped in and zipped them up.

When Nick opened the door, Devereaux stood with a white napkin slung over his sleeve. "I wondered if perhaps you two night owls would like to have a little *petit dejeuner chez moi. Café au lait ou thé?*" he asked, as though it was already understood that his invitation would be accepted.

Maggie and Nick looked at each other in a mix of bewilderment and irritation. "Neither," Maggie said severely. "You woke us."

Nick, surprised at her frankness, recouped with, "Oh, sorry. This *is* a bit of a surprise . . . nice of you to invite us, but, as you can see, we're just not really functioning yet."

"The *petit dejeuner* can wait," Devereaux responded. "But I hope you will stop by later for a little chat. It is so nice to have pleasant young Americans in my building."

"Sure," said Nick, shutting the door. "Will do."

"It is so nice to have pleasant young Americans in my building!" Maggie mimicked. "When I see that man, a gaggle of goose bumps attack my body. I don't like him!"

"Have you met him before?"

"Yeah. He followed me up here last night. He's like a weasel—always on the alert. He's too large to slink, but I keep imagining that he's slithering around down there somewhere. Besides, my being here is none of his business."

The joyful moment was gone. A chill had invaded the room with Devereaux's entrance.

"You look great when you're irritated," Nick said, changing the subject to something more personal.

Maggie smiled. "I feel like a mess, but I do need to talk with you. I came over last night because I was so concerned about the chalice. You didn't answer your phone, and I just had to know it was all right. Also, I'm dying to tell you about the amazing experiences I had while we were apart."

Nick finished dressing. Maggie pushed toothpaste around her teeth with her finger and splashed her face with water. They spent the next two hours exchanging stories. Maggie told Nick about her emotional connection to the amazing cave where Mary Magdalene had lived in the first century, about Rennes-le-Château, and her vision at Montségur.

"How was it traveling with Israel?" Nick asked, grimacing.

"Fine. He was helpful, comforting—everything I needed, he provided. I couldn't have asked for a better companion—unless it could have been you, of course."

"I wish it could have," Nick said dejectedly. He went on to tell Maggie about meeting Devereaux and seeing his ancient alabaster jar, and about yesterday's frightening assault, being rescued from his attackers, and then being detained in a wealthy home.

"Someone hurt you?" Maggie cried. "Let me see your head." He lowered his head so that Maggie could see his injury. She brushed her hands over Nick's head softly. "I can feel it! My god! Who did this? Have you seen a doctor?"

"I was on the Champs Élysées yesterday afternoon, and two guys tried to mug me. I haven't seen a doctor, but," Nick hesitated, then grinned at her. "I'm fine. It only hurts when I laugh."

"Liar! That's a whopping lump. Oh Nick, What's happening to us? I'm worried."

Nick laughed half-heartedly, "I think our movie just turned into a film noir."

"Right," Maggie said. Anyway, tell me about the people who took care of you. Were they really from the Priory of Sion?"

"I'm convinced they are. In fact, Thérèse told me some incredibly interesting stuff about their bloodline."

"Thérèse?"

"Uh-huh."

"That was the name of the woman I met last week at Napoleon's Tomb. Tell me more about her."

"She was quite beautiful—slim, thirty to thirty-five. She had black, shoulder-length hair." Nick thought a moment remembering his strange evening with Thérèse. He smiled. "She laughs easily. At least she laughed at *my* jokes."

"Oh, not too sharp, I see," Maggie teased.

"Thanks a lot!"

"Your description sounds like the same person I met before we left. She has some kind of a connection with Hércule."

"Yeah, and there's a family connection between the Priory and Mary Magdalene. I can't remember Thérèse's exact words. She said originally they were Jews and were descended from Mary Magdalene and Christ. What do you make of that?"

"Oh, Nick. I don't know what to think. What have we gotten ourselves into? People are following you and hurting you. This creep downstairs is breathing down our necks. Why?" Maggie looked confused and frightened.

Nick motioned toward the bathroom.

Maggie walked to the safe and unlocked it. She pulled out the carefully wrapped chalice. She twirled it in the light from the window. The sun's rays seemed to hover over the bejeweled golden object, sending kisses of light to each jewel that then disintegrated into bright-colored mirages on the bare floor. Maggie drew the chalice to her chest, as though it were a child and rocked with it there close to her body. Nick watched her silently.

"Oh, Nick, what have we done? Is this chalice a jinx? I almost feel as if there is a tapestry weaving itself around us?" She replaced the vessel in its hiding place and locked it securely again.

Nick came over and put his arms around her. "God, I'm happy to have you here. It can't be a jinx because now you're here with me. I felt lost when you were off with Diamond and Hawkins, and I didn't know what was happening. And I agree, things are getting more intense and tightly woven. Yeah, it is like a tapestry—like the ones we saw at the Cluny."

"Nick, did anyone call the police about your assault?"

"I didn't. I couldn't have recognized anyone, and what could the police do, really? Nothing."

"Well, I wonder if it was really something random or not? It's worrisome. I guess whatever we've stepped into has already begun. We don't seem to have a choice but to play out our roles as the story unravels."

"Hmm," Nick grunted. "But we must play them cautiously and with as much discernment as we can muster. We have to be shrewd . . . discriminating . . . on top of the game." Nick knew he hadn't exactly lived up to his own advice yesterday, but he didn't want to mention that to Maggie.

Maggie agreed, "You're right." She paused and then said, "Well, let's go see your persistent neighbor who comes around being neighborly at eight thirty in the morning." She pulled Nick by the hand as she moved to the door and down the stairs.

Marcel Devereaux welcomed them warmly, bowing formally as Maggie moved past him. She found the salon quite delightful. Though plain, the room was full of light from the tall, floor-to-ceiling windows, and the furnishings were distinctive, but not obtrusive. The floral design of the large paprika-colored Persian rug reminded her of the unicorn tapestries they had seen, though the carpet's figures looked Asian rather than old French. Devereaux served them *café au lait* and *croissants au chocolat* and pears with *crème fraîche*. Small knives with curved embossed handles that fit one's fingers lay beside their plates. Hmmm, Maggie thought, this man has exquisite taste. Maybe he's not as bad as I thought. Yet her body bristled, as it had last night, whenever Devereaux spoke.

"Nick, do you collect anything of value?" Devereaux asked.

"You asked me that the other night. I thought we settled it. I told you I collect parking tickets." Nick laughed, and Maggie smiled wryly at the joke. Devereaux looked stern and humorless.

"Yes, well," he said. "A friend of mine said he saw you over by St. Sulpice in one of the shops there."

"I was on a shopping errand for a friend," Nick answered. "I didn't know I was well enough known in these parts to be recognized by a Frenchman."

Devereaux smiled politely, but continued his questioning. "And you, Mademoiselle. Do you fancy owning some of life's finer things?"

"Yes, of course, I enjoy beautiful things. Who doesn't?"

Devereaux smiled ingratiatingly. Maggie gave Nick a wide-eyed let's-get-out-of-here look.

Devereaux stopped directly in front of her, looked into her eyes, and said, "Are you acquainted with a M. Hércule St. Clair?"

Maggie jerked slightly and several drops of her coffee splashed onto her lap. "Is he the man who has the antique shop on rue des Saintes Pères?" she asked, her voice rising. She grabbed her napkin and attacked the stain on her pants. "I stopped in that shop one day, but I didn't meet anyone by that name," she said, looking up at Devereaux. Pausing to gather her wits, she added, "I would certainly like to meet him, though. St. Clair is one of the family names on my mother's side. It's strange that you should ask."

Nick rose. "We have an appointment, Maggs. We'll be late if we don't hurry."

Maggie rose. "Thank you so much for a delightful *petit déjeuner, Monsieur*. You are very kind." She was thankful to be leaving and not to have to answer any more questions about Hércule.

Devereaux wished them a pleasant afternoon as he walked them to the door.

When they stood outside the building, Maggie asked, "What did he mean? Someone saw you shopping? And who would be watching you of all people? I wouldn't think anyone would know you from Adam."

Nick winced at her tone. "Because . . . when you were in Provence and Languedoc with Hawkins, I went to St. Clair's and asked to see some old goblets or chalices."

"You did what?" Maggie's voice was incredulous. "You didn't say anything about that this morning. Was Hércule there?"

"No. Another man, Alain DuClos, was there. He turned out to be the same guy that apparently engineered my capture. They, of course, called it a rescue."

"Nick! How could you do such a dumb thing? You asked for *chalices*? I don't believe it!"

"Just hold on! It turns out to have been helpful. Otherwise, I wouldn't have seen Henri Diamond snooping around St. Clair's shop."

"Henri Diamond. He doesn't have anything to do with the chalice. You must have gone nutty while we were away!" Maggie looked at Nick with amazement. "Besides, Henri was with us in Provence."

"Was he with you yesterday? or the day before?"

"Well, no. Henri said he had to come back to Paris for business."

"I have more to tell you about what I learned about the Priory of Sion, but I can't do it now because I have an appointment in thirty minutes on the other side of town. Can we have dinner tonight?"

"I promised Israel I'd have dinner with him."

"Oh, for god's sake. Why? Did anything happen between the two of you while you were gone?"

"Nothing unusual. We can make dinner a threesome, and you can tell us both more about what you've learned about the Priory."

"Are you sure you want him to know about this? I don't think it's a good idea." Nick sounded adamant.

"Well, he is a historian. He has mentioned some kind of a connection to the Priory and the St. Clairs. Maybe he can help fill in the blanks."

"That is our secret. Damn it, Maggie! We can't tell anyone." Nick said emphatically. "Oh, I'm so glad to see you and have you back here, I'll do anything you say. But I don't think we should share much information with Hawkins." Nick kissed her solemnly and then dashed hurriedly down the street.

CHAPTER THIRTY-FIVE

Rachel

THE DINNER FOR three did not occur that day. Nick's appointments took up most of the afternoon and early evening, and Maggie didn't feel as though she could face Israel alone now that she was back in Nick's presence. Perhaps Nick was right when he said that they should not involve another person in their grail mystery.

Maggie used the day to recuperate from her ordeal at Montségur by visiting and taking photos of some of the Black Madonna sites in Paris. Maggie appreciated Paris's most venerated Black Madonna (*La Vierge Noire de Paris*)—*Notre Dame de Bonne Delivrance* at the Church of St. Etienne des Gres, carved from a single block of limestone and the wooden *Notre Dame de Toutes Aides* at Chapelle de L'Abbaye aux Bois. But her favorite was the small wooden sixteenth century *Notre Dame de Paix* at the Church of Nuns of the Sacred Heart, a small wooden Madonna surrounded by brilliant gold and blue. Being near these Black Madonnas gave her a special feeling because of their connection to Mary Magdalene, who some believe to have been the woman honored by the Black Madonna statues. And she could also sense the intermixed aura of magic and deep faith that surrounded these revered carved images. She loved this assignment.

Maggie fell asleep soon after returning to her hotel. In the middle of the night, her sleep became troubled and she awoke. Odd, she thought, but I feel that someone else is here in the room. Maggie sat up to look around. Startled, she saw the Montségur woman's pale gray eyes staring at her from the foot of her bed. The woman wore the same handspun woolen cloak that Maggie had seen in her vision. The woman spoke in a harsh voice: "How could you let me take baby Joseph alone? You were supposed to come with me. You knew what had to be done. Yet you stayed behind while I took the risk of saving the grail and your child." Maggie was astounded to hear the woman in her vision speak. She spoke in a language that was neither French nor English, but to her surprise, Maggie understood it.

The misty figure looked directly at Maggie. Her clear, high-pitched voice fluttered with emotion as she said, "I did not want to make that dangerous descent alone, with all the pope's men waiting at the foot of our mountain ready to slit my throat. I understand you were frightened, but I wanted you to come with me. I needed your help. And I wanted you to be saved, too. I kept yelling to you, 'Come with me! Come with me down the rope!'"

Maggie listened, tears welling in her eyes. Maggie could feel terror in her heart. Fear permeated her body, as though it was coming from her soul. Warning her. Putting her on alert. She didn't dare climb down the rope. She wanted to save the grail. She wanted her baby. She wanted her friend. But she couldn't do it.

She could feel the pain and the loss—the terrible loss of her best friend Rachel and the baby. Was it really her baby? Her stomach muscles tightened. Maggie tried to answer. She wanted to explain in Rachel's language, in what must be Occitan, but no words came. She couldn't speak the language anymore.

Rachel faded in and out, sometimes appearing clearly and sometimes a part of the shadows of the darkened room. A cool draft seemed to accompany her visage. Maggie concentrated hard and the image continued.

When Rachel saw the tears in Maggie's eyes, she too began to cry. "I was frightened, too. If only you had come! It was so hard." Then she exclaimed, "But we made it. Joseph and I were free from those papist bastards who squashed our people and our beliefs to get to our treasure. And they didn't get our treasure. I saw to that!" She paused. "How much do you remember?" Rachel asked.

The words were coming slowly now. Maggie heard her own voice say, "Not much. When I was at Montségur, faces came to me—people I knew, the familiarity of the place—that made me feel I'd been there before."

Rachel twisted her long brown braids into a coil at the back of her head as she spoke. "You've been out of time—in a limbo of sorts until this lifetime. But now you must relive the experience and learn from it. I'll help you." Rachel continued. "You have to work harder. You have to get this. There's a place where people like you go—not because you were bad, but because you didn't do the job you were born to do. You were to save the grail and to carry on the holy line for posterity. We're always responsible for our lives. Remember that cave we found when we were children? The baby and I hid there for five days amid the stench of burning flesh and the jubilant jeers of the bloodthirsty troops. We walked to Quillan where a farmer's wife took us in. Eventually, we made our way to Rennes-le-Château and then, much later, to Lyon and Paris. Joseph became a wonderful son to me, and he carried on the family line through his son René and his daughter Sophie. As far as I know, we were the only ones who survived that dreadful night and the burning the next day. No one was safe, not even the perfecti—the holiest ones."

Maggie asked, "And the grail?"

"Safe within the St. Clair family. Always. Thank God I didn't have to watch you die . . . and all my friends and family! I had a dream about you in the cave. They called us the Church of Love, but, in my dream, the parfait pushed you forward first. I think they wanted to punish you for getting pregnant, and here was the perfect opportunity."

Maggie began sobbing hysterically. The fear, the brutality, and the pain in her soul from the loss of the child—it was all coming back. Someone grabbed her and dragged her outside the castle, hooked her vestment onto a seven-foot pole, and began placing firewood at her feet. Maggie saw herself swinging wildly, screaming, and flailing at the air and her persecutors. She prayed to the holy couple. The prayer came back to her:

> Holy Christ and the Magdalene,
> Our Messianic King and Queen,
> Bring the Light to me now,
> Purify me as I join you in Eternity.

The flames licked at her bare feet and at her skirts. The heat from the flames rose up around her in scalding waves. Fanned by the wind, her flaming underskirts beat against her legs. At first there was searing pain, then nothing but the panic of not being able to breathe as the smoke from the fire choked her lungs. She screamed for her child, though she knew he was gone. Death closed in upon her. Her spirit rose above her burning body. She called to Rachel and saw her hidden with the child in their familiar childhood cave. Why hadn't she had the faith to go with them? She was the mother of one of the children of the *sang real,* the royal bloodline of Christ and Mary Magdalene. They say that giving birth changes one dramatically, yet her fear had held her at Montségur. She was supposed to be the caretaker of the grail, not Rachel. How could she have failed so miserably?

The unbearable heat—she had to do something. Unconscious to what she was doing, Maggie threw off the covers and tore away her nightgown until she lay naked, still sobbing—great gasping sobs that rent the silence of the room. Then she heard the music. Lilting music sung in a strong contralto voice: *Sur le pont d'Avignon, On y danse, On y danse, Sur le pont d'Avignon, On y danse, tous en rond.* Now that she thought about it, the song had been echoing in her head for days.

Maggie sat up and saw Rachel's image twirling gently. Rachel plucked Maggie's scarf from the bedpost where Maggie had thrown it. Sometimes the scarf seemed to be twirling on its own, and sometimes she was sure she could see Rachel dancing with it. Rachel said, "Remember? Your favorite song—it always cheered you up."

"I remember now. I remember everything. But I don't want to. I don't want to be here remembering."

"Your soul has been asleep. But I have awakened its scarred surface. Weep, Maggie, weep. This is your chance to atone." Rachel hummed the familiar tune again.

Gradually, the music calmed Maggie, and her tears subsided. She felt a strange sense of peace.

"Oh, Rachel. I'm so glad you escaped that terrible day. Did they ever find you?"

"Yes, in Paris. It took years, but the Inquisition was tireless in its pursuit. Someone must have told them that I knew where the grail was. It was perhaps not as bad as burning, but still horrible. We Cathari knew so much. We knew that Christ did not die at the Crucifixion, but lived on for many years. The Catholics did not want that story told. From early on, their control silenced Thomas, Eusebius, Josephus, and other historians who knew the truth. And of course, in my case, they wanted the grail."

"Did you tell them?"

"No, of course not! Do you think I would succumb to their torture after all I'd been through?"

"How did you die?"

"Painfully. On the rack. They broke all my bones. The Black Friars—an appropriate name for evildoers. They would have killed me whether I told them our secret or not. That's what they did to all their victims."

Feeling Rachel's pain, Maggie shivered. "Oh, Rachel, if only I could have saved you! If I had come with you . . ."

"You couldn't have saved me."

"Oh, my dear Rachel, why am I here now?"

"You have been given another chance to redeem yourself in this life. You have been led here, and I have come to help you understand."

"But have I not suffered enough?"

"No. You have lived many lives. From Atlantean times to our life together at Montségur to this life, some were ignominious and some were glorious, including the one when you were close to Christ and the Magdalene. But despite the wisdom you have accrued over these many years, you still have things to learn . . . and the grail is in danger." Rachel pulled her cloak tightly about her as if suddenly chilled. "I have been given the task of watching over the Sion Grail. Whenever it is in danger I appear. You may see me again." Then she was gone.

Maggie felt like she was about to suffocate. There was no air. It was dark. Was this a tomb, like Lazarus's? She couldn't free her legs. She sat up and found her damp cotton nightgown wrapped tightly around her legs. In a panic, she struggled to uncoil it and free herself. Her own acrid sweat from the night of tumultuous dreaming enveloped and sickened her. She looked about the room. There was a fragrance in the room she hadn't noticed before. *Chevrefeuille*, she thought, the honeysuckle that, reaching for the sun, interwove itself among the branches of the bushes that clung to the Montségur hillside. She and Rachel climbed down to where it grew thickest and made wreaths of it for their hair every spring. But now the fragrance drew from her a feeling of unbearable sadness.

The remembrance shocked her. Had she really lived at Montségur before? It all seemed so real to her. It must be so. There was something both comforting and frightening about the realization. The world she lived in had now expanded beyond anything she had previously dreamed. Wow!

In her wonderment, Maggie tried to recapture snatches of the vision, but it was disappearing quickly. Her mind locked on today and it refused her entry.

CHAPTER THIRTY-SIX

Suspicion

NICK HAD AWAKENED to loud voices arguing in the flat below. He recognized Devereaux's shrill angry voice, but he couldn't identify the other voice. He yawned, stretched, grabbed his robe, and made himself a cup of tea. Warming his hands with the steaming cup, he moved to the window. The voices stopped. He saw a short, stocky figure moving rapidly around the corner of the building and out onto the street. In his surprise, Nick spilled his tea. Henri? What connection could he have with Devereaux? Then it dawned on him.

Nick shaved and dressed with more than his normal efficiency. He needed to find Alain DuClos quickly. He called Maggie. "Maggie, I've got some news for you," said Nick.

"I just woke up. I'm still a little foggy. What news?"

"I can call you back later."

"No. Tell me now."

"Okay. This morning I saw Henri Diamond leaving Devereaux's flat. There were sounds of an argument. I don't know exactly what it was about, but I suspect that Devereaux is the guy who's after the St. Clair chalice. I'm going to try to get more information about him. I'll call you later—hopefully, by four this afternoon."

He hung up the phone and looked at his watch. It was 9:15. Nick headed out the door. He stopped before closing it, wondering if he should move the chalice to a different spot. But he knew he had to hurry and, at this moment, he couldn't think of a better hiding place than the safe. He grabbed his raincoat to fend off the drizzle outside. One last glance showed him that everything in his apartment was in order.

When he arrived at St. Clair's shop, it was already 10:00 AM. Alain DuClos looked up as Nick entered. DuClos's "*Bonjour*" was welcoming.

"*Bonjour*," Nick replied. "I'm happy to find you. I need to talk with you," he said, almost whispering.

"Really?"

"I know who is after the chalice."

"Oh." DuClos's voice showed no emotion.

Nick leaned against an armoire. DuClos did not move or make any effort to find Nick a chair. "I'm renting a flat near the Hotel de Ville on the Rive Droite. A neighbor of mine is a collector of *objets d'art*. He's the one. At least I think he is." DuClos said nothing. Nick continued. "His name is Devereaux, which sounds French, but he has a distinct German accent."

Finally, DuClos moved. He rose, walked through a side door, and returned with a chair. "*Asseyez-vous, s'il vous plaît.*"

Relieved and grateful, Nick sat. "Thanks."

"So? Have you met this gentleman?"

"Yes."

"What do you know about him?"

"Not a lot. I believe he has other residences besides his Paris apartment. He is a collector who is interested in ancient treasures. He showed me an alabaster jar that could have been first or second century—an amazing piece. I have no knowledge or sophistication in these matters, but I could tell that the piece was special. Have you heard of him?"

"*Oui,*" Alain responded. "I have. He may be the person who frightened Hércule a week or so ago, although I do not know why he would be so interested in *our chalice*. He usually buys through contract employees who pose as unsophisticated buyers but know the market well, and know precisely how to barter to get a good value. Why have you come to the conclusion that he is the one?"

"It is curious, really. My friend Maggie and I went to Chartres a week ago. We met a man there, Henri Diamond, who knew a great deal about Mary Magdalene." Nick knew this didn't fit well with the rest of his story. "Uh. Maggie is very interested in Mary Magdalene.

"*Oui, je connaîs de M. Henri Diamond.*" Alain DuClos nodded for Nick to go on.

"Do you remember the day I came into this shop? Well, I saw Henri Diamond enter the shop right after I left. I don't know what Diamond said to you or what he asked about, but it struck me as just a bit odd that he was now seeking something in the same shop as I. It could have been a coincidence, but it made me wonder." Nick's voice trailed off.

"*Ah, oui* . . . a peculiar coincidence. I remember. I was suspicious of both you and Diamond that day," said DuClos. "I know Diamond well. Continue."

"I followed him up to St. Sulpice. I talked with him and then I was hit on the head. You already know all about that. It might have been a random accident, but somebody could also have wanted to get me out of the way. Your people were obviously watching either me or him."

"*Oui.* And then you were taken to my home with a wounded head."

"Yes. I can't believe that he would have anyone hit me. I don't think he is capable of anything like that."

"How innocent you are!"

Nick flinched, but said nothing.

DuClos saw Nick's reaction: "I am sorry. Forgive me. I didn't mean that you're an idiot. Our people were watching both of you. We know this man. He is a go-between for several collectors. They call them 'pickers.' They find what you need for a fee. I must try to remember what exactly Henri Diamond said to me that day."

DuClos became quiet. "Yes. He asked about medieval art objects. He said he was particularly interested in gold items. Eh! I remember I did suspect something then, because that is not his usual pitch, but I suspected you as well. Now, after the fact, it seems so simple."

"My flat is above Devereaux's. This morning, I heard two people arguing, and immediately afterward, I saw Henri Diamond leave Devereaux's flat. There *has* to be a connection between the two of them. I suspect that it has something to do with the chalice."

"Of which you know nothing? Right? Isn't that what you told me just last night?"

"Right." Nick said sheepishly.

Alain DuClos rose from his chair. He was almost a foot taller than Nick. He circled Nick with a sardonic look on his face—the hawk hunting the field mouse. "So much for the American's truthfulness! Now, whom do I trust—yesterday's American or today's?"

"It's the truth. At least, as I know it so far."

DuClos sat down and looked at his shoes. Then he looked up at Nick. "Wait. Hércule will have information on this Devereaux. He has a file on all prospective customers. I'll get it."

Relieved, Nick said enthusiastically, "Good!"

Alain returned with an envelope that held a small dossier on Devereaux. "Hmmm. Apparently, he grew up in Alsace-Lorraine. He has a home outside of Vienna and one near Strasbourg. Devereaux's father was a Nazi soldier. I wonder where Hércule found that. There's no family connection to money of the sort that he has available to spend, so he must be a very clever dealer. Oh, here's a list of some of his pickers. *Bien sûr*. Henri Diamond." DuClos laid the envelope down. "But why is he pursuing our chalice?" He paused, pondering. Then he looked straight at Nick again. "And you still have no idea where the chalice is?"

Nick hesitated. He and Maggie needed help with this. He didn't know if he should trust this man. He had no reason to, but he was panicking about their responsibility and the value of their charge. He had to trust someone. He couldn't go to the police with this story. It didn't really make sense, and he had no real evidence against Devereaux. Nick asked Alain, "How are you connected to M. St. Clair? Why isn't he here running the shop? Please, I need to know this."

"He's my uncle. I help when he needs me. He is usually never away for more than a day or two. I do not know where he is, but I am very worried about him. But this is certainly not your business."

"The Priory. You're both involved?"

"A curious remark. What did Thérèse tell you?"

"It doesn't matter. I know where the St. Clair chalice is, and I can take you to it."

"Give me a few minutes to properly close the shop. *Ça alors!* Do you think that Devereaux knows where it is?"

"No, but he's been sniffing around. Someone may have seen Maggie or me at the shop, and he knows we're friends. I'm afraid that if he hasn't already, he'll figure it out soon."

Alain pulled on his jacket, grabbed his keys, shut off the lights and the hot plate, and opened the door for Nick. "*Allons-y.*"

A few blocks away, Devereaux pondered yesterday's breakfast guests and their behavior. Even though it didn't totally make sense to him, Devereaux couldn't let go of the idea that the Americans had something to do with the chalice he desired so intently. He just couldn't fathom why. But if he were right, he needed to assess all the possibilities.

Where would they have hidden it? He asked himself. Would they have put it in a bank in a safety-deposit box? This would obviously have been the safest thing to do. Were the Americans likely to have done such a reasonable thing? No, he thought not. They are too romantic and entranced with the French scene. Their minds wouldn't be functioning like that.

Devereaux was pleased with his deductions. Certainly, he was not a stupid man! Had he not excelled in all levels of school? Had he not, as a youngster, won all the available prizes? His parents expected him to excel. His mother was easy to please, but no matter how hard he tried, he was never able to meet his father's expectations. He groaned, remembering. But he was not one to dwell on sadness and regret. Devereaux knew he had learned from his past trials, and that had led him to higher levels of success. He looked around the apartment, feeling rather pleased. He was wealthy now. His parents had never achieved anything close to what he had.

Yet there was a part of him that wanted still to please and to outdo. His father had always wanted to find the sacred treasure at Rennes-le-Château. It was rumored that the grail was buried there along with other holy objects. He'd been sent there as a young German soldier under Hitler, but although they had dug up the entire area, his detachment had failed to find anything of value.

Devereaux began to suspect where the grail was hidden. There was little question of it now. And he would soon possess the St. Clair chalice. He would see to that. He would definitely surpass his father.

CHAPTER THIRTY-SEVEN

Waiting

A**S MAGGIE DRESSED,** she obsessed about Nick's phone call. What could Nick be planning to do about Devereaux? And what should she do? Should she go to his apartment and retrieve the chalice? Maybe Nick had already done so. Should she try to find him? Perhaps she should try to locate Hércule, but she hadn't heard from him for more than a week. She had to take some action. But what?

She stopped for a few minutes in the hotel breakfast room to eat a croissant, but her worry prevented her from enjoying it. She just couldn't sit around waiting. Who could help her? She gulped her *café au lait* and pulled out her cell phone. She dialed Israel's number.

"Yes?" His voice sounded distant and uninterested.

"It's Maggie."

"Oh, Maggie. What can I do for you? The newspaper has been my morning's conquest so far. Are you my next?"

"Oh, shut up! This is no time to be clever." She hated this damned cavalier attitude.

"Okay . . . Sorry." Israel sounded taken aback. "What's up?" he asked cautiously.

"I'm worried about Nick. He left me an ominous message this morning."

"What did he say that was so ominous?"

"I don't think we should talk on the phone. Can you meet me at 10:30 at the Café Beaubourg? It's near the Pompidou."

"Done. I know it well."

When Israel arrived, Maggie was waiting inside the café, warming both hands with a bowl-shaped cup of cappuccino. She looked up as Israel entered. He smiled at her slowly, almost knowingly. She caught the look, and it made her angry. *He thinks he's got me all figured out!* She felt a warm flush spread up from her throat. She glared at him. But seeing Israel also brought forth feelings she'd been trying to lay aside.

"Are you mad at me? Why the look? What's happened?" Israel reached for Maggie's hand as he seated himself next to her and motioned to the nearest waiter to bring him a cup as well.

"Oh, Israel . . . so much . . . and all of it distressing. I hardly slept last night. And today, I'm feeling desperate." She paused.

Israel squeezed her hand. "Why?"

"Nick left me a message saying that he's going to find out more about this strange guy who lives in the apartment below his. Devereaux is his name. I just met him yesterday. I couldn't stand him. He's unctuous, pretentious, and stony cold . . . he gave me the creeps!"

Israel took both of her hands in his and waited for her to continue.

"He's Alsatian or Austrian or something. He acts very proper—he bows and all that. He collects art objects." Her nervousness at seeing Israel again lessened as they talked, and her tone leveled as she went on. "His apartment had charm, but it was too fastidious—not a thing out of place—sanitary like a bathroom. Well, not *my* bathroom. And I just didn't like him."

"So what's so terrible about him? Why is he a threat to you?"

"Oh, Israel!" Maggie said. She put her head in her hands. "I know I asked you to meet me here. But I don't know how to explain this without giving away our secret. Damn! I am incompetent. I hate lying and secrets!"

Israel's expression was calm, but curious. "You really don't have to explain to me. I can tell you're very upset, and it's enough reason for me to be here with you."

"Nick and I had so little time to plan, and we didn't know our way around the city. We thought no one would suspect us." Maggie said.

"Suspect you? Of what?" Israel asked.

Maggie ignored his question. She wanted to tell him, but she still didn't dare. She sighed. "Oh, Israel. I'm frightened. We can't lose it!"

"Lose what?"

"You must think I've gone batty," Maggie said. She paused for several moments and then decided to go ahead. "Nick and I—we're keeping something of value for Hércule St. Clair. I don't know if you remember—I mentioned that I was related to the St. Clairs on the plane. It turns out that he's my great-uncle. It seemed like an innocent and helpful gesture, but it's all gotten very complicated. I'm afraid for Nick. I don't know what to do." Maggie looked at Israel imploringly. Maggie fidgeted with the napkin, folding it into tight, tiny balls, which she twirled from palm to palm. Had she said too much? They had established trust on their trip. Perhaps telling this much would be all right.

"Something of value, you say." Israel asked, "You don't mean the Sion Grail? That fabulous, ancient, gem-laden piece? He'd never give that away."

Astounded, Maggie asked, "You know about it? How could you? We haven't told anyone about this! And you know Hércule?"

Israel laughed. "It seems that we're related, Mlle. Forsythe—probably very distantly. I'm a member of the Sinclair clan, and I guess I'd be eligible for membership in the Priory. My father's descended from the Scottish

Sinclairs. We've known about the chalice for years. My father actually saw it one time when he visited here. I received a letter from Hércule before I left, but I was coming to Paris anyway. I haven't had a chance to look him up yet."

"Related? I don't believe it! You got the same letter? But you warned me about the St. Clairs like they were evil or dangerous or something."

"Oh, *then*. I was kidding—to see how you'd react—and you didn't, which spoiled my little game," Israel smiled.

"God!" Maggie said, "And I've been conflicted as to whether I should confide in you about the chalice! Have you ever seen it?"

Israel shook his head.

Maggie continued, "Besides being beautiful, it's very special. When you hold it, it feels almost human—like it can talk. And it feels holy—and it's *my* responsibility. If Devereaux is after it, we need to do something to stop him—and quickly."

Israel put his arm around her and said firmly, "You're the lady who should decide what the next step should be."

Israel's arm was reassuring. Maggie knew he was right, but this all felt so frightening.

"Hey, you're trembling, Maggie," he said. "Come on, you're not the moaning and groaning type. I would've thought you'd be chomping at the bit for action."

Maggie pulled away from Israel. "Are you making fun of me?"

Her question apparently surprised him. "Well, no . . . not exactly." He paused, looking chagrinned. "In a way I *was* making fun. I'm sorry. Really. I just want to help you."

"I need to act. But I . . . I don't know anyone else here in Paris but you and Nick and Hércule. I must try to reach Hércule." She stopped. "I'll do that first."

Maggie dialed the number that Hércule had given her.

"Allo," a deep voice answered.

"To whom am I speaking?" she asked.

"François St. Clair."

"But this is Hércule's cell number. I need to speak to Hércule St. Clair."

"He is not here, Madame. He left this phone here at the shop. But perhaps his nephew Alain could help. Can I give him your message?"

Maggie hesitated, wondering if she should give her message to this man she didn't know. "Tell him that Maggie Forsythe called. There's trouble. I must talk with him."

"Where can he reach you, Mademoiselle?"

"I am at the Café Beaubourg, but I will be leaving here shortly. I am going to 77 rue de Beaune. The number there is . . . wait a minute." Maggie looked in her purse for Nick's number. "Oh, never mind, what am I thinking? Have him call my mobile. The number is 01-44-51-89-44. Have him call that number as soon as possible."

"*Oui, Madame. Ayez de la patience, Madame.*" The phone clicked.

Maggie turned to see Israel standing behind her leaning against the stair rail. "Hércule's not there," she said. "He seems to have disappeared just when I need him! Oh, damn! His nephew is supposed to call me, but we can't wait for that." Her heart beat loudly in her ears, and the bitter milky coffee made her belch. Pushing her empty cup away from her, Maggie said, "It's at times like this that I wish I smoked. It would give me something to do besides stressing out."

The rest of the café was ominously quiet. Then her cell rang. Maggie leaped from the table. As she opened her phone, it blinked: Call ended. "Hello. Hello." She said in vain. "Damn it!"

"Not him?" Israel asked.

Maggie shook her head. She grabbed her jacket and motioned to Israel with her head, saying, "*Allons-y!* Who knows when we'll hear from Hércule's nephew? The Sion Grail is in danger."

When they arrived at Nick's apartment building, Maggie sprinted for the door and up the stairs while Israel paid for the cab. She fumbled in her purse for the key to Nick's flat. When she opened the door for a moment, the room looked as she'd seen it last. Nothing appeared out of place. A sense of relief flooded over her. As Israel came through the door behind her, she turned to him. "It's okay," she said. "At least I think it is. Oh, thank God! I didn't want that pompous jerk to get our treasure."

"I'm glad that it's become *our* treasure." Israel smiled. "You see, all that nervous energy may have been wasted. You really should check the hiding place, though—just to be sure."

"Right. I was just going to." Maggie moved to the bathroom and kicked the cabinet door under the sink. As it flew open, she saw that the little safe had been compromised, and the inside was bare. "Oh, no!" Maggie exclaimed. "It's stolen! How can it be?" She began searching under the sofa, opening closet doors and drawers. Her hands flailing the air, she cried, "This is my fault! I should never have agreed to take care of this centuries old thing. Oh, God! Why is this happening?" She pressed her head between her hands. "Is Devereaux some kind of a mind-reading bloodhound? I can't believe this!"

Although Israel looked around nervously, his voice was calm when he spoke: "There must be some explanation. Perhaps, it wasn't Devereaux who took it at all."

Maggie looked at Israel as though her head had suddenly fallen off. She said angrily, "Devereaux's the one. That was Nick's message. Who else even knows it exists? Who would connect Nick to it? How could they have found it? Oh my god, keeping the chalice safe was *my* responsibility. I've let Hércule down." Maggie began pacing back and forth, wringing her hands, and shaking her head as though she couldn't believe what she was experiencing. Between sobs and groans, she was thinking frantically: Who else knew that they had the chalice? Had anyone seen her with it that day at St. Clair et fils? How could this possibly have happened?

She sobbed, "Nobody's screwed this up for centuries, and then *I* come along and Pow!—the famous Sion Grail disappears!"

Israel interrupted her. "Maggie, maybe Nick arrived before we did and took it to a new hiding place."

"Do you think that's possible? Oh, God, I hope that's what happened. I'll try him again. When I tried earlier he didn't answer." She dialed Nick's cell. It rang a dozen times. There was no answer. "Damn!" Maggie said, angrily tossing the phone down. "Damn, damn, damn! I can't stand not knowing what's happened to our precious grail!" She began to feel nausea creeping up from her stomach and a dry retch followed.

Israel walked to Maggie and put his arm around her to stop her from shaking. "I wish I could help."

Maggie left his arms and walked back to the safe where the chalice had been hidden. She looked at the interior intently as though she expected it to begin speaking to her and divulging its secrets. Then she went to the front hallway to see if she could find other signs of activity. She noticed that Nick's raincoat was half off its hook. She pressed the damp sleeve to her cheek, savoring Nick's smell. She looked quizzically at Israel. "Nick's raincoat is wet. He's been here."

CHAPTER THIRTY-EIGHT

Ownership

HENRI DIAMOND HAD to hurry, but he also had to be careful in how this game would be played. Nothing could go wrong today. Devereaux was sure that the chalice he so desired was in this apartment, and Diamond had been given the job of finding it. While the renter was out, the locksmith Devereaux hired had made a duplicate key for the door and had let him in, along with two toughs in Devereaux's employ—a shorter burly man with a permanent sneer and a tall thin hunched-over guy with a little moustache and an unlit cigarette in his mouth. He hated these ruffian types, but Devereaux had insisted they come along for muscle, should that be necessary. They were searching the apartment for the chalice when they heard voices and footsteps. Panicked, Henri shouted, "Get out on that balcony. And don't come in here until I give you a signal." He hid in the apartment's small kitchen, watching through a crack in the door. To his surprise, Henri saw Nick Payne come bounding into the entryway. Following Nick Payne was the man he'd seen recently at St. Clair's shop—DuClos. A woman was with them. He'd never seen her before.

DuClos immediately shut the door behind them. "One can never be too careful," he said.

Henri saw Nick slip out of his damp raincoat and throw it casually at one of the hooks in the foyer. Then Nick slipped into the bathroom, and a few minutes later he came out holding a velvet wrapped object.

Wow, Henri thought, Devereaux got this one right. This may be easier than I could have imagined.

"Thank you, God." Nick sighed in relief. "I am so thankful the chalice is still here. Maggie would've killed me if it had been stolen."

The woman stood to Nick's left. She trembled.

Nick asked, "What's the matter? Are you cold?"

She said, "I suddenly felt a chill." She looked to the tall, floor-length French doors that led to a narrow balcony. "A door is open." She walked toward the balcony as Nick began carefully unwrapping the chalice from its casing.

"Alain! Thérèse! Voilà!" Nick said in a loud whisper. Nick pulled the golden jewel-encrusted chalice out into the light and thrust it high in the air as if toasting a king. "Behold the Sion Grail!"

Thérèse screamed. Nick and Alain turned as a swarthy muscular man burst into the apartment from the balcony and grabbed Thérèse around her ribs with his left hand, a gun in his right. In seconds, from behind, a tall, thin, and hump-shouldered man leaped into the room and pointed another gun at the group.

Nick and Alain stood motionless. The woman's eyes were wide with fear.

Those idiots! Henri knew using them would be trouble. He'd hoped to do this without anyone seeing their faces. The dummies were supposed to wait for his signal. Now he had to act.

Henri pushed open the kitchen door and stepped firmly into the room. He whistled loudly and commented, "*Elle est magnifique! Et maintenant, elle est à nous!*"

"Henri!" Nick shouted. "Why are *you* here? What is this? Remember me? We met at Chartres. I just talked to you two days ago at St. Sulpice."

Henri marched abruptly up to Nick and grabbed the chalice from him, saying, "*Le donne à moi!* Give it to me."

"No! No! This is Maggie's and mine. No! Stop! What the hell are you doing here, Henri?" Henri could feel Nick's fists battering his arm. The tall one came to his rescue with a blow to Nick's head from behind. Nick's head smacked against the floor as he fell.

Thérèse screamed, "Don't hit him! He's already hurt."

When Henri turned to look at Nick, someone yelled "*Arrêt !*" In his peripheral vision, Henri saw Alain's legs disappear out the door as he headed for the stairs.

"Follow him!" Henri shouted. The thin man raced down the stairs in pursuit.

Across the room, Thérèse struggled to free herself from the hairy knuckles that enclosed her midsection. She hunched her shoulders forward and suddenly jammed her elbows back into her guard's ribs, throwing him off balance for a second. He released his grip.

Henri raced toward her captor. "Don't shoot!" he yelled. He was losing control of the situation.

Thérèse darted across the room toward the door, but the repulsive hands reclaimed her and shoved her so hard against the wall that her head cracked the glass on a Monet print. Thérèse touched her head to feel for blood and slumped to the floor. Her guard pulled her to her feet and looked straight into her face. "Sorry you came along now, aren't you?" he growled as he tied her hands together with the belt from his raincoat. He asked Henri, "What do you want to do with her?"

Henri clasped the chalice tightly. "We'll take her downstairs with us for now. If she goes to the police, she could be trouble."

To Henri's surprise, the woman pulled herself up and hobbled directly toward him. Her voice was surprisingly sharp and confident as she said, "You have no reason to hold me. I have not harmed any of you. I have no intention of calling the police. I have no argument with you. As far as I am concerned, you can keep that silly object. I certainly don't want it. I only came along to see what the American was talking about. It's not worth someone's life!" She looked defiant. "You, Monsieur, must know that I am Thérèse de Beaufort. My family will look for me, and they will contact the police if I don't return by nightfall. You will be in big trouble if anything happens to me. Let me go!"

"*Taissez-vous!*" Henri interrupted her. He recognized her family name. He hated this whole business. Why didn't Devereaux do his own dirty work? This woman *was* a woman of consequence, but he knew they couldn't just let her go. For a moment, he considered granting the woman's request, then abruptly he said, "Take her downstairs. We'll let Devereaux decide her fate."

His compatriot came up behind Thérèse de Beaufort and tightened the belt around her wrists until she winced. He pushed her out of the room and down the stairs.

Thérèse turned and yelled as she stumbled ahead of him: "*Assez, Con! Quel casse-couilles!*" Henri Diamond shut and locked the door. He'd botched this job. What would Devereaux say now? At least he had the grail.

CHAPTER THIRTY-NINE

The Dance of the Grail

HENRI DIAMOND ORDERED the two men to take Nick's unconscious body to a back bedroom. "We'll tie him up good," said one of them. Upon entering the salon, Henri sent Thérèse to a chair on the far side. He laid the velvet package in Devereaux's lap. He watched with apprehension as Devereaux began opening the treasure.

Devereaux looked up and nodded at Henri. His fingers eagerly uncovered the chalice. When it was out of its coverings, he inspected every inch of it. This beautiful vessel fit exactly the description he had read about in the archives of the Bibliothèque nationale de France, and he was convinced that he now held the Sion Grail in his hands. Devereaux leapt from his chair and held the golden chalice to the sunlight. Reflecting the light, its embedded ruby, emerald, and sapphire jewels spread colorful streaks across the room.

"Here you are, my lovely. At last! My darling! My love! We will dance together." Devereaux moved in erratic swirls around the edge of the room holding the chalice as though it were his dancing partner. For a large man, he was graceful. It seemed to Henri that Devereaux's feet barely touched the polished wood floor as he twirled around the room, but he still looked ridiculous and crazy. Finally out of breath, he stopped and looked at Henri.

"Henri, you *are* truly a gem. You have brought my love to me. How can I repay you?"

Diamond frowned. He clenched his jaw and rubbed the thumb of his right hand back and forth across the ends of his fingers.

"Oh, yes. You will be well paid."

"Now!" Diamond's angry monosyllable cut the air. "I want to be through with this. I am not your thug. I only agreed to help because . . ."

Devereaux moved toward him and put his free arm around Diamond's shoulders. "I know you have problems. You have the debts from the old wife's illness. I know, my friend. But aren't you interested in my new treasure? Here!" Devereaux forced the chalice into Henri Diamond's hands.

"This is history, my friend. You who are so filled with the details of history—here is something real that you can touch. This is not a conjured up story, or some historian's research. Here is history we can admire and touch and even drink from." Devereaux's tone became insulting. "You Jews in your stupidity do not acknowledge Christ as the Messiah. But just think: it's possible that the holy man may have drunk from this same vessel."

"Guillaume!" he called loudly. The younger man entered the room and stood at attention. "Bring us some wine. My friend, M. Diamond, wants to celebrate with me. Something a bit sweet and red, I think—like a communion wine. Yes, a communion wine would be very appropriate. You choose from the best in the cellar."

Henri set his face in a look of unconcern. He had steeled himself many times to the insults and whims of this wretched man. He hated Devereaux's ways. He hated doing his bidding. He hated the intrigue and the violence. If his hatred could kill, Devereaux would surely have been dead long ago. Henri wished he could be free of him.

In his haste, Guillaume ignored the dust that clung to the opened bottle that he handed to Devereaux for approval. Devereaux took a monogrammed handkerchief from his lapel pocket and wiped the inside and the rim of the chalice and then the bottle itself. After Guillaume poured the wine, Devereaux delicately sipped the sweet, fragrant liquid. "*Parfait!*" he declared, again holding the chalice high.

Before Henri could move, Devereaux, laughing gleefully, pushed him down into a chair. "Open your mouth," he commanded.

"What are you going to do?" Henri asked.

"Just open your fucking mouth!"

When Henri reluctantly opened his mouth, Devereaux poured a stream of rose-purple liquid into it. Henri coughed and sputtered at this rude invasion.

Devereaux said, "There, my little Jew. Here is his once-Jewish blood given for thee."

Devereaux, obviously excited with his bit of theatre, began to bounce back and forth from one foot to the other like a marionette, wine splashing.

Had Devereaux gone completely mad? Henri, revolted by Devereaux's distasteful display, pulled away. He watched Guillaume rush to the kitchen to find something to remedy Devereaux's excesses.

"From now on, only I will drink from this, my lady's lips." Devereaux filled the chalice and, head back, poured the wine into his mouth, letting it run sensuously down his cheeks. When the chalice was empty, Devereaux set it down. The metal clinked on the glass surface.

"Ah," he said, "if my father could only see me now. All those stories he told of his search for the grail in Languedoc for his Fuehrer! Bonaparte looked for it too. Hitler didn't deserve this magnificent piece. I am as royal and deserving as Hitler or Napoleon." Devereaux chuckled to himself, "Besides, neither of them found it and I did."

Lifting the chalice again, he addressed it. "Thank you for giving me such pleasure, my beauty. And my thanks go also to you, my brilliant Diamond, for this grand accomplishment."

Henri noted that there was something stranger than usual about Devereaux today. His eyes were shining and unblinking. It seemed to Henri that Devereaux could look right through him. Henri wondered if the chalice or the wine had somehow affected Devereaux. Silly thought! He looked across the room to the woman at the other end. He wondered what she was thinking about this little drama. She looked aghast. Devereaux didn't seem to notice that he had a witness, and a stranger at that.

Henri looked to Guillaume. His horror-stricken look belied his reaction as he saw his normally reserved and fastidious employer change into a demonic idiot sashaying around to silent music. Diamond suspected Guillaume would not dare to question Devereaux's behavior.

Devereaux's voice interrupted Henri's thoughts. Looking at Guillaume, Devereaux yelled, "Bring me my bank drafts, Guillaume."

Guillaume did as he was ordered. When he returned with the book of checks, Devereaux scrawled an amount and his name with a flourish, walked to Henri and handed the draft to him. He smiled beneficently at Henri. "There. Any complaints?"

Ten thousand euros! Henri never dreamed he'd be paid so handsomely. He said only, "*Merci.*" Nodding his acceptance, Henri placed the draft in his inner jacket pocket. I'd better get to the bank soon, he thought.

"Now, I want to hear every detail of our successful rapprochement with our lovely grail."

Devereaux motioned him to two side-by-side chairs, and Henri began the play-by-play description of the capture of the grail. Devereaux listened and smiled until Henri mentioned Alain's escape. "Not acceptable. Not as clean as I would like. We cannot allow someone out there tattling to the police about this. You must find him for me, Henri."

Henri nodded, fingering the check in his pocket.

"So we still have two of the witnesses. Now, what shall we do with our captives?" Devereaux looked to Henri for advice.

"Just let them go. The woman has connections. She could bring you trouble if you keep her here. The man who escaped could also involve people of importance or the authorities. The American is harmless. He can't go to the police. The chalice was not his. It will be impossible to explain why he had such a valuable thing in his possession. It won't make sense to the police. They will think he stole it. Even if they find out you now have the chalice, hardly anyone knows the damn thing exists. If you keep these two witnesses, you'll be up for kidnapping as well as burglary." Diamond's voice was calm, but severe. "You're in enough trouble already. Don't compound the problem. And for god's sake, don't kill anyone!"

Devereaux listened. Then he turned to Guillaume. "What do you think, my dear?"

Guillaume suddenly became very animated. Henri noted that Guillaume's normally sedate façade had been replaced by a jittery excitement. He grinned as he said breathlessly, "*Comme le chat!* Remember what we did with that cat that bothered us? The cat does not bother us anymore."

Birds of a feather, Henri thought. They're both twisted.

"*Mieux!*" Devereaux turned to Diamond and said mockingly, "I like Guillaume's idea. But for now, put them both in the back bedroom. We will decide later as to the ultimate resolution of this problem."

Henri looked away from Thérèse's imploring gaze and the accusations he saw there as he untied her and led her to the assigned room. He couldn't bear to think about what might happen to her.

Henri bit his lower lip as he hurriedly left the apartment. How do I stop this devil? He has too much power over me. I must find a way to be free of him and this nasty business.

CHAPTER FORTY

Links

"OH, WHERE IS Nick? What shall we do?" Maggie looked at Israel. "Do you think we should wait here?" she asked. She looked at her watch. They had already been at Nick's flat for close to twenty minutes.

Israel tried to be reassuring. "We have to find out what's happened, but we don't have to wait here. In fact, it may be dangerous to stay here any longer. They could come back."

Maggie wasn't listening; she was berating herself for the loss. "It seemed so easy—no one would suspect *us*. And who could have imagined that someone so focused on getting the grail would even exist? I'm the silly woman who left the St. Clair's ancient family heirloom in a rusty safe! Why didn't we take it to a safety deposit box? Why were we so stupid? And now . . . it's gone! What will the Priory of Sion do to me now?" Maggie's voice broke, and the tears that she'd been holding back filled her eyes and began racing down her cheeks. "Gone!" she croaked.

Israel moved to the window to check out the area. Spotting something, he called quietly, but commandingly: "Maggie. Maggie. Come here."

Maggie walked quickly to the open window; her eyes followed Israel's pointing finger to a figure with a slight limp hurrying down the street on the opposite side. Opening the window, Maggie yelled, "*Henri! Henri! Attention! Ici!*" Receiving no response, she darted toward the door. "I must talk with him. Why is Henri here? This is too strange."

Israel held her back. "You can't catch him. By the time you get downstairs, he'll be in the metro."

"It was Henri, wasn't it?"

"Yes, it was Henri."

"He didn't even look up. His head was burrowed in his collar, and he just kept walking."

Israel said, "He must have heard you. I can't imagine why he wouldn't respond. Apparently he doesn't want to talk with you." He released Maggie and, pushing her chin up, he said, "Come on. We haven't eaten all day. Let's grab a bite somewhere."

"No, I couldn't eat. My stomach wouldn't accept food. I want to go back to my hotel in case Nick, Hércule, or Alain DuClos tries to contact me. Oh, God! What will Hércule do when he finds out?"

As they left the building, Maggie noticed a tall thin man standing outside Devereaux's flat. He looked away as they passed him, a puff of smoke from his cigarette swirling off in the opposite direction. That's interesting, she thought. I saw him sitting in the park today when I left my hotel.

Alain DuClos arrived via the metro at Jean Desmarais's office at half past noon. He flopped into a chair, gasping. "*Mon dieu, je me suis fatigué!* I've been running. Have you a cigarette? I left mine in my car, which is now across town."

Jean, his balding fortyish friend, dug through the pockets of his coat and pulled out a squished pack of Gauloises and threw it in Alain's lap.

"There. You can kill yourself with those! I may be gaining weight, but at least I'm not killing myself."

Alain ignored his holier-than-thou attitude. "What an unbelievable morning! I need to relax."

"Why come here?"

"You can help me."

"How?"

"With your know-how, mostly, and I might need a little brawn as well."

"*Moi?* I'm not exactly the brawny type. I'll need more explanation."

Alain described the morning's events, ending with his escape.

"So what have they done with Thérèse and the American?"

"I don't know. The American was out cold, but Thérèse was still all right when I left."

"Perhaps they will let them go. Would they harm Thérèse and the American?"

"*Certainement.* They both know who has the chalice. They wouldn't want them to go to the police."

"Well, this sounds pretty extreme. But, Alain, you know that this kind of high drama is not the Priory's forte. Yes, we've had our quiet little political dealings, and we know people always wonder about what we're up to, but this . . . a rescue would be pretty risky for our organization. What if the press should get hold of it? We don't want that! We can't sacrifice years of secrecy."

"I know, but we're in it now. It will be just as dangerous to back off as to proceed. The grail is extremely important. It's been with one of the Priory's members since our beginnings—eight centuries. They don't know its exact origin, but Mary Magdalene herself or the Knights Templar may have brought it from Palestine. Even discounting the chalice's obvious enormous value as an antiquity, it is a symbol of our line and heritage. We can't let it go to a ruthless megalomaniac."

Jean nodded, put both hands on his hips and said firmly, "You're right."

"Devereaux could be dangerous. We've got to get Thérèse and the American out of there." Alain paused. His voice very serious, he said, "We could lose both the grail and our charming compatriot."

"Thérèse? *Your* charming friend, you mean." Jean laughed.

"Enough. We need a plan. It looks as though Hércule gave the grail to an American named Maggie Forsythe. Hércule wouldn't have done that if he hadn't had faith in her, and she may also have a connection to the Priory. Hércule had me do some family research on her, and he was very pleased with the results. Hércule told me Mlle. Forsythe has a bit of the *audacieuse* in her, so I think we might be able to use her to find out about the goings-on at Devereaux's. Also, according to Nick Payne, there's a strong emotional connection between Mlle. Forsythe and Nick, so, it's a good bet that she'll do anything to help get him and the chalice out of there."

"But won't Devereaux suspect her?"

"Why? He knows of their friendship, but I doubt that he knows she has any connection to Hércule or the grail."

"But now that he's got the chalice, why would Devereaux even talk to her?"

"I can't predict what this guy will do, but we've got to do something to get Nick and Thérèse out of there." Alain smiled. "Using Maggie could be the answer."

"I can imagine what the other Priory members will have to say about that!" Jean exclaimed.

"At this point, I don't care how McLaren or the others react."

"Will we have to sacrifice Thérèse and Nick to get the grail back into our family's hands?"

"I hope not. But we have to act . . . and soon!" Alain DuClos stood and prepared to leave.

CHAPTER FORTY-ONE

The Priory Meeting

ISRAEL DROPPED MAGGIE at her hotel and went on to an appointment he'd previously scheduled. Maggie dashed up the four flights of stairs to her hotel room. Panting, she opened the door. Aghast at the sight before her, she whispered, "Oh my god!" Her bikini panties were draped prominently over a lampshade; her clothing lay strewn about as though a whirlwind had spun in through the window and laid waste to the room. These were *her* things. No one had the right to touch them. She felt violated.

But more importantly, someone had obviously been here looking for the grail. Why did they suspect her? If Devereaux was behind this, as Nick suggested, could it truly have been that dumb little mistake she made when he asked if she knew M. St. Clair and she spilled her coffee?

"This is *not* my fault!" She kicked the bedpost and whimpered in pain. "Ow!"

She'd discovered part of her family here in France, and she had hoped to build a relationship with them. She wondered what Hércule's reaction would be to the missing chalice. Would he hate her or feel his trust had been misplaced? Would they want her to spend the rest of her life paying for this amazingly valuable thing?

Maggie looked around her room in dismay. Should she call the police? She suspected the man they'd seen outside Nick's and again in the park nearby, but she hadn't paid enough attention to give a definitive description of him. He must have come here first. How could they get in?

She called the reception desk. She said crisply, "Send someone up here immediately. My room has been disturbed. Someone went through all my things. Did you see anyone this afternoon that wasn't a guest?"

"Madame, there are many guests here, and they change daily."

"Don't you watch who comes in and out?"

"We cannot see the stairway from the desk. But only you have the key to your room. Are you missing anything valuable?"

"I don't know yet. I don't want anyone going through my things. What kind of security is this?"

"We do our best, Madame." The concierge hung up.

"Great! Thanks for all your help!" Maggie said angrily as she slammed the phone down.

She began clearing the mess, stuffing her underwear into a drawer. "It feels like my whole life is a mess—not just this room," she muttered.

When the room was back in order, she flopped on the bed. Alain DuClos still hadn't called. Maybe Nick would be back in his flat by now. She dialed his cell again. She let it ring until she could no longer stand it. Why hadn't she heard from him? Nick had said he would call her. He wouldn't say he was going to do something and then not do it. Not Nick.

"Oh, dear God, please let him be okay," she said aloud.

She thought about calling Israel. But after the initial pleasurable reaction, she knew she couldn't face the conflict between her feelings for him and her worry about Nick. It was just too complicated to deal with now.

A knock on her door startled Maggie. "Madame! Madame Forsythe!" Wearily, she answered, "Yes."

"A gentleman waits for you in the lobby. Come down, please."

Maggie looked at her watch. "Who is it? Did he give you a name?"

"*Il me donne une carte pour vous, Madame.*" The maid handed Maggie Alain DuClos's card.

"Oh, yes. Thank you. Please tell M. DuClos to wait. I will be down immediately." She paused before shutting the door. "Why didn't you just telephone me?"

"The concierge wanted me to let you know personally."

Maggie shut the door. She splashed her face with cold water, brushed her teeth, and put on her favorite navy jacket before heading downstairs. Despite her upset at the disaster in her room, now Maggie felt energized at the prospect of learning what happened to Nick.

Alain DuClos sat in the small waiting area off the stairs. He greeted Maggie with great seriousness. He took her hand.

"*Bonjour, Madame. Je m'appelle Alain DuClos.* You came to St. Clair et fils yesterday. I am here in Hércule's stead."

"Good. I have been trying to reach Hércule for several days." Maggie liked DuClos immediately, but his eyes gave her the strange impression that they could see in all directions without a turn of his head.

DuClos said, "Shall we go? My driver's waiting. We can talk in the car."

They entered the gray Citröen that waited at the curb. "*Allons-y!*" Alain told the driver. He turned to Maggie, "Nick will be fine. The Priory will see to it." He gave her hand a squeeze.

"Priory? Oh," Maggie gulped as she took in the significance of what was occurring. She asked, "What do you mean—Nick will be fine? Has something happened to Nick? My god! What? Is it something terrible? I haven't been able to reach him and he promised to call me."

"*Oh, pardon.* You wouldn't know," Alain DuClos apologized. He recounted his escape and the capture of Nick and Thérèse at Nick's apartment.

Maggie swallowed hard. She didn't want to lose it in front of this stern Frenchman, so she tried not to blurt out her feelings and concerns. But she had to ask about Hércule. "I've been trying to reach M. St. Clair. Do you know what's happened to him?"

"No. But I suspect that Devereaux is holding him somewhere. Probably they have been trying to get the chalice's location out of him. I hope he'll let Hércule go free, now that he has what he wants. And there's a possibility that Diamond could get Hércule out of there. We'll see."

Diamond. Yes. She'd seen him that afternoon. What was his connection? Maggie wondered. Then she thought of Israel—perhaps he could help. She began, "My friend, Israel Hawkins, though not an actual member of the Priory, belongs to the clan through the Scottish Sinclairs—or so he told me. I thought . . . Oh, I don't know . . . Perhaps he could be helpful. Would there be any harm in his coming with us?"

DuClos's hawklike eyes pierced right through her; she couldn't tell what he was thinking. "I see. Have you been spreading this story of the missing grail to the world?"

Embarrassed, Maggie said, "No. I assure you . . . *only* Israel and Nick. You've already met Nick, right?"

"Yes. Well, what can I say? I've heard of M. Hawkins, but I haven't yet met him. We can certainly use more manpower. We are only a small group. Where is Mr. Hawkins staying?"

"At the Pierre."

"Here is my mobile. Call him. If he's available, we'll pick him up." He handed the phone to Maggie and she dialed.

"Israel. It's Maggie. Nick is missing. I'm very worried about his situation," her voice wavered; she continued, "Alain DuClos and I are en route to a meeting of the Priory of Sion. Could you join us? We'll pick you up. Good. We'll be there in fifteen. A gray Citröen."

After picking up Israel, they drove to an elegant home in an *arrondissement* near the center of Paris, stopping just after passing the rue-de-Faubourg-St. Honoré. "Is this your home?"

"No. It belongs to a friend." Maggie wondered, Is this the same house where Nick had been protectively held after the incident near St. Sulpice? A maid dressed in black answered the door and ushered them into a long foyer. Its crystal chandelier, though unlit, reflected the light from the two windows on each side of the door to the walls of the room. Alain led them up a curving mahogany staircase lined with what looked like valuable paintings.

Thick velvet drapes partially covered the windows, giving the long second-floor room the aspect of early evening, rather than the bright afternoon sunlight they had just left. A heavy carved table occupied the center. An intricate tapestry depicting a medieval scene with troubadours entertaining gentry completely covered one wall. Percival and the grail? Maggie wondered. She wished she could inspect the tapestry in more detail.

Alain pulled Maggie and Israel aside before entering the room. "This is something of a formality," he said. "These are our senior members, and they are not always the most pleasant. Please reserve judgment for now."

Four seated men and one woman watched their approach. Four of the six looked older than Hércule. Maggie was shocked. How could this group save anyone? She wasn't sure some of them could even walk. If Nick needed help, this wasn't the group to provide it. She was sure of that.

They entered and were seated. Alain began introducing the members to Maggie and Israel. "Hélène Cocteau." Maggie held out her hand and smiled at the woman whose wispy white curls were gathered in a chignon at her neck. She wore the most amazing earrings Maggie had ever seen—brilliant diamond teardrops swung from double gold rings. They clinked together in a bizarre kind of melody at the woman's slightest movement. A throaty, whispered *"Enchantée"* accompanied a demure drop of the woman's head. The men in the room seemed somber in contrast to this bejeweled woman.

Next to Mme. Cocteau sat Jean Desmarais, a man of about forty with balding dark hair, a broad figure, and a ruddy complexion. Though his name was French, he had a British look to him. If this had been Edwardian England, Jean would have been the perfect portly innkeeper.

At the far end of the table sat a fragile-looking old man with a goatee. The skin on his face had a translucent, paperlike quality. He looked to Maggie as though he might be glued in place, but when they approached, to her surprise, he rose to his full height of five foot two and bowed to her. When he took her hand, his hand shook in a palsied movement against hers. "Didier Rousseau," Alain announced.

When Alain introduced François St. Clair, he smiled sweetly, almost innocently, at Maggie. She had the sense that he must have been the studious, nerd brother—the one who didn't get the girls.

Morton McLaren frightened her the most. He was an old billy goat of a man with a Scottish accent—not French in any way. There was nothing suave about him, either. "Hmm," he said. He nodded at her, but did not rise or offer his hand. "What's she here for?" he barked.

Maggie decided Alain DuClos was the friendliest of the bunch. At least he wasn't half dead.

When Alain introduced Israel, his manner indicated that Israel was one of his fast friends. The other Priory members regarded Israel coolly, with the suspicion an outsider can arouse, but Maggie saw that they respected Alain and his opinion.

Maggie and Israel sat quietly on either side of Alain. The introductions completed, Alain told his story of the capture of the grail and of Hércule's earlier mysterious disappearance. Maggie suspected they had already been briefed. She gasped in disbelief when he told of Henri Diamond's role and gasped again when she heard that Nick had been knocked unconscious. Israel reached over and took her hand in his.

Alain explained that Maggie was Hércule's grandniece and that Hércule had given her the chalice for safekeeping. Again her fears came upon her. Would they blame her for its loss?

François St. Clair asked her, "Why did you accept this responsibility?"

Mme Cocteau added, "Couldn't you have said, '*Non*'? Hércule must have been very persuasive." She shook her head in disbelief.

Before Maggie could answer, Alain interrupted, "What's done is done. We need to move on. We must recover the Sion Grail, and we have to find Hércule and our friends. We are here to decide how we can make this happen. We suspect they are all being held by Marcel Devereaux."

"First, I want to ask this young woman some questions," growled McLaren. "What kind of idiot would hide a precious antique in a Paris flat right above a man known to be a collector of antiques and an unscrupulous one at that?"

Maggie looked at Alain. "I . . . I didn't know . . ."

McLaren continued, "No, you didn't, did you? Do you know how long that precious object has been within the Priory?"

"Yes, I . . ."

"No, you don't! You know nothing of our history and what this treasure means to us. That chalice is a symbol of our family line."

"I've only recently learned that I am a part of your bloodline, and I know the grail is extremely valuable. I'm very sorry this happened, but I'm not responsible for the chalice's being stolen," Maggie said quietly.

Another voice interrupted. It was Jean Desmarais. "Do you know this Devereaux?"

"I met him yesterday. I immediately disliked him."

Hélène Cocteau interrupted. "My dear, we are not interested in who you like or who you don't like. *Pouf.*" The haughtiness in the woman's voice jarred Maggie.

"And your friend, Nick—did he know this Devereaux?" Mme. Cocteau asked.

"Well, they were neighbors," Maggie responded. "Nick said he'd met Devereaux a couple times, but I wasn't present at those meetings."

Desmarais asked, "And your friend Nick knew Devereaux was a collector of *objets d'art?*"

"Yes, I believe Devereaux told him that he collected valuable artifacts, but we didn't think Devereaux would have any way to connect us to the chalice."

"You two were very stupid, weren't you?" McLaren cut in.

"Outsmarted, perhaps—not stupid." François St. Clair said quietly.

"You and your friend Nick were in on this with Devereaux, weren't you?" McLaren added. "He could have hired you to deceive Hércule. Hércule's the double fool!"

Alain bristled. "Stop your foul Scottish noise! You don't know what you're talking about. Are you into the whiskey this early?"

Maggie was surprised by Alain's outburst, but also pleased by it. She didn't like the Scot. How did he fit here? He could be part of the reason Israel had cautioned her about the St. Clairs. They must both be from the Scottish Sinclair line.

McLaren looked angrily away at Alain's remark. "There's another important issue," Alain continued. "Hércule disappeared within a day after placing the grail in Mlle. Forsythe's care. None of our sources have been able to locate him, but my suspicion is that Devereaux's people have been interrogating him someplace. Now that Devereaux has the chalice, our hope is that he will let Hércule go. Let's hope he is still alive!"

Maggie gasped. It had not occurred to her that Hércule and Nick could possibly be dead.

McLaren spit out his next words. "Hércule was stupid . . . involving this little tart and her friend—what a ridiculous idea. When his wife was alive, he had some sense. Now he's gone off his nut because of this young woman."

McLaren pointed at Israel. "Who is this? What's he doing here?"

Although Alain had introduced Israel along with Maggie at their entrance, he hadn't explained Israel's presence. "This gentleman," he said, tapping Israel's shoulder, "came at Mlle. Forsythe's and my request. He is here to help us regain the Sion Grail and rescue our friends."

"Too many cooks spoil the broth," grumbled McLaren. "You're all stupid."

Maggie couldn't stand it any longer. She stood and, looking squarely at McLaren, said, "I am outraged at your behavior toward us. What have you ever done to deserve this grail? You've lived a long time, and you've got the right bloodline, but that doesn't make you smarter or more able. None of you have shown me anything that makes me want to help you. Perhaps you don't deserve to keep the grail."

Israel pulled at her sleeve. "Sit down," he whispered.

Maggie sat. She looked down the line at the Priory members. She'd been rude, she knew, but what could these old fuddy-duddy relics accomplish on their own? She didn't get a sense of power here. Arrogance, yes, but not the kind of cohesiveness that she would have suspected this group might have.

Alain stood. "Priory members, please. I can understand your suspicions, but Maggie and Israel are here to help us. We are not here to assess blame. What's done is done. We're here to come up with a plan. We must locate Devereaux and the St. Clair chalice. We must find out what has happened to our friends, Thérèse and Nick Payne."

Someone clapped. The sound came from the end of the table. Everyone looked at Didier Rousseau. A faint, clipped "Bravo" followed, accompanied by two distinct and serious nods of his head.

Jean Desmarais and François St. Clair both said, "*D'accord.*"

Obviously irritated, Morton McLaren said, "I don't like this. You fools are all too easy."

"Oh, hush up!" said an equally irritated Hélène Cocteau. "Let's do get on with this."

Maggie felt relieved. Perhaps something could still be accomplished.

François St. Clair exclaimed, "This Devereaux will not stay here in Paris. He may already have left. We have to move quickly."

"Perhaps we should call in the police?" Hélène Cocteau offered.

Alain DuClos hesitated, "We don't have any kind of proof that Devereaux is even involved. Right now we need more information."

But Hélène wondered aloud, "Who can we send? Does anyone know this Devereaux?"

Didier Rousseau clapped twice. They turned to him again. "Already asked and answered," he said tersely. He pointed to Maggie and nodded again. The group turned to her.

Jean Desmarais looked at Maggie. "Could you get into Devereaux's flat?" he asked.

Maggie looked from face to face around the table. "Yes," she said, "I believe I could." The calmness and clarity of her voice surprised her. She wanted to do this. She needed to do this. The potential danger for Nick and Hércule renewed her determination.

McLaren interrupted, "Why not Alain? He'd be better than an American know-nothing."

"Either Devereaux or his friend could easily recognize me. They've probably both been to the shop. That won't work," Alain said firmly.

After further discussion, the group developed this plan: Maggie was to go to Devereaux's to find out if Nick and Thérèse or Hércule were being held there. Her visit was to be timed, and if she did not leave Devereaux's flat within thirty minutes, Hélène would call to retrieve her *cousine*. Within the allotted time, Maggie was to find out as much as she could about what had happened to the chalice and to Hércule, Thérèse, and Nick.

CHAPTER FORTY-TWO

Reflections

IN HER HOTEL room, as she tried to relax and prepare herself for her assignment the next day, Maggie's thoughts retreated to her family. Garth, her physician father, adored her. As his only daughter, Maggie knew she held a special place with him. He showered her with toys and gifts, but his patients and his research ruled his time to the detriment of his family, and he was often unavailable to her. She'd always wanted more time with him.

Glory, her mother, loved and nurtured her up to a point, but as Maggie grew into a beautiful child, Glory began withholding her love. Maggie hadn't understood why. She remembered getting boxes of cookies from her mother at college, only to find a letter enclosed complaining about some unforgivable little sin she had committed (like not thanking her aunt for a gift she'd hated). After she'd read the letter, she couldn't eat the cookies. It took Maggie years to understand why she could never please her mother. Now, much later, after discussions with friends and a therapist or two, she figured out that she had dethroned her mother from her position as queen of the family, and that Glory's actions were jealous ones.

They'd called her home from college when her mother became seriously ill. She hadn't understood their relationship then. At the time, she felt that her mother wanted to tell her that she loved her . . . she could feel it in the way her mother's cold hands clutched hers. But her mother was too weak or too sick to say the words that Maggie wanted to hear. Many times Maggie had wished that her mom could have said, "I love you, Maggie. I am proud of you. I know you will do well." Her mother died before she and Maggie could make their peace.

Tears streaming, Maggie suddenly realized that she wished she could have seen through her mother's illness to the woman who lived inside, to her beautiful essence. But the disease and the petty problems between them kept it from her. Now Maggie could see that her mother was whole and loving inside, regardless of the illness and jealousy that interfered.

"Maggie."

The sound of her name jolted her. The room was suddenly bathed in a phosphorescent glow. Maggie squinted, but she could discern nothing except the eerie light; then she could see Rachel, her body a glowing contrast to the dark night that seeped in the window. Rachel's long braids were tied on the top of her head and hung like hoops around her ears. Her blue homespun skirt seemed to flow around her ankles even though her body didn't seem to move.

"You called me?"

The word "no" formed in Maggie's mouth, but she stopped before uttering it. She didn't want to deny herself this opportunity to talk with Rachel again. "Yes," she said simply, "I did."

"You were thinking about your parents and their love for you." Her spirit body seemed to whoosh in toward Maggie.

Maggie grabbed a corner of the spread and used it to wipe away her tears. "How can you know about me and my parents?"

"I can know everything now that I'm on the other side. And what I see is that you've not trusted God because you didn't trust your parents' love. You based your understanding of their love on what they showed you, not on what you truly knew inside. Now you realize that they did love you. When we were together at Montségur, you didn't trust me and you didn't trust God, though we were taught that God could work directly through us." She paused. "Before you were born, you made a contract with your parents to learn from them. And you made a contract with me. But you didn't keep it."

Tonight Rachel's voice sounded different—softer, gentler. Maggie listened, rapt.

"You and I knew that the world outside of us is not always the truth. It is only a resonance of who we are at the moment. It captures our energy and plays it back. But because we are constantly changing inside, our outside world changes, too. We always have the choice to change our lives and our beliefs. If we look, we can see perfection in everything that happens. Why do you not know that? Despite several lifetimes on earth, you keep experiencing the same lessons."

It took all of Maggie's concentration to understand Rachel's remarks. "I see," Maggie said after some moments. "Perfection is a hard word for me."

Rachel smiled. "Yes. But this is not about becoming a perfect person. It's about seeing that somehow everything that happens to you has some piece of perfection in it. Think about your mother's death."

Maggie said, "I felt guilty that I hadn't spent much time with her before she died. I was young and busy with my college life. I didn't know she was so ill. At the time, I wanted her to show me more love than she did. Even though she didn't say the words I wanted to hear, just being with her as she lay dying brought me closer to her. I could feel the love without the words."

Rachel nodded. "I'm here to awaken your memory and to help you better understand relationships. Tell me, did you come to any conclusions about your relationship with your mother and father?"

Maggie's earlier tears returned as she spoke, "I've spent years hating my mother. I hate the way she treated me. It wasn't fair—not at all. I could never please her no matter how hard I tried. I did try. Then she became ill, and it was too late."

"You missed the goodness in her."

"Yeah, I did. When I was a little girl, she always sang to me as she combed my hair, so I would forget about the snarls and how they hurt. She wouldn't have done that if she didn't love me. When I think about my mother's illness, I don't know if I could have changed it. It was hers. But I could have seen it differently. Just seeing it now is a miracle, really. I've been fighting the idea that my mother didn't love me for so long. And I haven't looked for the good part of my father, either. Recently, he gifted me with a glorious chic dress for no reason other than to surprise me and show me he supported me taking this trip. Because he's hurt me in the past, I let that blur my entire picture of who he was."

"I'm glad you're seeing things differently now," Rachel said. "That's good. You have a choice in how you view your relationships with those dear to you and in how you view what happens to you. Look for the wholeness, the rightness in everything. It is always there."

"And now, two wonderful men are in love with me . . . at least they seem to be . . . and I don't know exactly what to do about that. And . . . I've had the responsibility for this valuable grail and, on my watch, it's been stolen. It's the worst thing that's ever happened to me!" Maggie wailed. "There couldn't be any rightness in that."

Rachel's voice was softer now. It reminded Maggie of tiny seashells softly crashing together under the surf. "Be grateful for the love of two men. An answer for that will come. But you are anguishing over a piece of metal, Maggie? In time, you will see there is rightness in whatever happens to the chalice."

Outraged, Maggie said, "A piece of metal? What are you saying! It's much more than that! It's ancient . . . treasured . . . holy. Why are you belittling it?"

The phosphorescent figure wavered. "Think about it," Rachel whispered. Then the darkness outside the window sucked the diaphanous image of Rachel's body into it. Maggie raised her hand as though to wave good-bye, then lowered it. She smiled at her automatic response. The grail had brought her Rachel and these new insights. She was thankful for that.

She tried to grasp the wisdom in Rachel's statement about the grail. Suddenly, something came loose in her. She felt holier and more complete, and it didn't seem strange to feel that way. "Maybe we're all a little holy," she said quietly.

CHAPTER FORTY-THREE

The Plan

AT 3:10 PM, Maggie arrived at Devereaux's flat. She rang the bell several times. No answer. Then she knocked. Guillaume opened the door and looked questioningly at her.

"Madame?"

"Is M. Devereaux in? I would like to speak with him."

"I am sorry, Madame. M. Devereaux is out for the afternoon and perhaps the evening as well. I do not expect him until much later, if at all."

"Oh no! I'm trying to locate my friend Nick Payne. He lives upstairs. He mentioned that he knew M. Devereaux. Did you meet him?"

"Yes. We have met."

"Nick called me early this morning saying he'd be back in the afternoon by 1:00 PM, but I checked his apartment and he isn't there." Maggie stepped closer to Guillaume and lowered her voice. "I thought perhaps you or M. Devereaux might have seen him." Maggie hoped she sounded confiding. Guillaume did not react. While maintaining eye contact, she tried to see beyond him.

"I have not seen M. Payne. As I told you, Madame . . ." Before he could finish his sentence, Maggie abruptly pushed past him and moved quickly into the salon.

Guillaume followed her crying, "Madame! Madame!"

Maggie stopped in the center of the empty room and scanned it. It appeared to have been recently used. Two corners of the Persian rug were curled and its fringe was awry in several places. Maggie saw what appeared to be wine spills on a glass table and on the polished floor. "You must have had a party here."

"*Oui, Madame.* How discerning you are. M. Devereaux was celebrating a new acquisition."

"Was Nick Payne here for the party?"

"*Non, Madame.* M. Payne was not here. We had a small gathering earlier. I am negligent in not having cleaned the remainders before this, but I have been occupied with my other duties."

Maggie spotted a glass case between a tapestry and a large seventeenth-century landscape. She moved quickly to it. "Oh, is this the new acquisition?" She pointed at a goblet, which appeared to be quite old, but which was obviously not her chalice.

"No, Madame. I am sure that M. Devereaux would be very pleased to see you, but, as you can see, that is not possible. I am sorry not to be of further help, Madame." He motioned toward the door.

Calmly, Maggie sat down in the chair near the wine spills "I'll wait," she said determinedly. She could feel Guillaume's irritation.

"But, Madame, you must have other engagements. It will be late before M. Devereaux returns. It is not proper for you to stay here with me."

A slight laugh escaped her throat. "I'm not worried about you, Guillaume. I'm sure you are a gentleman. You know, I think I left something here yesterday when M. Devereaux hosted Nick and me for brunch. It's a green hand-painted pin—Russian, I believe—a gift from a special friend. There is a rose in the center. I was wearing it that day, and it's disappeared. Have you seen anything like that?" Maggie got up and began lifting chair cushions and looking on top of and under furniture.

"I have seen nothing like that!" Guillaume looked nonplussed and helpless, and the set of his mouth told Maggie that he was angry. She returned to the chair.

Guillaume sighed. "If you insist on waiting, I will bring you some wine, Madame." He paused. "Or tea, if you prefer?"

Maggie moved her hands in the universal sign that said, "It doesn't matter." Guillaume left the room. Her eyes searched the room for other traces of what might have occurred earlier. Maggie walked back to the glass case to take a closer look at its contents while she waited. Inside, near the mirrored back, was a small jar with a curved, chipped lip. Its brown velvet case had slipped down around its circular base. An empty wooden box with a hinged lid sat next to it. Maggie smiled. Nick had told her about the ancient jar. She wished she could reach into the case and touch it. What stories could it tell her? As she stood there mesmerized, she heard a muffled sound—a groan or a cough not distinct enough to identify. Someone else is here. Nick? Hércule? Her excitement grew.

Guillaume returned. She wished she could get him to leave her alone for more than five minutes. Did he suspect her? Probably.

"I thought I heard someone groan," she said.

Without hesitation, Guillaume replied. "Ah, yes. A noisy drunkard was outside on the street earlier." He wrinkled his nose in distaste. "He's probably still there. No matter how good the neighborhood, we cannot keep them away."

Guillaume handed Maggie a glass of wine and moved rapidly out of the room, saying, "I have some business to attend to."

Maggie wondered if she could trust what Guillaume had given her. She set the glass down without tasting it.

Something here made her uncomfortable. The walls were calling out to her in a sort of hysteria. She felt queasy. She wasn't frightened, but she didn't like this place. She wondered how she could get to the other rooms in the apartment. Though Guillaume had left the room, she couldn't be sure how soon he would return. Then she heard Guillaume's footsteps descending to a lower floor. Now she could look around.

Maggie immediately removed her shoes and placed them in her nylon bag. In her stocking feet, she could almost skate down the hall floor that she hoped led to the bedrooms. She opened the door to the first room—a small study with a nineteenth-century desk, an elegant antique where Alexandre Dumas might have written one of his adventure stories. All it needed was an ink well, a plumed pen, and a curling shaft of watermarked velum.

The room on her left, whose door was slightly ajar, held an ornate sleigh bed with a cream coverlet and two large carved armoires. A tufted chaise longue, upholstered in an amber-colored *matelassé*, was angled to take advantage of the view out the tall windows.

She approached the two doors at the end of the hallway. On the left, Maggie found a rather prosaic bathroom with hexagonal white tiles and utilitarian fixtures. She tried the door on the right. Locked. She rattled the doorknob and pushed to see if it would open. No luck. "Nick?" she called softly. "Nick, are you there?"

She listened. She thought she heard breathing. She had to see who was in that room. But how?

She heard Guillaume's returning footsteps echoing on the polished floor. Maggie dashed into the bathroom and flushed the toilet, turned on the water in the sink, and wet her hands. She put her shoes back on and came out of the bathroom shaking her semi-dry hands to find Guillaume waiting for her just outside the bathroom door.

Before he could speak, a phone rang. Guillaume hurried off. He took the call in the study with the door shut. Maggie could hear his laugh, a descending cascade of chortles, but she couldn't catch the words. Even with the door open, she knew she might not have been able to understand. Though her French was quite good, sometimes when she couldn't see the face of the speaker, her mind refused to understand the bursts of sound. She tiptoed quickly to the locked room, rattling the handle again. "It's Maggie," she hissed as loudly as she dared. No response. Disappointed, she walked slowly back to the salon and settled in the blue chair near the table with her wine glass. Within a few minutes, Guillaume reentered the room.

"M. Devereaux will not be returning tonight."

Maggie looked suspiciously at Guillaume. "You said he was just making business calls in Paris this afternoon."

"No, Madame. I said so only because that is usual when he is in Paris. He frequently has business interests that take him away from Paris and social obligations as well. M. Devereaux is a very unpredictable man."

Liar! You know where he is, Maggie thought. She stood up. "Well, I am disappointed at not being able to discuss with M. Devereaux a priceless and very old *objet d'art* that is at my disposal. I was sure he would be interested. *C'est dommage.* Too bad!" she repeated in English. "If you find the brooch I described, please give it to Nick when you see him next."

She moved through the front entrance hall like a queen discarding last year's crown. She hoped this show of bravado would conceal the frantic concern that was in her heart. She had not found Nick or Hércule. Maybe she had. It was hard to know who was in that room.

Sounding relieved, Guillaume offered an obligatory, but curt, "*Au revoir,*" as she passed.

"*À bientôt,*" she said to herself. This was not finished.

That evening, when Maggie returned from Devereaux's apartment, the Priory of Sion held another meeting. Maggie described her visit to Devereaux's flat to Alain and the other members. "Although I didn't see Nick and Thérèse, my guess is they are being held in the room at the end of the main hall. I heard groans coming from there. It was the only locked room on that floor. I was able to look into all the others."

Despite her helpful information, the meeting dragged on for longer than Maggie would have liked. The French way of dotting every *i* and crossing every *t* and addressing each other with unnecessary politeness irritated Maggie. Why couldn't they just get out there and do something? Her troubled sleep the night before, followed by her frustratingly unsuccessful confrontation with Guillaume, had drained her energy. Her head ached, and the overpowering disappointment with her efforts enveloped her. She thought, "God! If they don't decide on some action soon, I'll have to find someone else to help me. Something has to be done soon!"

Noticing her distress, Israel took her hand. "We'll get through this together," he said.

She felt his strength in the tendons of his fingers. She loved the feeling. It's amazing how good holding someone's hand feels. She smiled appreciatively. How concerned Israel seemed. It really wasn't his problem, yet here he was.

Alain was summing up the situation and their planned response. He turned to Israel. "Hawkins, are you in or not? We have to act quickly. We are not dealing with a rational man. Who knows what this deviant will do next. We need to see if they have Hércule and see that the American and Thérèse come to no further harm."

"*D'accord,*" Israel said as he shook Alain DuClos's hand. "I'll go with you," Israel volunteered.

Surprised, Maggie looked at him. Israel didn't seem like someone who would seek adventure. Maggie wondered if he was motivated by his interest in her or if he was just one of those wonderful people who gave of themselves whenever they were needed. Or maybe the cosmos of intrigue they were all experiencing was drawing him in as well.

"Maggie," Alain called.

Alain's calm tenor voice broke through to her. "What?" she responded.

"Hawkins will take you back to your hotel. We'll call you when we have some news of our friends."

"No!" Maggie sputtered. "No way! I want to help. I want to be involved. I want to find Nick and Hércule as much as or *more* than you do."

Alain said, "You're not needed for this foray." The severity of his message was softened by, "We won't forget about you. We'll keep you informed."

"Wait!" Israel interrupted, "Maggie has to come with us. Alain, I don't think you understand how important this is to her. I'll see that she is safe, no matter what happens. But I can't help you unless you include her in whatever we do."

Alain looked thoughtfully at Maggie. He shrugged. "*Ça va.* It is against my better judgment, but she may join us. However, she must stay out of our way if things get dangerous."

She smiled at Israel. Thank God, Maggie thought. And thank Israel. I would have died if I'd been left behind and not be able to be involved in Nick's rescue. She prayed silently: Thank you. Thank you. Please keep Nick safe.

CHAPTER FORTY-FOUR

Catacombs

D EVEREAUX PHONED AT 5:00 PM. "Guillaume?"

"Oui."

"What's happening with our visitors?"

"They're in the back bedroom."

"Still? Haven't you dealt with them? They can't be found at my apartment. And we don't want them talking to the *flics*. Get rid of them."

"But how? I don't know where to take them."

"You idiot! Take the two of them to the catacombs. With seven million bodies there, no one will notice a couple more."

"I hate that place. You know I can't stand to be closed in. I get frantic. Besides, I don't know my way around down there. I'll get lost!" Guillaume's whining voice was shaking in concert with his body. Just the idea of that place!

"Do I have to come back and take care of this myself? Call Diamond. No, on second thought, he's too weak. Call Heinrich. He'll know a special entrance where you won't be watched. He knows his way around inside, too. He'll tell you what you'll need to get them down there. Perhaps Heinrich's boys can help. I want this done before daybreak. Do you hear?"

"Yes."

"And Hércule St. Clair? What have you done with him?"

"He's where we left him—in the wine cellar. He's not doing too well. He won't eat. He doesn't move about. It's not my fault. He's just too old."

"We don't need him anymore. Have Diamond take him home."

"What if he talks?"

"He won't, you silly fool. Tell him he'll never get his chalice back if he breathes this to anyone. Tell him he's a dead man if the police hear of this. The St. Clair grail is ours now. I am keeping it with me until things settle down."

"Where are you?"

"Out and about. You can reach me on my mobile, and I expect you to call at 8:00 AM tomorrow with the news of exactly how you disposed of Payne and that woman. Do you understand, my imbecile? That is an order!"

"*Mein fuehrer* will not be disappointed." Guillaume hated their game. The German words froze in his mouth. He hated having to call him that. There were times when he hated Devereaux and his stupid games so much he could hardly breathe. Arrogant bastard! He had tried refusing to play this game on previous occasions, but Devereaux's punishments had taught Guillaume to comply. He had to keep remembering the perks of this job. Guillaume was silent.

"Bye, bye, darling." The phone clicked.

Merde! How am I going to get rid of these ridiculous interlopers? Guillaume pondered. Call Heinrich! I hate Heinrich. I hate all Devereaux's occult birds. Damn! What do they want with Christian relics? It doesn't make sense. Devereaux seems to think this chalice has some kind of magical power that will elevate him to his political dreams. All their satanic rituals haven't gotten them anywhere yet—just some pretty boys for Heinrich. Now this. Ach!

Guillaume walked down the hall to check on his captives. He peered through the keyhole. The woman was seated on the floor leaning against the chaise holding the man's head in her lap. He could see that she had worked her hands free and pulled the tape off her mouth. Thank God she hadn't screamed when that woman was here!

He decided he'd just scare them now, before he got Heinrich involved. Guillaume rattled the door handle and yelled, "Your death is at hand!"

That ought to keep them quiet, he thought. He picked up the phone and dialed. "Heinrich. I need you. Now! Bring some help . . . and a map of the catacombs. Devereaux wants us to dump two interlopers there. Get here as soon as you can."

Guillaume walked quickly to his room at the other end of the house, pulled coveralls from the top shelf of his closet, and climbed into them. Past experience had shown him that disobedience to Devereaux's orders did not serve him well. Now where had he put Devereaux's damn gun?

Nick drifted in and out of consciousness. He was floating. Then his cloud touched down on a landscape of rolling hills. The cushion under him moved. "Agh, my head!" he groaned, surprised that he had a voice and that it worked. "Where in hell?" His eyes searched the apparently vacant room. A woman's face bent over his.

He blinked. Who? Had spiders spun cobwebs in his mind? Then, suddenly, he understood.

"*Bienvenue.* Welcome back." Thérèse's enthusiastic words were spoken softly.

Nick pressed his forehead—as though pressure could relieve the intense throbbing in his skull. The scene in his apartment with Thérèse, Alain, Henri, and Devereaux's henchmen bubbled up.

"Okay. I'm beginning to remember. Where the hell are we?"

"We're in the large apartment downstairs. I understand the owner's name is Devereaux. They dragged us down the stairs. You were out cold. I was in the salon at first, where I saw the weirdest celebration I've ever seen. Devereaux was drinking from the Sion Grail and dancing with it as his dancing partner. It was almost as if the wine or the chalice had infected him. The bizarre frivolity that followed doesn't seem to fit with what I would imagine would be his normal personality. I wish you could have seen it."

"You know," Nick said, "it's almost as if I did. I could hear some of it, but it came to me in snatches from afar—like in a dream." Remembering his own experience of drinking from the chalice and making love to Maggie, Nick paused and looked at Thérèse and asked, "Is it possible that the St. Clair grail could have caused his weird behavior?"

"I've only heard stories of the powers of the grail. If the stories have any truth, then—yes, the wine from the grail could change a person in some way."

"I have to think about this," Nick said. If that were true, could that mean the night he and Maggie . . . Oh no. She wanted it too. He was sure she did. It couldn't have been their drinking from the chalice.

Thérèse interrupted. "Don't you want to know the rest?"

Nick looked up. "Sure," he said.

"That funny Diamond was there. Later they put us in here." Thérèse paused to let her story sink in. "Once, I heard a woman call your name. I wanted to answer, but I hadn't yet freed my hands to take the tape off my mouth. I finally managed to wriggle out of the tie-backs, but by then, the person was gone." She held out her hands. "Look, my wrists are black and blue!" Thérèse's voice faltered.

Nick leaned as far back as he could and turned around until he could look into Thérèse's eyes. "It must have been Maggie. She's got balls—more than I imagined."

"*La tête?* How is it?" Thérèse patted his head gently, almost imperceptibly.

"Ever have a locomotive running back and forth inside your skull? It makes it much harder for the brain to work. That's my current excuse. I'm having a hard time understanding why all this happened over Maggie's grail."

"Maggie's grail? What are you talking about? No! It is the St. Clair family's and the Priory's, not Maggie's."

"Well, temporarily it was hers . . . ours. I wish neither of us had ever seen the damn thing!"

"Do you think I like this?" Thérèse said, irritated. "The grail has great significance to the Priory families. Hércule was very foolish to give it to an outsider. And this Devereaux—he's more a thief than a collector." Nick heard anger in her voice.

Nick commented, "When I first met Devereaux, I would not have suspected that he was capable of this. He gave the impression of an honorable man."

Thérèse shrugged, pushed Nick gently aside, and rose to her feet. "People are not always what they seem," she said.

Sitting up, Nick looked at his watch. "How long have you been holding me?"

"Too long. I tried to find a way out of here, but there's only that one window. The latch is rusted, and the frame is swollen. It won't budge. So I gave up. I decided the best thing I could do was to comfort you."

"Have you heard anything going on out there?" Nick pointed to the door.

"Only that one woman. That prissy guy came by and rattled the door and yelled that he was going to get rid of us. I heard him talking about the catacombs."

She waited for the message to sink in. Her voice became frantic. "Are you feeling any stronger, Nick? Could we force the door? We've got to get out of here! We can't just stay here and wait to be killed."

Nick wondered if his legs could support him. He had to try. He struggled unsteadily to his feet, putting his hands on the seat and then on the back of the chaise longue to steady himself.

Thérèse paced back and forth across the faded pastel Aubusson rug. "Alain must suspect we are here. If only he would come! Where can they be? Have they forgotten us?" She slumped into the room's only chair. She began sobbing noisily.

Nick understood that all her pent-up fear was coming out. "I know," Nick said, "This is more difficult than any of us could have imagined. It's not fair, is it?" He moved his hand gently up and down her spine, just barely touching her through the soft silk of her blouse.

Thérèse wiped her wet face with the sleeve of her silk blouse and nodded wordlessly. She sniffed trying to restrain each sob. Then, suddenly, as though possessed by a different being, her back stiffened, and through clenched teeth, she growled, "*Je déteste cet homme! Je déteste ce Devereaux!*"

Surprised, but happy that Thérèse had recovered from her emotional outburst, Nick followed her lead. "Me too! I quadruple that."

Thérèse looked dubious at Nick's choice of words.

Walking gingerly so as not to shake his still-painful head, Nick looked around the room for a weapon to use if and when they could manage to get out the door. Nick pointed. "Hand me that clock over there."

Thérèse got up, went to the table, and lifted the ornate clock. "Ugh! This is heavy."

"Yeah, that's the idea. Now get over there." He pointed to the other side of the room.

CHAPTER FORTY-FIVE

Escape

ALAIN, ISRAEL, AND Maggie arrived at Devereaux's apartment building late that night. Alain tried a set of standard keys on the door, while Israel and Maggie kept watch through the building's doorway for any activity on the street or within the apartment house. "Eh! This old key works in the main lock, but there is a deadbolt above. I don't have a key for that. This place has a terrace on the other side. We can get in that way." They walked around the building and climbed up onto the terrace; a row of French doors opened onto it. "This ought to be easy," said Alain. He slipped a credit card from his pocket and worked it swiftly back and forth through the door's latch. Alain signaled success making a circle with his thumb and forefinger, and they moved stealthily into the salon.

Alain's flashlight circled the room. It stopped on a glass case on the opposite wall. "Hawkins, watch at the door to the hall. I need to check this out." Maggie followed Alain. Israel followed his instructions.

"Aha!" he said under his breath. Was the St. Clair chalice there among the treasures? No. But wait. His gaze stopped at a chipped alabaster jar that was just barely visible beside an open small wooden box.

Maggie whispered, "I caught a glimpse of that old piece when I was here yesterday. What do you think it is?"

Alain put his finger to his lips to shush her. To his surprise, the catch holding the carved wooden frame of the glass doors released, and the right-hand door swung open. Why hadn't it been locked? Someone here was careless. "Aha!" he muttered again as he quickly removed the jar. He popped it into its box, pressed it into his coat pocket, and returned smiling to Israel. "Now, we can teach M. Devereaux a lesson."

"What the hell do you mean? Forget Devereaux. Aren't we here to look for Nick and Thérèse?" Israel asked.

Maggie was as taken aback as Israel at Alain's strange move.

"Shh," Alain hissed.

They heard a loud pounding on the entrance door. Exchanging looks, the three pressed themselves against the wall at each side of the door that led from the salon to the entrance hall. They saw a barefoot Guillaume rush to the door, unlock the deadbolt, and open it. Alain remembered the two men who entered as the same two he'd seen at Nick's apartment. They were dressed in rubber boots and coveralls. The muscular one said, "André is going to help."

"*Bon!* We have to hurry. I have to report to Devereaux just after daybreak."

"Where is he?"

"I don't know. But I can reach him on his mobile."

The crash of breaking glass interrupted their conversation. All three in the hallway looked toward the rooms at the end of the hall. "*Comment?*" Guillaume began running to the room where Nick and Thérèse were being held. He reached the door and suddenly remembered he didn't have the key in his coveralls. "*Merde!*" He strode rapidly down the hall. The other two followed him. "Keys," he said, embarrassed. "Damn keys!"

As Guillaume approached, Alain, Israel, and Maggie quickly backed into the darkness of the salon. By craning their necks, they could see Guillaume pass in the hall and then return to open the door to the room where the sound came from. Guillaume was too occupied to notice them. He saw that the room was strewn with broken glass, but he didn't yet see Nick and Thérèse, who had wrapped their hands with the heavy quilted drapery tiebacks. Each held sharp fragments of glass in both hands. As Guillaume stomped into the room, a large shard of glass pierced his foot. He jumped up and down screaming furiously as he ground the glass deeper. One of Devereaux's thugs pushed him to the floor saying, "Idiot! Get out of the way!"

Thérèse nodded toward the stocky man who had roughed her up earlier that day. "That one's mine!" She flew at him with furious abandon. Her right hand slashed across his face leaving a gaping wound from his left cheek across his lips to his chin. Her left hand cut through his right wrist just below the sleeve of his coveralls. His mouth choked with blood, the man gurgled, but determinedly held his foot out and sent Thérèse sprawling. She hit the floor close to the entrance and began crawling toward freedom.

At the same time, Nick lunged at the taller man, cutting a bloody swath across his neck. Unable to speak, the man grabbed Nick and held him tightly. Nick punched at the belly in front of him with his glassy fists, swearing with each blow. The man's blood dripped from his neck onto Nick's upturned face. As the man toppled, Nick fell with him. After they hit the floor, the man's hold relaxed.

Seeing Alain, Thérèse grabbed at his pant leg. He leaned over and helped her to her feet, brushing off the glass shards as best he could. His hand behind her, he led her out of the room to where Maggie stood frozen and staring, aghast at the violence and blood. Maggie pulled off her cardigan and used it to clean Thérèse's wrists.

Israel pulled Nick away from the bleeding man. He didn't bother to check to see if the man was dead. Guillaume sat on the floor muttering and crying.

With Alain leading, they exited the open terrace door. Israel jumped down and then helped Nick. He caught a glimpse of Maggie's relieved face. Alain handed Thérèse gently down onto the front car seat. As they entered his waiting car, Alain tapped each on the back and said, "Bravo."

Israel shook Nick's bloody hand. "I can't believe what I just saw. God! You two were ferocious. You didn't need us at all."

Maggie's arms encircled Nick. She could taste the blood on his cheek. "Oh, Nick, I'm so relieved that you are alive. My god, you were spectacular in there!"

Nick kissed her face several times. Then he shook his head. "It all seems unreal. I don't believe it myself."

Thérèse was crying softly, "*Incroyable. Oui. C'est trop!*" She sat up suddenly. "But wait. You must still look for Hércule. I heard Guillaume say that he was being held in the wine cellar. He has been there for days. We must get him out."

Alain nodded to Israel. "Wait here. If someone comes out, take off. But wait as long as you can." He tossed the car keys to Israel.

"Take off to where?"

"Where we had the meeting."

Alain rushed back into the house. He found the stairway off the kitchen that led to the wine cellar. He found Hércule propped unconscious against a water heater. He had been tied, but the ropes had slipped away from his frail collapsed body and were now in a tangle around him.

"*Sacredieu!* Those bastards almost let the old man expire." A rat scurried across his foot and across Hércule's lap. "You're in good company," Alain said to the rat as his boot searched it out. "Hércule! Hércule!" He shook the drooping head and limp body several times, hoping there was still life in it. "Let's go, old man. We'll take care of you. We'll get you home." He struggled to get Hércule into an upright position so that he could lift him like a flour sack onto his shoulders. He tied Hércule's arms around his neck with a piece of the rope, reached for his haunches, and headed to the stairs. Upstairs, he heard halting footsteps and Guillaume's voice: "The bastards! Heinrich's dead. What should I do? It's Devereaux's fault. And he's not even here to help!" Then he began to scream mindlessly in pain and confusion.

Alain waited until it was quiet again, then he quickly climbed the stairs with Hércule on his back. He searched the hall at the top of the stairs, saw no one, then moved as fast as he could out through the French doors where they'd entered earlier. At the car, Israel helped him lift Hércule gently down. Alain untied Hércule's hands and eased him into the back seat next to Maggie and Nick just as Henri Diamond drove up. He got out and approached Alain's car. Alain pointed to the unconscious Hércule leaning against Maggie's shoulder. "Did you do this?" he said as he grabbed Diamond's collar and pulled him close. Alain's arm lurched back as though to slug Diamond.

"No. Please. I know nothing about this. Guillaume called and asked me to come here to take M. St. Clair home. I was surprised to see Hawkins and Nick here, so I stopped."

"Right! You're such a good guy. *Alors, c'est fini.* You've caused enough trouble. You better look to the others in there—it's a bloody mess. The police will be very interested in this. Kidnapping is no small crime, and I know you were involved." Alain let Diamond go and jumped into the front seat. "*Allons-y!*"

Israel jammed the car into gear, and they roared away. Alain called the police from his cell, telling them about the evening's events.

Nick comforted Maggie by putting his arm around her. He could feel her shaking. He was as yet unwilling to think about what had just occurred.

When they were clear of the neighborhood, Alain turned to Nick and Thérèse and said, "We have to find a safe place for you to stay tonight . . . a place where you can rest and clean up. I think Mme. Cocteau's is the safest. I'll call her and let her know we're coming. We'll drop you there. I'll call the police and leave an anonymous message. After that, Israel, Maggie, and I will deal with Hércule. I have something to show him."

Puzzled, Israel looked at Alain. "Isn't this enough for one night?"

"Don't worry, my friend. I'll wait until another day when he's himself again."

Hércule's eyes flickered open. Maggie whispered in his ear, "*Tu es avec des amis, Hércule.*"

To the others she said, "I think he's coming to."

Alain turned around. He handed her a bottle of water. "See if you can get him to drink. He's probably dehydrated."

Maggie gently pulled Hércule's head into a more upright position and wet his lips.

"What?" Hércule asked dazedly without opening his eyes.

"Here, drink this. Swallow. That's right."

Hércule coughed.

She tried again with more success. He seemed to welcome the liquid, but his eyes remained shut.

"*Tu as soif?*" she asked.

Hércule nodded.

Maggie began to fuss over him, wiping his brow with his ascot. "We must take him to a hospital. He looks so frail."

Hércule stirred. Barely audibly, he said, "*Pas de hôpital! Seulement chez moi.* Get me home. I just need to rest."

Alain turned to him. "Hang on, Uncle. We will have you home in your bed soon. We'll make you some soup. I have a wonderful surprise for you," Alain said, "but, it will have to wait until you are well again."

Hércule's face brightened. "The Sion Grail? You've got it?"

"No, not yet. Something else."

Hércule slumped over. "I didn't tell them where it was."

"We know. Devereaux has it, but we'll find him."

"It's my fault. I am too old. We need new blood in our organization." Suddenly Hércule's head shot up. "Mlle. Maggie? Did Devereaux and his men find her? Is she all right?"

"I'm fine," Maggie said, putting her arms gently around Hércule.

He turned to look at her. "*Grâce à Dieu!* I was so worried that they would hurt you, too." He closed his eyes again.

CHAPTER FORTY-SIX

Maison St. Clair

THEY DROPPED NICK and Thérèse at Mme. Cocteau's. Alain replaced Israel at the wheel of the Citröen. "We've got to get Hércule home quickly," he said, careening the car adeptly through Paris's narrow streets.

"Hércule," Maggie said quietly. "I tried to reach you many times. I am so relieved to see you." She took both of his hands in hers.

He smiled faintly. "And I to see you," he said.

Alain shook his head. "That damned Devereaux! He held this sweet old guy prisoner in hopes of getting the location of the Sion Grail from him. *Quelle con!*"

Alain drove to the *dix-huitième* and turned onto a narrow street that led off to the left as they entered the Madeleine section of the city. He stopped the car in front of a two-story eighteenth-century mansard-roofed house. He felt in Hércule's pockets for his keys.

"They took them," Hércule said, frowning. "But there's a spare over the lintel."

Alain helped Hércule out of the car, and he and Israel half-carried him up a narrow flight of stairs into a drawing room. Ornate furniture that might have once graced his shop now lay strewn about in complete disarray.

Hércule gasped, "*Sacrebleu! Qu'est que c'est?*" He began to cry as he viewed the room.

Alain muttered angry oaths as he and Maggie helped Hércule to his bedroom. "I'll undress him. See if you can find some bouillon in the kitchen."

While Alain fed the soup to Hércule, Maggie and Israel straightened up the mess in the salon.

"He's asleep," Alain said when he returned.

"They did the same thing to my hotel room," said Maggie. "Awful people!"

"Those bloody bastards!" Alain sighed and ran his hand through his hair as he sank heavily into a chair. "The Priory was never set up for this kind of thing. When we started nine centuries ago, perhaps tit for tat was the warrior's way, but *now* I don't think it works."

"Maggie tells me there's a history of violence connected to the Sion Grail," said Israel.

"Yes, unfortunately that's true." Alain looked quizzically at Maggie and said dryly, "You've been talking again, I see."

Maggie blushed, embarrassed.

"Well, perhaps Devereaux will now experience that mysterious negativity as well," Israel added.

"We can only hope," Alain said grimly.

Israel saw Alain fingering his bulging coat pocket. He pulled out the wooden box he had taken from Devereaux's cabinet. He opened it carefully and gently extracted the alabaster jar. Alain held it up for Maggie and Israel to see. "A little something extra—I think we've got Devereaux now!"

Israel looked baffled. "What do you mean? I saw you take that old broken pot, but how can that solve anything?"

"Ah, my new friend, you are not as experienced as I am in the ways of the antique-obsessed. This is a *chef d'oeuvre*. Not that it was designed by a master, but," he paused for dramatic effect, "it is old enough to have been used by *the Master. Comprends-tu?*"

"No," Israel said. "I don't get it."

"You will. Just wait. When I show this to Hércule, he will know how it fits in the puzzle of the *Prieuré de Sion*."

CHAPTER FORTY-SEVEN

Zurich

DEVEREAUX ENJOYED THE view of Lake Zurich and the distant Alps as he sipped his martini in the bar at his hilltop hotel, the Zurichsberg. The normal Zurich haze had cleared, allowing full enjoyment of the city's most spectacular view. He hoped Guillaume had everything under control in Paris. Guillaume was usually capable, if sometimes a little self-centered.

As Devereaux gazed across the lake, he remembered that when he was eight, his mother and father took him to Zurich to visit his mother's cousin. As a special side trip, they had taken a train around the lake to a small village on the other side, where there was a monastery and a church. The church reminded him of a down-at-the-heels fairyland. Though badly in need of repair and restoring, faded religious frescos in pink, yellow, and green covered the ceiling. Inside, gold and white cherubs cavorted overhead, while trumpeting angels gathered along the columns to flirt with the worshippers.

He remembered an altar near the entrance that was banked with bouquets of flowers—gifts to a statue of a dark-skinned woman holding an equally dark infant Jesus. How strange it had seemed to his young eyes.

The Black Madonna and the babe wore golden crowns and were dressed in clothing that might have been worn in a fifteenth-century Spanish court. Devereaux sighed. Why was he remembering this church and this statue now? He'd been to Zurich many times before and never thought of them.

When the waiter returned, Devereaux asked, "What do you know about that monastery across the lake?"

"The Abbey of Einsedeln? Benedictines run it. It's well known. There have been pilgrimages to see its Black Madonna since the Middle Ages. Have you seen her, Sir?"

Devereaux nodded. "Yes, as a boy, with my parents. I find it difficult to believe there could really have been a *black* Madonna." He grimaced at the distasteful thought.

"That doesn't bother us. Some say the dark skin comes from the soot of the candles lit to her over many years. Her color makes her special. If you've not seen the Romanesque church recently, you should see it on this visit. It's been beautifully renovated." The waiter pointed out across the sunny terrace. His stance stiffened. "Would you care for another drink, Sir?"

Devereaux nodded yes, and the waiter returned to the bar.

Devereaux's cell phone rang. It was Guillaume.

"*Oui. C'est moi.*" He listened as Guillaume told his story. "What? They escaped? *Merde!* Idiot! How did this happen? I don't believe your stupidity! How could you let me down, Guillaume? You had your instructions and you failed. They know who you are and who I am. No one must trace this chalice to me. You will pay for this!" Devereaux's voice rose to a frantically high pitch and loud volume, "Do you understand? Anyone that knows I have this chalice must be silenced! You must find them and get rid of them. I told you to take them to the catacombs. It's still the best place. Remember the World War II bunker where we had our meetings—like the Nazis? Take them there. I don't care if the entrances are sealed. Heinrich will know how to get in."

As Guillaume explained, Devereaux listened impatiently. Then he exclaimed, "What? Heinrich is dead and André is near death? Dead? How did that happen? Who did it? Unbelievable! Well, get Diamond to help you. He owes me. Call my mobile when you've got it arranged."

When he hung up, Devereaux noticed others in the bar watching him. He looked disdainfully at the gawkers and stuffed the phone in the pocket of his jacket. He uncrossed his legs and, irritated, pulled at the hems of his slacks. "What are you looking at?" he said to no one in particular.

His mind in a flurry, Devereaux hastily left the bar. How could those incompetents have let Payne and the woman escape? Would they tell the police? Doubtful. The Paris gendarmes wouldn't care about a theft from an American who didn't even own the object. He'd asked Diamond how his American neighbor became the possessor of this treasure, but he'd not gotten a satisfactory answer. It didn't make sense. Could Payne have bought it from old St. Clair? No. He didn't look like he had taste or money. Ridiculous thought.

Despite Guillaume's troubling news, Devereaux smiled to himself. What a breeze it had been! There, right in his building—just waiting for him to come to rescue her from the Priory and their dubious holy heritage. She deserved to be with the master race. Hitler knew that. His troops had searched for her at Rennes-le-Château. Himmler supposedly knew a lot about the esoteric. Yet he hadn't found this gem. Only Devereaux could do it! He thought of his little Neo-Nazi group and shrugged—a bunch of do-nothings. I wouldn't sully this lovely chalice by sharing her with them! She is for me alone.

Although he felt a shortness of breath from taking the stairs, once in his room, Devereaux took the chalice from its velvet case. As he held it, the late afternoon sunlight's rosy hues gave the chalice a special luminescence. He'd begun to believe that the chalice was a being with its own personality. "You are happy to be here with me, aren't you?" he asked. Now that his mother was gone, this lovely would be the only female presence in his life.

Devereaux had to set the chalice down abruptly on the cocktail table. "See what you've done! You have my heart palpitating just looking at you, my lovely," he blurted out as he bent to sit for a minute. Strange? He'd been holding the chalice, and now he could feel his heart beating rapidly and spasmodically. He felt a tingling and then the pain. He clutched at his shoulder. It felt like something heavy was sitting on his chest. Devereaux groaned and grabbed frantically for the inner pocket of his jacket. His fingers scraped at it until a silver engraved pillbox fell out onto the floor. He dove for it. On his hands and knees, he scrambled to it, and opening it, he popped three tiny white nitro pills under his tongue.

"Damn!" Devereaux's voice echoed through the spacious room. Dizziness overcame him. His knees buckled and his head hit the floor.

Guillaume massaged his swollen bandaged feet. Agh. What a night! Getting Heinrich, André, and himself to the hospital after the disaster had taken all of his cunning. He'd smashed the windshield in Heinrich's car to make it look like there was an accident, with Heinrich and André in the front seat. He threw some extra broken glass on the floor of the car, then dragged them into the car and propped them up, while he squeezed in beside them and drove to the hospital emergency room. What an ordeal! All the questions and the pain . . . it was awful. And he still had the police to look forward to. He'd seen their blue lights flashing as he drove away, but they hadn't come back to question him.

Devereaux didn't appreciate my cleverness. Damn him! And now my beautiful feet are ruined. He didn't even ask about me. He doesn't even care! I could have died last night. I'm not ready to die. Damn! I hate Devereaux for what he's done to me! He put me up to this.

Guillaume began limping around his room as he mulled over his unfortunate situation. His job and his relationship with Devereaux were on the line. In the main, he liked his job. He liked traveling wherever Devereaux's fancy took him, and he had grown accustomed to their sophisticated lifestyle. Also, he had a fair amount of freedom. No, he thought, that's not exactly true. There's always the need to please Devereaux—to cater to his whims, to do his dirty work. That's what he hated most. But sometimes Devereaux's tasks relieved his own anger and animosity—like killing that lousy, noisy cat that had been annoying them with her scratching and yowling. He really enjoyed that.

"Silence them. No one must trace the chalice to me." That had been Devereaux's command. But Guillaume had no idea where to find the dark-haired woman who had been held in the back bedroom. He'd heard her say her name was Thérèse de Beaufort, but that didn't mean anything. He'd never seen her before, nor did he know anything about the other two men who showed up last night. And then there was the red-haired woman who'd come snooping that afternoon—Mlle. Forsythe. He probably was expected to find her and silence her as well. "Silence them. No one must trace the chalice to me." That had been Devereaux's command. What a mess! This was impossible.

Though he dreaded Devereaux's response, Guillaume decided to call him again. He needed some guidance. He dialed Devereaux's cell phone. It rang seven times with no answer. Perhaps he's having a late dinner. Oh, well. I'll try tomorrow, he thought. But Guillaume knew he had to *resolve* this tomorrow, or Devereaux would have his hide. Despite the hour, he called Diamond.

Diamond refused to give Guillaume any information. "I do not wish to further participate," he'd said; and he'd been very emphatic. Diamond warned Guillaume. "You don't need more blood on your hands."

CHAPTER FORTY-EIGHT

Vanished

WHEN THE MAID at the Zurichsberg hotel entered Devereaux's room, she saw a man in a sports jacket lying on the floor; the spilled contents of a pill bottle surrounded him. A burned-out candle's wax had splattered over the table on which sat a magnificent jewel-encrusted chalice. As a maid at the Zurichsberg, Ilona had experience dealing with residents' health crises, but instead of focusing on the man, she was drawn immediately to the chalice. She'd never seen so beautiful an object before. Ilona knelt carefully and put her ear to the man's open mouth. His chest moved slowly in and out, and she could hear the faint shush of his breath. He made stifled gagging sounds, like the ones she made when the doctor put one of those wooden sticks on her tongue. She was relieved that the man was alive, but intuitively she sensed that the man on the floor was not a good person.

Crouching made her back and her knees hurt. With one hand on his chest, she leaned across to the table and picked up the chalice. How lovely it was. The chalice felt so powerful. She could feel it vibrating in her hands. The surprising intensity unbalanced her. She fell backward onto her bottom and dropped the chalice on the floor. Straightening herself, she took it in both hands. Suddenly, myriad images flooded her head—a nattily dressed older man, a priest in a seventeenth-century cassock, a beautiful woman with long braids who held the chalice close under her cloak, a long elegant table with a king at its head drinking slowly from the chalice. The back of her neck buzzed with a peculiar feeling. She patted at it with one hand. She said, "Amazing! Who are these people?" She set the chalice down. Shaking her head, she said, "I don't want to see anymore."

From her childhood, Ilona had had psychic abilities. As was the Romany custom, she learned to read palms and crystal balls, and she knew both the pasteboards and the Tarot cards as well. At this moment, Ilona knew instinctively that this beautiful object should not belong to this man, He was not someone who should have such a sacred object. And the vessel was holy, she was sure.

It had been many years since she'd allowed her clairvoyance or her clairaudience to function. The priest had told her to bury her gifts inside her and not let them out. He'd said it was not behavior that the church would approve of. That had frightened her. She loved the church, and she wanted to please it with her holiness. But her native psychic gifts were overpowering her desire to be good. She picked up the chalice again. She couldn't stop the pictures . . . they swam around her. She saw the chalice being passed between longhaired men at a table with a red-haired woman sitting next to . . . who was that? The name Jesus came into her head. Could it really be that these messages were from the one she loved so much? Could her psychic senses, now rusty from disuse, really be right about this?

"Is this the grail?" she asked aloud.

Devereaux moaned. Ilona looked at his body, but he was only an irritant to her at that moment. She knew she had to deal with him, but her fascination with the grail was overpowering.

Holding the chalice, she felt guided to stand and walk to the mirror that hung on the wall over the desk. She saw a face wrinkled and leathery from years of hard work and suffering, coarse gray hair that still curled itself in ringlets around that face, and sharp black eyes that looked as if they could see through a wall of stone. She had been beautiful once—only a trace of it remained—but she no longer cared that her beauty had faded. Her once smooth bronze complexion was paler now, allowing her to pass for an Italian or a Savoyard. As she held the chalice next to her worn face in the mirror, her skin seemed to lose its wrinkles and become smooth once again. "What kind of magic is this? What could make me look so young again?"

Messages were coming into her head. She heard, "Save me! Take me away. Take me away from this man." Was it her imagination? Then a cloaked woman with braids that she had glimpsed earlier while holding the chalice appeared. The apparition spoke, "I know you no longer steal, but you must take this chalice to safety." Rachel's voice was stern.

As the vision disappeared, Ilona moved quickly. She slipped the chalice and its case under her apron. This was a sacred object. Ilona made a sacrosanct pledge to do as the woman in the vision had told her. She called the manager's office to alert them of the collapsed man, explaining that she had to leave because she was afraid to stay in the room with a dying man. Then she scurried out of the room to the linen closet where she hid the vessel under a stack of white towels embroidered with the hotel's crest.

When Devereaux slowly opened his eyes, he saw a man leaning over him and pressing a stethoscope to his chest. Devereaux's shirt was unbuttoned. Where was he? Who was this man? Then he realized he was in his hotel room in Zurich. Another man stood nearby holding a small, open bottle. Devereaux recognized him as the hotel manager. He had previously complained to him about his room not being on the side with the view. Devereaux could smell ammonia. He hated the stink of it. He coughed. The man with the stethoscope waved to the hotel manager to back up.

The man with the stethoscope leaned over him. "Monsieur Devereaux? You are very lucky. Did you take some of these pills?" he said, pointing to the bottle. "They saved you this time."

Confused, Devereaux looked around. He groaned. "Who are you?" he asked.

The hotel manager explained. "This is Dr. Neumann. I called him immediately when the maid found you." The hotel manager nodded toward a frumpy gray-haired woman Devereaux hadn't noticed.

"We should take you to hospital for observation. You may have had a mild heart attack or TIA," the physician said.

"What's that?" Devereaux asked.

"A small stroke," the doctor replied.

Devereaux wondered, What time is it? How long have I been unconscious? Sun streamed across the floor. It must be late morning or early afternoon. Devereaux raised himself on his elbow, but he could not quite see the tabletop or the chalice. The doctor pushed him gently back. "You mustn't strain yourself. You're still weak."

Devereaux's arm flailed at the doctor with enough force to send him stumbling backward.

"Don't tell me what I must do," Devereaux said sharply.

Looking aghast at Devereaux's rudeness, the manager said, "Please, Monsieur! The doctor tries to help you."

Devereaux ignored him. He needed to see the tabletop. He motioned to the manager to help him. With assistance, Devereaux regained his feet. When he saw the empty table, a strange gurgling scream left his lips. "Aaagh! No! She can't be gone! Where is she?"

"You had a companion last evening, Monsieur?" The manager's tone was calm and respectful.

"Yes. No. I . . . I am missing something." He pointed. "It was there on the table." Devereaux noticed that the velvet case was missing, too. He looked to the manager. "How dare you come into my room and take my property while I was unconscious! I certainly hope you put it in the hotel safe."

The manager looked confused. "Put what, Monsieur?"

"A valuable antique chalice." As soon as he said the word *valuable*, Devereaux thought better of it. He didn't trust hotel employees. He didn't want to indicate the object's value. "Nothing of real worth, of course—a family item—but to me it is irreplaceable."

Emotion overcame his need to be cautious. He wailed, "I . . . I can't lose it. I've gone through too much." Devereaux's hands shook.

The manager asked, "Can you describe this valuable item, Sir?"

"A jeweled chalice—gold—a bit dented. Quite an unusual piece." His hands continued to shake

"Jewels! I will surely question the staff, Monsieur," the manager responded. "You can be assured of that."

The doctor looked at Devereaux in alarm. "I will call an ambulance."

Devereaux shot back, "No, I won't go. You can't make me."

The doctor shook his head. "You may have a second attack. You'd be much safer in a hospital."

"Pshaw!" Spittle dripped from Devereaux's lips. "I'm not leaving until this idiot finds my antique." He turned to the manager. "Find that chalice! Now!"

"Monsieur Devereaux, if this behavior continues, you will have to leave this hotel. We do not countenance such actions." The manager, looking severe, left the room. The maid followed him. The doctor dropped a packet on the table, turned on his heel, and marched toward the door. He turned before exiting and said, "I've left you some tranquilizers. You may need them." He slammed the door behind him.

Devereaux limped to the nearest chair and flopped into it. He could hardly believe that after all his efforts to become the owner of the Sion

Grail, while he slipped out of consciousness for a few minutes, his beloved treasure disappeared. The bitter irony. Unimaginable! What could he do now, with the chalice stolen from him? Could someone have followed him here and gotten into his room while he was unconscious and taken his precious chalice? The stress of this disturbing situation had replaced his fright about what was happening in Paris. But now, it returned. Had Guillaume silenced those Americans? Were the police involved? Devereaux phoned Guillaume. No answer. A feeling of fear and emptiness crept over him.

CHAPTER FORTY-NINE

Priory Secrets

THE NEXT MORNING, at Maggie's insistence, Alain picked her up on his way to Mme. Cocteau's to check on Nick and Thérèse. The maid directed them into a sunny breakfast room decorated in yellow and blue. When Nick entered, Maggie ran into his arms.

"Oh, Nick. I'm so relieved that you're safe. It's wonderful to see you! I've been so worried." Maggie shook with excitement at seeing Nick again.

"I lost the grail, Maggie. I let you down," Nick looked at the floor.

"It's not your fault. Devereaux's crazy. Oh, I'm so happy to see you!" Maggie felt like jumping up and down.

"I'm happy to see *you*!" Nick kissed Maggie and tightened his hold on her.

Alain brought in a tray with three cups, a pot of coffee, a pot of steamed milk, and a plate of *beignets*. Alain yelled to them. "Come on, you two. It's time for my morning *café*. Nick, you must be starving. Where's Thérèse?"

"Still asleep, I guess." Nick said, as he and Maggie sat down opposite Alain.

Alain shoved the pastries toward Nick. "Did you know they were planning to kill or drug you two and then dump your bodies in the catacombs under Paris? I overheard them talking about it. It's a devil of a place to find your way out of. The grid of an underground graveyard goes on for miles in all directions. The Nazis had a bunker down there during World War II. I'll bet that's what inspired Devereaux."

Maggie shivered. "God, that's unimaginably awful! You didn't tell me that, Alain! Do you think Devereaux will keep trying to silence us in one way or another?"

"Let's not talk about that." Nick pushed the plate away. "I can't eat. Just coffee."

Alain chomped on a *beignet,* then commented, "You were resourceful in your escape, but lucky, too. It was you, not Hawkins or I, who made it happen."

"Thanks." Nick sighed. "I can't think of myself as a hero. I'm too horrified at what we did to feel good about it. They were men I didn't know, and we slashed them up pretty badly." He put his head in his hands.

Maggie reached over and took his hand in hers. "It was survival, Nick. You had no choice in that awful situation."

Nick asked. "Do you think they lived? What do you suppose happened after we left?"

"I called the gendarmes," Alain responded. "Hopefully, they arrived shortly after that. We could check the hospitals to see if any of Devereaux's boys have checked in. Devereaux's companion seemed to be upright and walking. He would be the one to take care of the other two. What story he told the hospitals or the police, I couldn't guess."

They were all silent for several minutes. Then Nick said, "I hate what they are and what they planned to do, but I'm also appalled at what we did to them. It seems unbelievable when I think about it now."

Alain nodded. "It was life or death. There was no other way." He reached across and touched Nick's hand.

"I guess that was it," Nick said quietly.

The enormity of what had happened the previous night brought a pall on their conversation as they each relived their experiences. Then Maggie nudged Nick and said, "Now that we've got Alain all to ourselves, I want to ask him about the Priory."

"Yeah, I'm curious about your connection with the *Prieuré de Sion*, too. Thérèse told me something after I'd been conked on the head the other day, but I was so foggy at the time, it didn't all register," Nick said.

"Ah. The big question. What is it all about? Well, it can't hurt to tell you some history. The Priory's ultimate beginning was the marriage between Mary Magdalene and Jesus."

Nick and Maggie looked at each other. They knew about this, but they didn't want to interrupt Alain. He continued. "A prominent British genealogist claims to have traced the line. He says there were three children from the union—Damaris, born in 33 CE; Jesus II, born in 37 CE; and Joseph, born in 44 CE."

Maggie said, "You know I've heard some of this before, but only in a speculative kind of way, not with any detail. Can it be true?"

"There really are no records from that time, but yes, it could be. You know the story that Mary Magdalene came to France to escape persecution in Jerusalem, along with Lazarus; Martha; Mary Salomé, the mother of James and John; and Mary Jacob, the Mother Mary's sister?"

Maggie and Nick nodded.

"The genealogist claims it was the baby Joseph that came to France in Mary's belly and from whom the Merovingian kings descended. Others claim there was only one baby, and it was a girl named Sarah. That fits better with the ancient worship of the Black Madonna, often called Sarah. And Sarah means 'princess' in Hebrew. That could be another clue."

"I knew about the group voyaging from Jerusalem, but not about the babies. I thought Jesus died in 33 CE or thereabouts. Two of the children you mentioned were born after that. How is that possible?" Maggie asked.

"Well," Alain responded. "There is a theory that Jesus did not die on the cross . . . that he was resuscitated and spirited away . . . which could explain his so-called 'rise from the dead.' Also, husbands and wives in the Hebrew culture at that time did not always live together year round. After the time spent for procreation purposes, if conception occurred, the couples would separate for several months."

"Is there any documentation of this marriage?" Nick asked. Although he'd always been open-minded about religion, this seemed a bit extreme.

"Not exactly, but the Gnostic Gospel of Philip which was found with the other Nag Hammadi scrolls in Egypt in 1945 openly discusses the relationship between Jesus and Mary Magdalene. Philip says that 'Christ loved her more than all the disciples and kissed her often on the mouth.' Then there's Mary Magdalene's erotic anointing of Jesus using her hair. In those times, when a woman anointed a man with oil of spikenard it symbolized espousal. That custom came down the ages as a sacred marriage rite from the ancient goddess-worshipping Mesopotamians." Alain reached for the coffee pot and the steamed milk and refilled their cups.

"Fascinating. Of course, the four gospels tell none of this," Maggie said sarcastically. She'd learned not to trust the church long before.

"Of course not," Alain exclaimed. "The church deliberately removed the statements in the gospels referring to Jesus and Mary Magdalene. Mary Magdalene had become symbolic of the divine feminine, and the church fathers wanted to do away with any kind of goddess worship. They didn't want women to have any power. They tried to hide another of the Gnostic Gospels, the Gospel of Thomas, from the world, but it eventually resurfaced. That gospel's message is that God's light or the true spiritual light is found in everyone. That idea certainly did not fit with building a hierarchical institutional religion. I believe the early church fathers portrayed Christ as celibate to set an example. But that was not normal for a rabbi. Rabbis married. In fact, all Jewish men at that time were expected to find a wife by their twentieth birthday. They were honoring God's command to 'be fruitful and multiply.' Many believe that the wedding at Cana was Jesus's wedding to Mary Magdalene."

"It makes sense," Nick agreed. Having succumbed to the plate of pastries, he brushed the *beignet* crumbs from his lap.

Alain continued. "At any rate, over six or seven centuries this *sang real* or royal bloodline came down through the Merovingian kings, who were the first organized rulers of an area that included what is now France. There's also a theory that Arthur, Lancelot, Gawain, Morgaine, or the British knightly crowd that inspired those legends were also direct descendents from Mary and Jesus's son Joseph."

"But aren't those just fictional characters?" Nick asked.

"Not according to the British genealogist. He's researched their lines, too."

"Hey," Maggie interrupted. "I was just thinking, if you break down Mer-o-vingian, you have *mer*, which in French means either 'sea' or 'mother'; and *vingian*, which could mean 'of the vine.' So the vine could be the line of Mary Magdalene who came to France from across the sea, or it could refer to the blood line of Mary Magdalene, the mother—the initiator of the line."

Alain nodded to Maggie. "Of course, you're right. Very clever. Mary Magdalene preached a different Christianity than the Roman church. Her message spread throughout the south of France, and many followed her teachings for more than a thousand years."

Maggie couldn't resist asking, "So originally this was a Jewish line?"

"Yes. Obviously, Christ and Mary Magdalene were Jews. You know the fleur-de-lis, France's symbol?"

Maggie responded. "Sure. You see it everywhere—on fabrics, china, trinkets."

"Here it is," Alain said as he pointed to the design on the blue and yellow napkins at their table. "The fleur-de-lis began as the royal emblem of King Clovis, an early Merovingian king. It represents the iris or lily. But some believe it's a graphic image of the covenant of circumcision symbolizing the promises of God to Israel and the House of David." Alain paused and looked at his watch.

"Interesting," Maggie commented. "Were the men who founded the Prieuré Jews?"

"No. They were French Catholics. Godfroid de Bouillon, the founder, was a Crusader in Jerusalem and a descendant of the Merovingian dynasty. The Prieuré's original headquarters were at the Abbey of Notre Dame du Mont de Sion in Jerusalem or, as you would say, Mount Zion. Of course, the word Zion is symbolic of Israel and its people."

"I'd supposed Sion was for the city in the south of Switzerland," said Nick. "I never tied it to Zion."

Nick's mind was sifting through a myriad of questions related to the information he was being given. "And the Knights Templar," he said after a few minutes. "Where do they fit in?"

"About twenty years after the Priory was organized, two of its members created the Knights of the Temple to defend the Priory and the Christian faith. Then in 1138, the pope decreed that the Templars owed allegiance to no one but the Catholic Church. So in essence, they became the military arm of the church. The *Prieuré* eventually divorced themselves from the Templars, but not before the Templars returned to France with the treasure some say they found buried under the Temple Mount in Jerusalem, the original site where Solomon's Temple once stood."

Maggie said, "Absolutely fascinating. It's amazing that a vestige of that ancient society still exists." And to think that I might become a part of that ancient society. Maggie sighed at the thought. She felt overwhelmed, but happy to be a part of all this.

Nick had been fidgeting more the longer Alain continued to speak. Finally, he interrupted. "You know," Nick said, "I'm really interested in all this, but I'm feeling very anxious about my things in my flat. I need to go back there and reclaim some very important documents or my time and efforts here will have been wasted. Everything I've been working on for several weeks is there—my computer, my notes, my interviews, my documentation, and most importantly, photos of my kids. I keep their photos with me wherever I go. Plus, I need a change of clothes."

"I can give you clothes." Alain looked over at Nick's shape and laughed. "Well, no, on second thought that may not be possible. We're not similarly put together. We can buy you clothes. But returning to your flat could be dangerous. I would definitely not recommend it. You've already had a very close call."

Maggie added, "Alain's right, Nick. I don't want you to go back there. Please, please don't take any more chances."

"I have to go, Maggie. If we send someone else, they wouldn't know where to find the important stuff, and I must take the work I've done here in Paris back to California. Kaiser will never believe this crazy story of why I don't have anything to show for my time here. I'm going back there. That's final."

"Devereaux may still be lurking about. It's hard to know what he will do. He could pop up at any time. We'll have to watch for him and assure ourselves that his boyfriend is also not around," Alain said. "Both are dangerous. When Devereaux finds out that you escaped, the guy whose assignment was to get rid of you is going to be in big trouble. To make amends to Devereaux, he'll have to find a way to even the score."

"What else can Nick do?" Maggie asked, looking to Alain for help.

"Maybe we can get Hawkins to go over there for you. Or Maggie could go." Alain suggested.

Nick was adamant, "Neither! Guillaume saw Hawkins last night, and he's also onto Maggie. Besides, I would never put Maggie in that kind of danger. She's really special to me, you know." Nick winked at Maggie. She smiled and squeezed his hand.

Alain chuckled. "I rather suspected that. I'm trying to think who else we could send. Thérèse needs to stay safe after her difficult experience. Most of the other Priory members are too old. Hércule needs to recuperate from his ordeal, and McLaren is too damn difficult. He'd make more trouble than we're already in." Alain picked up their cups and plates, carried them into the kitchen and quickly returned.

Nick said simply, "*I* have to do it."

Maggie interrupted. "Maybe we're making too much of this. It feels like we're watching a film noir. I don't like Guillaume, but he didn't seem violent to me. In fact, he struck me as kind of a nerd, though a good-looking one."

Alain nodded, "*Alors*. Guillaume may be incapacitated; his feet looked pretty bad last night. Let's try it. Maggie, you can wait in the car when we get there. Nick, you, and I will go in together. I'll keep watch for Guillaume or Devereaux while you get your things." As he spoke, Alain shrugged on his jacket, and Nick grabbed his from the back of his chair.

"No way!" Maggie stood abruptly. "If you think I'm letting Nick out of my sight, you're crazy. I'm going in with you. I won't be left out this time!"

Nick sighed in relief. "*Merci, mes amis.*"

"*Allons-y, amis!*" Alain stood and motioned to the others to follow. "Let's go. We shouldn't waste any more time. We can continue this conversation as we head down to my car. We don't want to give Guillaume time to recover. I can tell you both more as we drive," Alain said as he guided Nick and Maggie down the stairs, out into the street, and to his car. As Alain switched on the ignition, he mentioned, "We Priory members value our heritage, but the Priory today has evolved into something quite different. We have supported various political movements, and recently we've given our support to a unified Europe. Now, many of our members are too old to be effective. That is why I sent out the letters seeking our relatives in other parts of the world. We are very small, but we have members from various religions. However, mainly we are Christians, hopefully in the finer sense of the word."

"You seem so to me," Nick said quietly.

"*D'accord!*" Maggie added.

Alain adroitly steered the car out of its tight parking place with the skill of an experienced Parisian driver, and the car careened ahead. "That's enough history for now. We must hurry; we don't want to take a chance on Devereaux's returning," he said as he headed the car into traffic. Maggie looked at Nick with uncertainty, wondering if their mission would be successful. She said a silent prayer that they would all be safe.

CHAPTER FIFTY

Guillaume

A T THE HOSPITAL, Guillaume received a tetanus shot, several stitches in both feet, and pain medication. Guillaume was not one to bear his wounds stoically. This injury was a terrible affront. Anything that hurt his well-loved body angered him. And this was not his fault. It was the guy upstairs and that woman. "Damn those Americans!" And it was Devereaux's fault, too. "He abandoned me with all these problems. Damn him!"

Guillaume thought back on how he'd come to Marcel Devereaux. He'd had other wealthy gay sponsors, and he knew how to please them. He was willing to serve if the rewards were high enough. He'd never considered that his role with Devereaux was self-sacrificing, or that others might not consider it the plume in his hat that he did. He relished the opportunity to live sumptuously and travel. But Devereaux's leaving him alone now in this mess made him furious. How dare that giant prig do that! After all, wasn't he, Guillaume, the most valuable possession Devereaux had? Now he takes off with that old chalice. What can he be thinking? He doesn't value that over me, does he?

After he returned from the hospital, Guillaume sat down with a beer in the salon. He noticed one of the cabinet doors was slightly ajar. He limped as quickly as his painful feet would allow. Perhaps the pain meds were causing this aberration, this distorted reality—he always kept the cabinet locked. Had he forgotten in yesterday's excitement? Some of the treasures inside it were beyond value—at least that's what Devereaux claimed. According to him, Christie's or Sotheby's would sell them for a fortune if they were put on the market. Some of them, of course, could not be sold on the open market because of how they had been acquired.

Guillaume saw immediately that Devereaux's alabaster jar was missing. "*Sacredieu!*" he screamed. He searched the lower levels of the cabinet and behind it, but there was no sign of it or its box anywhere. He tried to remember what he'd done that day. He'd opened the cabinet door because he thought Devereaux would want to store the new chalice there temporarily. Then Devereaux had done his silly dancing thing and left with the damned new grail. Before Guillaume could lock the cabinet, that Forsythe woman had shown up, and he'd had to deal with her.

This was terrible! Devereaux's probable reaction scared the hell out of him.

How could he explain to Devereaux that someone had taken their most treasured piece while he was in the house? Could whoever took it have come while he was at the hospital? He couldn't even imagine how furious Devereaux would be if he found that it was missing. Devereaux cherished the jar beyond all his others, with the exception of the new chalice he'd just gotten his hands on. As he'd told the American earlier, his son had come into his life along with the jar. Guillaume had always doubted the veracity of Devereaux's tale; still, there was no one in the world, not even himself, whom Devereaux valued more than his adopted son.

Guillaume knew that he had to do something quickly to appease Devereaux. He would find out who took the alabaster jar. He would settle this before Devereaux returned to discover his negligence. And he wanted revenge for this wretched injury. How dare they injure his beautiful feet!

Guillaume phoned Henri Diamond. "An important piece from Devereaux's collection is missing. I need your help."

Henri Diamond refused. "You've made a mess of things, Guillaume. I've told you before. I can no longer be a part of this. Sleep in your own bed!"

Diamond's answer refueled his anger. Damn Diamond. *Quel con!* I don't understand why Devereaux keeps such a worthless type in his employ—and a dirty Jew to boot! Guillaume plopped down in the chair. His own father had been a collaborator with the Vichy government during the war, and though he had been tried and imprisoned after the war, Guillaume remained secretly proud of his father's anti-Semitic actions. His sympathies led him to Devereaux and his group, which was no consolation now. Curse that bastard Diamond!

So he waited. There was nothing else he could do but brood and moan and think about how he could get revenge. Revenge—that's what he wanted. He searched again for Devereaux's gun and found it. He didn't like guns, but he would use this if necessary. He sat down and tried to relax, resting his injured foot on a footstool. The drugs for his pain had kicked in. They made him sleepy, but Guillaume was determined to stay awake.

He had to be careful. He'd had seizures before when he'd been under stress. And they'd treated him with electric shock. He never wanted that again. He wanted to scream. What should he do? Cold water. Cold water. He ran to the bathroom, turned on the shower and stuck his head under it. Better. Better. Be calm now. Guillaume, be calm. But the water didn't stop what was inside his head. Everything was spinning. Maybe if he had a little sweet white dust. It always made him feel better. But there wasn't any, was there? Devereaux had caught him sniffing last week and taken all his joy away. *Merde!*

He heard a slight scrape on the floor above. "They're back! They're back!" he screamed. He leaped up from the chair forgetting his injured feet. Aah! Guillaume ran out of the room flailing the gun in his hand.

Maggie refused to stay in the car. "I almost lost you once, Nick. I'm not doing that again!" she said vehemently. Nick kissed her quickly and helped her out of the car.

Pleased that there was no sign of any activity at Devereaux's, the three quietly entered Nick's flat. Nick grabbed his laptop computer and retrieved the reports he had spent the past three weeks writing, his passport, his money, and photos of his children. Maggie helped him stuff everything but the photos in a laundry bag.

"You're making too much noise," Alain warned. They stopped in silence for a few minutes. "Hurry," Alain said, "We've got to get out of here before someone hears us."

Suddenly he whispered, "Someone's coming!"

Alain ran to lock the door, but it flew open with such force that he was thrown back into the wall behind it. Guillaume raged forth, hobbling in a strange kind of hop-leap. Nick froze, his hands filled with his mementos. Maggie stood behind him. Nick dropped the framed photos.

The tinkling sound of glass crashing on the floor further enraged Guillaume. Maggie heard several shots from a gun. Pictures fell from the walls and smashed to the floor. She felt the air of something whizzing past her head. Nick crashed into her and then fell forward onto the floor. Maggie screamed and quickly dropped down next to him.

Guillaume yelled, "*Merdeuses! Vous avez ruiné mes pieds—mes beaux pieds! J'assinerai chacun—tout le monde—n'importe qui—qui m'a blessé.*" He hopped from foot to foot, squealing "*Mes pieds, mes pieds.* You stupid Americans caused this!"

Guillaume ran crazily around the room yelling and shooting. He ran up to Alain and clicked the gun in Alain's face. It was empty. Alain grabbed Guillaume and pushed him down onto the floor. He pulled Guillaume's arms behind him and put his knee to Guillaume's back. Guillaume kicked savagely like a feral child. Alain held him as tightly as he could.

"Nick," Alain yelled, "get up. I need help with this wild man."

Nick's body lay still. Maggie cradled his head in her lap, his face looking up at hers frantically, his lips open and gasping, his throat spilling blood. With her lips close to his face she kept repeating, "Nick, I'm here. It's Maggie. Hold on. Please hold on. I love you."

Alain dropped his hold on Guillaume and got off him. Nick was more important than this nut case. He moved quickly to where Maggie and Nick lay in a pool of blood.

With each heartbeat, blood spurted from Nick's throat. "Do something!" Maggie screamed. "We've got to save him! We can't let him die."

"*Mon dieu, mon dieu!*" Alain said when he reached Nick and Maggie. "It's his carotid." Alain grabbed the scarf Maggie had coiled around her neck, pulled it off and tied it tightly around Nick's neck in an attempt at a tourniquet.

Guillaume raised himself, ran to the door and down the stairs. The cuts on his feet had reopened. They left a trail of blood.

Alain caught sight of Guillaume's retreat. He stood, pulled out his mobile, and called for an ambulance.

Maggie sobbed violently. Her body shook with each wail. Her mind had trouble comprehending what had occurred here. It was surreal—like the dream she'd had one night on the trip where a huge bloody chalice marched around her bed. Why? Why was this happening? Was it real? But there was a strange smell of something ending in the room, and she sensed that Nick was leaving her.

As Maggie's sobs dissipated, she looked up at Alain. "Is he d-dead?"

"He doesn't have long."

"Can't you do something? There must be some way to help Nick. We can't just let him go. Please. I'm desperate here!"

"An ambulance and doctors are on their way," Alain said, but he shook his head as though the situation was hopeless, and he turned away from Maggie.

CHAPTER FIFTY-ONE

Rescue

ILONA FASTENED THE shutters in her small apartment before she removed the chalice from its case. She closed her eyes and moved her fingers tenderly around the piece, feeling every little bump and crease, as well as the sharply cut gems, now rounded by years of handling. A tear formed in the corner of her eye in reverence for its beauty and the holy feeling it brought to her. She brushed the tear away.

When she opened her eyes, Ilona could see, even in the darkened room, that the chalice emanated a glow. Sarah will be so pleased, she thought. Ilona was sure this chalice should belong to her beloved Ste. Sarah. At one time, she would have been tempted to sell something this valuable. She could use the money. But fifty-seven years of life had taught her a few things, and now she only wanted to please the Lord and his angels. Yes, her sly Romany ways had come in handy, but she didn't use them often. When the hotel manager, the hotel detective, and the local police had questioned her about the missing chalice, neither her voice nor her face had betrayed her deed. Their questioning became an amusing game to her. She'd never forgotten her gypsy training in deception. She'd been taught to steal as a child. It wasn't something bad; it was simply her family's livelihood.

Ilona held the vessel close. Touching it sent her into a dream world where she wore a queen's crown. She imagined herself drinking fine ceremonial wine from it and then holding it high for her countrymen to see. When she set it down on her nightstand to rest her arm, the moment of delusional glory faded. *Her* countrymen? Right. *Gitane! Romani!* She hated the names they'd called her. Ilona had worked hard to elevate herself above the sting of the gypsy name and the connotations it brought. Yet in many ways, she considered her childhood experiences to be a blessing, as well as a curse. She'd loved having the freedom to move about and see many places. She smiled, remembering it.

And there had been wonderful times—like the summer her band had gone to work the ships in Marseille. It was steamy hot in the city that July, so the band had settled their caravans in the Camargue. There, they were miles away from the heat and the noise of the city, and Ilona could dance barefoot on the cool grass. And she had gotten to ride one of the *grai,* the small white horses that grazed in the fields nearby. It had been her favorite summer.

The highlight had been Ste. Sarah's saint's day, near the end of May, when gypsies from all over Europe gathered at the church of Les Saintes Maries de la Mer. In the cellar of the church was a tall and magnificent statue of Sarah, the young Egyptian servant girl who had accompanied the three Marys in their journey across the Mediterranean.

The boisterous, brawling gypsy crowd removed the wooden statue of Sarah from the church where she stood among what seemed to be hundreds of burning tapers. Ilona's older brother hoisted her onto his shoulders so that she could watch as the tall statue of Ste. Sarah, the Egyptian girl, was carried on strong dark shoulders into the Mediterranean in a hallucinogenic gypsy procession. She was the largest of all the Black Madonnas in Europe.

Ilona kissed the chalice and raised it high with both hands. "This is for you, Sarah," she said. This chalice should be with the Black Madonna in the Einsedeln abbey across the lake, whom Ilona had named Sarah after the

Black Virgin of her childhood. A holy thing should be in a holy place. The chalice would be safe there. She had no one else to trust. Ilona didn't know exactly how she could accomplish this, but her mind was made up.

Marcel Devereaux was furious. He had called Guillaume numerous times. Each time there had only been the same message on his answering machine. "Marcel Devereaux is not in. Leave your name and telephone number. All messages will be returned promptly." Hearing this message repeatedly was very irritating. Had those silly Americans brought some kind of trouble to Guillaume? Where could he be? It was not like him to desert his duty. My treasures must be kept safe. He thought fleetingly about calling the Paris police. No. It was far better that they not be involved—they might have other ideas about him. Devereaux decided that he would wait in Zurich for three days. Then, if the chalice had not been found, he would return to Paris to see to his affairs there.

Pacing wildly back and forth across his hotel room, Devereaux knew that his frustration was probably exacerbating his heart condition. He swallowed two of the tranquilizers the physician had left and tried to relax in the room's most comfortable chair. As he calmed down, he remembered the waiter from yesterday talking about the monastery he'd visited as a child. It wouldn't be crowded on a Tuesday. He decided to take the train.

It was a good decision. The green vistas that passed his moving window quieted his mind. Despite his seizure, he knew that it would do him good to get away. Climbing the hill from the station at Einsedeln, Devereaux felt strangely happy at the sight of the church. He stopped to gaze up at it from the entrance gazebo. Upon entering the monastery church, he sat down near the Black Madonna's shrine. Dizziness came over him. Thank goodness he was seated. He reached into his pocket for his little white pills. Nothing! Where were they? He hadn't used them since the previous night. Where could they be? Another irritant!

Somehow, however, gradually, the silence, the church's beauty, the golden cherubs ready for flight from the Romanesque pillars, the fragrance from bouquets of forsythia, daisies, and roses placed at the Madonna's feet, and the benign look on her dark face brought him tranquility. On a whim, he walked to the candles and dropped some coins in the slot. To honor his mother, he chose a candle from those in front of the Black Madonna and placed his with the others.

Remembering the love he had felt for his dead parents, Devereaux was dumbfounded that unexpected tears presented themselves. He pulled his handkerchief from his pocket and dabbed at them. Long-repressed emotions swept over him. It had been so long since he'd felt truly loved. He wished he could recapture the warmth and the softer feelings of those times.

As the cleverest, but least athletic boy, he'd suffered for years from the taunts of the other village youth. But he showed them all. He'd accumulated his collection of treasures, and, to showcase them, he had built a home high in the hills overlooking the Alsatian village where he grew up. His favorite treasures, however, were always kept with him wherever he was. It suddenly occurred to Devereaux that he left Paris so quickly that he forgot to bring the alabaster jar with him. "*Merde!*" His hoarse whisper caused a woman in the pew ahead of him to turn and give him a severe look.

Devereaux's thoughts returned to the missing grail. He pictured himself bringing the chalice to the church and setting it lovingly at the Madonna's feet. He felt humble and warmed by the sensation of this imaginary good deed. The church bell pealed out its announcement of an upcoming service, bringing Devereaux back from his reverie. What kind of perversion had that brief vision been? Give away his beloved grail to an already wealthy church? Ridiculous! He would never do a thing like that. He stood abruptly and brushed roughly past the other worshippers in the pew. He rushed outside to call Guillaume again.

Before entering the church, Ilona tied her diklo at the back of her neck. Her head should not be bare. As was her habit, she unconsciously touched the gold coin hidden under her dress. It hung from a chain about her neck. She never took it off. She bowed deeply before the statue she called Sarah and placed her small bouquet of lilies of the valley, iris, and fern respectfully at the statue's feet. "I have a surprise for you. You will see it soon," Ilona said excitedly. "It is a very holy object, and I want you to guard it from an evil man." After quietly telling Sarah about the gift that was soon to be hers, Ilona walked toward the pews that faced the main altar. Suddenly she halted.

Sitting at the rear of the Einsedeln church was the tall balding man from the hotel. What was he doing here? Terror gripped her. Had he seen her? Would he remember her? Her impulse was to leave quickly. The man's eyes were closed, though he dabbed at them with a handkerchief from time to time. He looked sad.

She had to chance him seeing her. This was her only day off. Ilona slipped quietly into a seat in the farthest pew to the left of the man, where, from the corner of her eye, she could watch him.

The chalice was wrapped carefully in a white box from the *charcuterie*. Ilona held it close to her side under her arm, covered by her red wool jacket. A mass would be starting soon. She would have to wait until the church cleared.

The man the hotel manager had called M. Devereaux suddenly stood up. He rushed rudely past the others in his pew and left the church just as the priest's incantation began. Ilona sighed in relief. He hadn't seen her. The holy chalice was safe—at least so far. Now she had to find the abbé and see if the monastery would accept her gift.

CHAPTER FIFTY-TWO

Death's Remainder

MAGGIE, IN SHOCK, rode in the ambulance with Nick to Hôpital St. George. She could never have imagined that anything like this could happen. She felt numb. She stared at the stretcher. How could this impossibility be real? She wanted to talk to Nick, but the ambulance made too much commotion with its wailing siren. Blue lights—a beautiful color for a terrible event.

The hospital was horrible: cold, tan stone inside and grayed granite outside, narrow hallways lined with gurneys waiting for new arrivals coming in to be healed or to receive final blessings. Final. God! What an awful word.

Alain and Israel had followed the ambulance to the hospital. They met Maggie at the curtained area where Nick's body lay. A policeman and a priest stood at the edge of the room. Aggravated, she thought, "Why is the priest here already?" Then she saw that a blanket the color of wet stucco covered Nick's body and an ominous white sheet covered his face. Maggie went immediately to him. She pulled back both the blanket and the sheet. Someone had closed Nick's eyes and cleaned his face. Several layers of white towels covered the neck wound. They had not changed his bloody clothing.

Maggie kissed Nick's cool cheeks, then his lips, and his forehead gently. One of her tears pooled in his eyelashes. "Did it hurt?" she asked softly.

She had to be with him now. She had to talk with him. She turned to the others in the curtained enclosure and waved them away furiously. They obeyed.

When she was alone, she pulled a chair up next to his bed. "Hi," Maggie said quietly. "You are always surprising me. Only this time . . . Only this time it's not your usual fun surprise." Her voice broke. "Damn! Damn, damn, damn! This is so hard to believe. I don't want to believe it. Maybe I never will. When I think of the pain you must have felt! You didn't deserve that at all. You're one of the good people of this Earth. You didn't deserve anything like this. I'm so sorry. If only we hadn't been involved with that dangerous chalice! Could I have stopped this if I'd done something differently? Oh, God, I don't know! I wish we were together someplace safe and you could still be your old funny self."

It occurred to Maggie that she was telling Nick how she felt about him. "You were my first, you know—a little late on the agenda, but special for that reason, too. No one else can claim that, and I will always cherish our lovemaking. At least the Sion Grail did us a favor there." She remembered that magical night. Even though she hadn't originally thought of Nick as her lover, his love had filled her emptiness. It changed her, she knew.

Maggie talked to Nick about the day two years ago when they'd walked to Muir Woods and discovered they really liked each other. She told him anecdotes about what fun they'd had at various times. It was comforting to just talk—she half-expected Nick to sit up and say something amusing. Her tears flowed in rivulets down her cheeks as she spoke, but she went on, sniffing occasionally. She had no sense of time; she didn't know how long she had been there talking with Nick. She was just talking to her friend, as she had often done, telling him of the events in her life. She told him about Israel and her feelings for him; she wanted Nick to know. Even though his life had left his body, Maggie felt it was important that she tell him what was on her mind. His spirit would hear and understand.

After she stopped talking, she sat quietly for a while until a strange, thrilling sensation interrupted her musings. A current ran through her body, accompanied by an unusual flowery fragrance that cut through the antiseptic and bodily smells of blood, sweat, and feces that surrounded her. She grabbed the end of the putty colored blanket that covered Nick's body in both fists and clutched it to her heart. "Why Nick?" she asked. "The grail was my burden, not Nick's. Can the grail have some way of discerning the good from the bad in the people who own it? But that would make Nick's death a sacrifice because he was good. None of it makes sense."

Maggie looked about. At first, it seemed that nothing had changed. The room was still. Nick's body lay on the gurney as before. But his spirit was here. She felt it. And she knew Nick would want to contact her, despite the fact that he would probably not have much spiritual energy after his horrible ordeal.

Maggie had picked up the bloodied photo of Nick's kids that he had in his hands when Guillaume's shots hit him. She had been too upset then to look at it. When she'd entered the hospital room, she'd absent-mindedly laid it on Nick's chest. Suddenly, the frame slipped off the bed and clattered to the floor. Startled, Maggie walked around the bed to retrieve it. In the photo, Nick had his arms around his two kids, Nora and Jack. They were smiling. Nick had probably just said something to make them laugh. They looked delighted to be together. "Oh my god! Nick's kids . . . What's this going to do to them?"

For a moment, Maggie was too choked up to make a sound, then she leaned down and whispered, "Don't worry. I'll take care of everything, Nick."

She paused and added, "Thank you for everything you've given me—all the wisdom, all the insight, all the fun." She stopped, remembering again their night of intimacy. It had been so wonderful and so important to her. "And all the love," she added. She kissed the photo and then hugged it to her chest. She blew several kisses around the room. She was sure Nick's spirit was here. Had his angel come to take him through the tunnel that they say leads to the light? She wiped her eyes with a corner of one of the towels that lay loose around Nick's neck.

Maggie pressed Nick's hands to her lips. "I will never forget you." The loudness of her voice surprised her—she was almost shouting. Why do we think that spirits are hard of hearing? She lowered her voice and repeated her last words. Then she turned and walked out of the curtained area.

CHAPTER FIFTY-THREE

Justice

L ATER THAT NIGHT about ten o'clock in the evening, disoriented from the excitement that had just occurred, Guillaume hobbled out into the street, not knowing where he should go or what he should do. Only a few people hurried by; no one seemed to notice him. Guillaume thought this strange because he had the sense that everyone would notice him now. He was on display to the world. He felt strangely jubilant, yet fearful. Would the police find him?

He stumbled over a drunk's body lying in the street. The sight of it triggered the gunshots again in his head. He wasn't quite sure why he'd done it. But he'd shown them, hadn't he? If only Devereaux could have seen him. Would he have approved? Was it real? He didn't know now. But he knew he needed to get away from here and his deed for a while. He headed for the metro. After that, he didn't know.

Guillaume traveled on the metro for hours, exiting and exploring unfamiliar stops, still flushed with excitement from the thrill of his actions. Never before had he done anything quite so wanton! For a second, he asked himself if he had really intended to kill anyone. Then the delirious surge overtook him again. It was like something he'd always wanted, but not known. He felt as excited sexually as in any sexual encounter he could remember. This was better than sex. It was so freeing! Several times he felt an orgasm coming on, and he let it force its way through him. He'd finally done something just for himself and not for anyone else. What a release! He'd do it again. It felt so good.

Sweaty and giddy, Guillaume stumbled back to his flat. He looked at his watch—3:00 AM. He was breathing hard. He couldn't seem to catch his breath. He looked furtively around in quick jagged glances before entering, but saw no one. Perhaps they hadn't alerted the police after all. He looked in the mirror before he showered. His face looked different, eyes bulging, but he saw a new determination there. He changed and quickly packed his favorite things. He placed the contents of the glass cabinet carefully in his bag, using his clothes as protective wrapping for Devereaux's treasures. He had recently found the password to one of Devereaux's Swiss accounts. When the bank opened, he would transfer as many dollars as he dared. Oh, why not take it all? Then he would be off to the airport for a flight to Argentina. His father still had friends there. He hoped they would remember him. Despite knowing that he had to hurry, Guillaume felt so giddy from this new burst of freedom that at times he had to stop all of his activities and sit clutching his knees to his chest, rocking furiously until his equilibrium returned.

He called a taxi and waited in silence. The silence bothered him. In his head, he could hear his mother's voice nagging him. He put a CD in the stereo. He would shut the voices out with music—Rachmaninoff—as loud as it would play. When he looked out, he saw the taxi waiting at the curb. He picked up the two valises and opened the door. Two men stood at his doorstep.

"*Bon jour, Monsieur,*" the tall plain-clothed officer from the Paris police said politely. "We've been waiting for you. You've had your little drama, and now . . ." He clamped handcuffs on Guillaume's closest arm, "*Nous avons beaucoup à discuter.*" His hand on Guillaume's arm felt like a wrench.

"*Oui,*" said the other, "*Beaucoup.*" He picked up one of the suitcases. "Ah, we will be very interested to see what you have brought for us. I hope these are *your* things."

Guillaume heard the irony in the officer's voice, but he couldn't make himself understand. This was not right. This was not how he had seen it happening. He had finally acted out his dreams, and he wanted to believe the story he had created for himself could still come true.

Guillaume struggled to free himself, swinging his arms and his head wildly in time to the Rachmaninoff, which still blared through the open door behind him.

"Psychotic fool," one of the officers said. He buried his fist in Guillaume's stomach. Then Guillaume felt himself being gripped tightly and shoved into the sleek black Renault that waited at the curb. Inside the car, Guillaume cried like a child—a whimpering, nasal cry. What would *Maman* say now?

CHAPTER FIFTY-FOUR

Messages of Death

WHEN MAGGIE HAD completed all the necessary police forms, she and Israel went to the American Embassy to register Nick's death, to make the arrangements for the return of the body, and to contact Nick's family about the tragedy. She also contacted Nick's employer, Kaiser Permanente, about his death and about how to handle the project reports he had done in Paris. She had Nick's reports in her possession now.

Maggie was still so shaken that she was physically unsteady, but somehow she managed to push through all the paperwork with only a few stray tears shed on the documents. The phone calls proved to be much more difficult, especially the one to Nick's former wife. The composure that she had exhibited earlier dissolved with the repetition of each new message. It hurt so much.

"Let me." Israel took the phone from her gently. Maggie just kept shaking her head and gasping back the sobs.

Her voice was weak, but it grew in strength as she spoke. "I promised Nick. I must be the one." She paused and looked directly into Israel's eyes.

"I appreciate your being here to give me hope and encouragement, but I must do this myself. I must be the messenger of death."

Maggie offered to accompany Nick's body back to the States, but one of his sisters planned to fly to Paris the next day to take over the chores of dealing with the body. Maggie was relieved that Nick's loved ones were responsible and caring people and that everything would not be left up to her.

The details finished, Maggie and Israel stopped for a bowl of soup and thickly sliced bread at a small café. "I can't handle another thing today," Maggie said. Her voice was weak. She knew she must look haggard and awful.

Alain had requested that Maggie and Israel meet him at Hércule St. Clair's apartment when all of the unpleasant but necessary details were completed. He did not explain the purpose of the meeting. They initially had agreed, but now Maggie had second thoughts. "Would you call Alain and see if we can postpone our meeting?" she said to Israel, "I don't know what it can be about, but I'm so exhausted. I just can't. I just can't!" Maggie's hands covered her face.

"No. Of course you can't. It was crazy for us to even consider it. I can't imagine what I was thinking when Alain brought it up. You need to rest. I'll take you to your hotel, and I'll call Alain. Don't worry about the meeting. We'll deal with it together tomorrow or whenever you're ready."

Israel helped Maggie up from her chair, and they returned to her hotel. He offered to stay with her, but she told him she wanted to be alone. Once in her room, she kicked off her shoes and collapsed on the bed in her clothes. She still couldn't believe that Nick was dead. Images of his laughing face and of the way he looked at the hospital alternated in her mind. Thank God she had not betrayed him by sleeping with Israel. She had been tempted, but thoughts of Nick had saved her. She would always love him.

Suddenly, overcome, Maggie reached down and pounded the floor in anger with her fists and wailed a keening cry she didn't know was in her. Her sweet Nick! This was so wrong—so unfair!

Her anger quieted, but Maggie's stomach ached from the tears and the trauma. To soothe it, she wrapped her arms about it and held it gently. She fell asleep in that position.

Israel returned to his hotel similarly fatigued from the stress of the awful event. He was concerned for Maggie, but he marveled at the courage she mustered in the face of this adversity. In the country where his mother had been born and after which he had been named, Maggie would have been a Sabra. He knew it was natural for her to be devastated now. Though he knew it was self-serving, he couldn't help wondering if Maggie would have feelings for him after this.

He had never fully understood the depth of the relationship between Maggie and Nick, and Maggie's feelings for Nick were an unanswered question. Had Maggie been in love with Nick? He didn't think it was quite like that, but he knew they had been close. If she had been in love with Nick, how would that affect the budding affection he and Maggie had felt for each other on their trip?

When he called Maggie late the next morning, Israel was glad to find that Maggie's voice now had some energy. She was ready to accept Alain and Hércule's invitation to meet. He was especially happy when she said that he was the only person in her life who she wished to have with her now.

CHAPTER FIFTY-FIVE

The Blue Book

AS SCHEDULED THAT afternoon, Maggie and Israel took the metro to Hércule's home to meet with Alain. At the door, Hércule greeted them warmly. He was dressed as neatly and precisely as Maggie remembered from their other visits. He led them to the reassembled salon on the second floor. Maggie seated herself on a settee covered in tufted rose brocade. Israel took a chair to her left.

"Would you like something to drink?" Hércule asked.

Maggie nodded. "Tea." A second later, she added, "As we had on our first visit in your shop."

Hércule smiled and looked to Israel.

"That's fine for me as well, Hércule."

Maggie's mind kept turning to Nick. As she surveyed the room, she wondered what Nick would have thought of Hércule's place. He would have liked its coziness and he would have loved all the books. Maggie smiled. Nick would have wanted to read them all. To avoid spilling the tears that were often there ready to be released, Maggie concentrated on the room and its contents. Despite the cluttered closeness of the room with its many antiques and family photos, it felt comfortable to Maggie. The richness and warmth of its *ménage* enveloped her in a feeling of sanctuary. She needed that now.

Hércule returned carrying a tray with a teapot covered by a tea cozy in a fabric of yellow and purple pansies and four delicate china cups, much like the ones they'd used at the shop. The tea cozy reminded Maggie of the flowers they'd seen in Provence. Alain, who had not met them at the door, entered behind Hércule with another tray bearing snifters that appeared to hold a liqueur. "Hello, you two," he hailed them. Alain handed out the snifters. Maggie took a cup of tea. She wasn't sure she wanted spirits, but she took a snifter and placed it on the nearby side table.

Once the cognac was distributed, Hércule sat down next to her. He spoke in French. His words were carefully chosen to soothe her overwrought emotions, and she could tell they were genuinely felt. He was extremely apologetic about the troubles that had come to her and to her friend Nick through his having given them the chalice for safekeeping. "*C'est impossible de te dire, combien de chagrin je sens,*" he began. "So much sorrow and so much pain have been caused by my fears and my actions. But now, perhaps all the sorrow that this historic grail has brought to our family is finished. *J'espère que c'est fini.* Although we valued the grail, perhaps it is for the best that it is gone from all our lives. However, it makes me furious to think that it went to such a man as Devereaux! The police contacted Alain and let him know that the madman Guillaume Joinville has been apprehended and arrested. He is now in their custody. That, at least, is a relief. However, they have not as yet located that devious Devereaux."

Alain said, "The Priory is working on that through our contacts, in addition to the efforts of the police. I'm sure all here today are relieved to know that his man Guillaume is no longer a threat to any of us."

Everyone nodded their agreement. Maggie said, "I know I won't feel truly at peace until we know Devereaux's whereabouts and that of the grail."

Alain added, "I'll drink to that, and to this spirited young woman who served her family well."

Maggie smiled graciously when the three men raised their glasses and drank. Alain had said "her" family. They were including her now, and no one seemed angry with her.

"You said *my* family?" She looked questioningly between Alain and Hércule.

Hércule responded. "Yes. I have a surprise for you. I don't know whether it can cheer you up after all this week's disastrous events, but we hope it will." He walked over to the shelves that lined the rear of the room and pulled from them a long narrow book with a royal blue leather cover centered by an embossed gold fleur-de-lis. It was similar in size to some of the journals Maggie's mother had kept, and its pages were tied together with a black silk cord on the left side.

Hércule sat down next to Maggie again. He opened the book to a page marked with a thin red satin ribbon. "This book contains family notes and records of the St. Clairs from around 1800 or so up until the late twentieth century. Of course, some information is missing during the war periods, but if you look here, you will see just when my long-ago great-great-aunt Annabelle left, in June of 1824, on her voyage across the sea to Quebec, where she married a farmer. She was a sort of mail-order bride. But closer than that, as I've recently told you, I have discovered that your grandmother was my sister who disappeared during the Second World War and ended up in Canada. We always worried that she might have been killed by the Nazis. Since that was not the case, I will never understand why she didn't tell those of us who loved her that she was alive and well. But now, after checking with the Canadian authorities, we found that to be true. So you see, you are my grandniece, and this family book is given to you from me, *ton Oncle Hércule.*" He put his arms around Maggie and hugged her.

Maggie was overcome with emotion. Hércule had hinted at this before, but it wasn't until this moment that the reality of her true connection with this family hit her. It pulled at her heart. She was a St. Clair. The grail could have been rightfully hers. "This makes me so happy. I hardly know what to say. I wish my mother could be here to share in this."

Maggie raised the journal to the light and read the words describing the family's distress when Annabelle St. Clair departed alone on a ship from Le Havre for Canada. She ran her fingers over the words as though she could feel them as well as read them. She thumbed through pages filled with various styles of handwriting in hues of black, purple, and brown. A much-used green ink blotter marked a page near the back where a dry pink rose had been pressed between the two pages that preceded the news of her great-great-grandmother's departure. Could her grandmother Hélène have put it there? Raising the book to her nose, Maggie noted that the faded rose had lost its fragrance, but the book had an odor of its own, a mix of hidden perfumed love notes, musty damp night air, candle wax, and the sweat and tears of many years.

"Do you like it?" Hércule St. Clair asked. "We have made an exact copy for you to keep." Alain handed Hércule a similar book, which he in turn handed gently to Maggie, saying, "I am so happy to see you smile again."

Maggie opened the identical blue book. Inside, Hércule had scrawled in his flamboyant script, "For my grandniece Maggie. With affection and appreciation, Hércule." Next to it was a photo of Hércule and her grandmother, aged about seventeen, with their arms about each other.

"The idea of giving you this family memento has inspired us to make other copies for each of our closest kin here in France," Hércule noted. He turned to Israel. "Alain tells me that you have a family connection with us as well—through the Scottish Sinclair line."

Israel nodded. "Yes, I had planned to respond to your letter, but other events precluded that from happening. However, I would be very interested in sitting down with both of you to learn more about the family history."

Alain broke in. "Of course, Israel. We'd be delighted to do that."

Hércule St. Clair shook his head—"Just don't expect too much. Everything in our past is not so good."

Maggie, who had been fondling the new blue book, smiled at Hércule. "Oh, thank you so much. *C'est merveilleux.* I can't wait to see if I can find out more about my grandmother and Annabelle St. Clair when I get back to the States. And I will let you know the results of my research." She added, "I treasure this gift. Now I feel that I am truly *une Française.* And am I also now a member of the Priory of Sion?"

Alain laughed. "*Bien sûr!* I told you we need new blood—new young blood. Now maybe even that cranky old Scot will have to accept you as an equal."

Maggie thought bitterly about how McLaren had treated her at the Priory meeting and grimaced. "I can handle him. I want to be involved in any way I can. I feel it's my duty as a St. Clair."

Alain smiled and added, "But of course, you will have to go through all the organization's required rituals before you can participate. And our secrets must be kept."

"*Oui, bien sûr.*" Maggie nodded. Though his tone was serious, Maggie wondered if Alain was pulling her leg.

Hércule smiled and said, "There is something else." He looked at Israel now. "After you and Alain rescued me two nights ago, the next day Alain surprised me with the gift of a very old alabaster jar. Do you remember his finding that?"

Israel nodded, amused, "Yes. Alain hinted that he planned to give it to you. Have you had it analyzed and appraised?"

"Yes. It is ancient . . . possibly first century. I do not know where you and Alain found this, but it is *very* valuable."

Alain gave Israel and Maggie a quick wink. He had not wanted to burden the older man with knowledge of how the jar came into their possession.

Hércule continued. "Not because of its quality—which is quite rough—but because of its age. It is of the period that could make it similar to the jar that was used to anoint the feet of the Christ by Mary Magdalene in that loving marriage ritual. A similar jar was found buried with her at St. Maximime, but it has been missing for some time."

When Maggie heard the name Mary Magdalene, she was instantly alert. She set the book down and looked up at the others. She said, "Really? I have felt absolutely surrounded by the spirit of that woman all the time I've been in France."

Hércule beamed at her. "Yes, my dear. I thought you would be intrigued by this, shall we say, unusual coincidence. However, one cannot say that this is *the* jar, of course. But it is interesting that it is from the period, to be sure."

"This is a real find for the Priory," Alain added, "even if we can only conjecture on its origin. Of course, we may not be able to keep it *in the family* as it were, but this object could be more important to us than the grail we have just lost."

Hércule nodded. "Will the Priory be able to keep it?"

Alain said quickly, "Depending on what happens to our friend Devereaux, its ownership could transfer to the Priory." He looked to Maggie and Israel and said, "Now, these two have had a devastating few days. I will take them to their hotels. I'm sure they have travel plans, but, hopefully, we will meet again."

Maggie gave Hércule a *bise* and a hug. "*Merci beaucoup, oncle Hércule.*" She laughed.

Hércule beamed.

The meeting had been so calming that Maggie forgot her intention to apologize again for the loss of the chalice while it was in her care. A relieved sigh passed from her lips. Her family had already forgiven her.

On their way back from M. St. Clair's, Maggie began to wonder about something that had been puzzling her. She said to Israel, "You know, do you think the members of the Priory knew that I had the grail in my possession? I meant to ask how all that transpired. Do you have any ideas about that?"

"Yes," Israel answered. "I asked Alain the same question. Apparently, after Devereaux demanded to see the grail, Hércule went to the Priory for assistance. He didn't tell them immediately that he'd given the grail to you, only that he removed it from the shop. But Alain suspected you were involved. He had Thérèse follow you on several occasions. Then, Devereaux's hacks kidnapped Hércule in an effort to get him to reveal where the grail was, and you know the story from then on."

"Hmm, I see. So the Priory has been involved all along?"

"Yes. Pretty much. Perhaps you should talk with Alain yourself. He can clarify what they've done," Israel suggested.

"Yes, perhaps I will. Someone from the Priory must have been following Nick that day when he was mugged."

Israel nodded. "Nick went to St. Clair's and asked about chalices. Wouldn't you follow him?"

Maggie chuckled. "Dear, sweet Nick! He knew how important finding my family was to me. How I wish he could see my beautiful book about my St. Clair family."

CHAPTER FIFTY-SIX

Connections

THE NEWS OF Nick's death and of Guillaume's arrest had already reached another of their French acquaintances. The next morning, Henri phoned. Maggie was surprised and suspicious when he told her that he had genuinely liked Nick and that he felt deep regret at her loss.

"Well," she hesitated, not knowing how to react. Wasn't Henri involved with that devil Devereaux? Despite that irritation, Maggie felt she had to respond. "I appreciate your sympathy, Henri," she said coldly. "But how did you know? It has not been in the newspapers, has it?"

"I have my ways. I knew M. Devereaux and his friend Guillaume all too well, I am sorry to say. Neither was a good person. Your friend Nick was. I was in M. Devereaux's employ, and I have played a role in your problems. I'm deeply sorry for that. This guilt weighs heavily on me. There is a hard line between what one must do for one's employer and what one believes to be right by one's own values. I did not want to be involved in taking the chalice from M. Nick's flat, but Devereaux forced me to be a party to it."

"*You* worked for him. *You* stole the Sion Grail. How could you?" Maggie wished she could reach out and grab Henri by the neck. "Look at what has resulted! My Nick is dead," she screamed into the phone.

"Yes, I know," Henri said quietly. "It is my shame. I loved the work. I hated the man. I never foresaw this terrible result." Though she couldn't see him, Maggie suspected Henri's head was bowed. "I hope you know that I had nothing to do with M. Payne's death. I had, in fact, that very day, severed all relations with Devereaux and his friend Guillaume because I was so upset with their treatment of M. Nick and the woman, Thérèse."

"It hurts me to hear that you had any connection to this, Henri. Nick was a wonderful dear person who didn't deserve to die. I loved him, and I miss him." The tears started to form again. "Damn!" she muttered.

Henri asked, "Did I say something to offend you just now?"

"No, Henri. I'm sorry. The damn is not for you. It's for Devereaux and this whole situation. I want to find him and let him know face to face what he's done. Damn him! I'm going to tell him head-on what disaster he's wrought with his scheming and thieving and . . . Nick!" She felt in her heart that Nick was dead because of her. Because of her! She needed to avenge him. Justice had to be done. Rage filled her throat. Her voice, accompanied by tears of pain, became louder and angrier with each word.

"Please don't cry," Henri begged. "Calm yourself, my dear. Devereaux is a very dangerous man. Do not even consider approaching him yourself. Wait until the police have him." Maggie could picture Henri's distress as he spoke. He continued, "I can understand your frustration with this hateful and arrogant man. I, too, would like to avenge myself against that monster."

"Then help me find Devereaux, Henri," Maggie pleaded. "You owe me big time." Her rage showed in her voice, but this probably wasn't a familiar French phrase. She hoped she could guilt him into helping her.

Henri muttered, "You're right. I know I owe you both as much as I can give. If I help you find him, perhaps it will ease my own guilt. I don't know for certain, but I believe Devereaux is in Zurich where he has a fence for some of his objects that were not purchased at auction or through verified sales. He often stays at the Zurichsberg Hotel there. There is a good likelihood that you may find him there if you feel you must personally confront him. But you must not go alone, and you must be very careful. Why don't you ask M. Israel to accompany you? And you should notify the Paris police of your plans. That would be the best. I will feel much better about your safety then—as long as you don't tell them where you got the information on Devereaux's possible location."

"I wouldn't tell them, and I'm sure Israel will come with me if I ask him. I will be careful." As angry as she was with Henri, talking with him helped.

"I know you are grieving. I can hear it in your voice, but perhaps I can suggest something that will help to soothe your sadness and occupy your mind while you are in Zurich." Henri said, "Do you remember the Black Madonna we saw together at Chartres?"

"Of course. I loved her! She was exquisite."

"There is another Black Madonna near Zurich at Einsedeln. You must see her. She has been waiting for you."

"Waiting for me? Why do you say that, Henri?"

Henri hesitated. "I'm not sure exactly. It just came to me."

"Where is this Einsedeln and what is it?" Maggie asked.

"It is a monastery with a small village surrounding it. It is perhaps fifteen or twenty kilometers from the city. People there will direct you."

A spurt of excitement at the prospect of seeing another Black Madonna bubbled up within Maggie. Despite the sadness in her heart, this reminder of her original purpose here in France felt like a positive in the midst of all the darkness she was feeling. And she did need something to ponder other than her hatred of Devereaux and her sadness over Nick's death.

Henri said, "When I met you, dear Mademoiselle, I knew immediately that you were special and that I must share my knowledge with you. I knew when I saw you staring at the Magdalene window at Chartres that you had a strong connection with Mary Magdalene. Although I do not know what the original Mary Magdalene looked like, she is often represented as a beautiful woman with long red hair. I picture her much as you look today. Of course, she would be in different garb—but, much the same."

Maggie's left hand gently touched her hair. It wasn't as long as the hair in the oft-painted images of her namesake, but it was definitely red. She smiled. "I sense that connection, too. You know, Henri, my first night in Paris, I had a beautiful dream about a baby alone in a forest seeking its way. I wondered at the time if the baby represented me. Now, I know that it did. God was showing me that I was on my path. And you, Henri, helped me see that. Thank you."

"*Ce ne pas necessaire de me remercier.* Perhaps some of the guidance I've given you will in some way make up for my mistaken involvement with Devereaux. Will you go to Einsedeln?"

"Yes, Henri. I will go. I need to get away from the gloom of Nick's death, and for me, Paris represents that right now. Nick's sister is coming to take care of Nick's body. I dread that meeting because it will bring back all the hurt and pain, but after that, I hope I can move away from this trauma a bit. A new city, Zurich, a chance to tell Devereaux what I think of him *and* a Black Madonna—that sounds wonderfully right for me now."

"*Bonne chance et au revoir.*"

The phone clicked dead in Maggie's hand. Perhaps she could forgive Henri in time. Maggie walked to the window of her fourth-floor room. Looking out at her bit of Paris, Maggie reflected about the funny little Frenchman. Despite his involvement in stealing the St. Clair grail, Henri had played an important role in what she'd learned about her namesake and in intensifying her connection to the Magdalene. It was so ironic. And he had dropped into her life out of nowhere. Or had he? Perhaps he'd been tracking her for Devereaux from the start, she thought, grimacing.

Whatever Henri's motivation, he had been helpful, and it still seemed that her life was being guided. All the recent events—it was as though she'd been positioned here for a reason. And Rachel had helped her, too. Maggie wondered if Rachel's spirit would ever return to counsel her. As much as she'd enjoyed that experience, she was content to be on her own now—and she was determined to find that damned Devereaux!

CHAPTER FIFTY-SEVEN

Confrontation

WHEN MAGGIE TOLD Alain about Henri's suggestion on Devereaux's whereabouts, Alain alerted the Paris police. He and Hércule advised Maggie to wait in Paris for police to act, but she was determined to go to Zurich to find Devereaux and the Sion Grail, if he still had it.

Israel insisted on accompanying her. "There's nothing to keep me in Paris. I was only here to feel a part of the city and to soak up its ambiance. I have done more than enough of that. Paris has been very generous to me."

Maggie looked at him with a sidelong glance, "Why do you say that?"

Israel grabbed her and shook her gently. "I found *you*."

Maggie wasn't ready for this. It was comforting having Israel with her, and the strong attraction to Israel was still there, but emotional energy remained from Nick's death. "Yes," she said quietly, "but let's put those thoughts aside for now. I'm happy you're with me. Let's leave it at that. I have mixed emotions about Paris. In some ways, I hate Paris—for what happened here to Nick. I'll never forget that. Yet I'm grateful to this city too—for meeting you, for finding a part of my family that I never knew existed—and for finding *me*. I feel like I'm a different person from the

Maggie who arrived here almost three weeks ago. I can't explain exactly how I'm different, but I feel it—it's a knowing."

"Well, I like you both—the before-Maggie and the after-Maggie. I suppose others will be along soon."

Maggie laughed. "You never know! But we need to get moving if we are going to find Devereaux and the grail."

Maggie told Israel, "If Devereaux is there, I want to see him alone. If the police beat us there, fine—if not, I want my say. Just remember this is my show," she warned.

Israel nodded acceptance, smiling to himself at her chutzpah.

Within two hours, they were on a flight to Zurich. They took a taxi from the airport to the Hotel Zurichsberg. Maggie had called from Paris to confirm that she was a guest, explaining that M. Devereaux was her father and that she and her fiancé wanted to surprise him. The desk clerk was happy to help and gave her his room number. Maggie hated the lie—especially one that connected her by family to this awful man, but she could think of no other way to get the information they needed.

It was close to eight o'clock that evening when Israel knocked on the door of room 217 of the Hotel Zurichsberg.

Devereaux, expecting the delivery of a dinner tray, yelled in a cross voice, "*C'est ouvert!*"

Maggie and Israel looked at each other quizzically. Israel turned the knob. The door was indeed unlocked. They entered the room, closing the door behind them. They scanned the elegant hotel room with its contemporary furnishings.

A sleepy, disheveled-looking Devereaux sat on the bed, dressed only in a sleeveless undershirt and wrinkled linen slacks with a monogrammed belt flapping at his waist. This was not the debonair gentleman that Maggie had met in Paris. Seeing Devereaux in his current condition, Maggie wondered if Devereaux's previous urbane manners had been merely a mask for an unhappy and despondent man.

Angered by the sight of Maggie, Devereaux pointed his index finger at her. "You! I suppose you have come to take my beloved chalice away from me? Ha. Ha!" he croaked. "You cannot have it. It's gone—stolen by some ridiculous thief!"

"There's irony!" Israel said sarcastically.

"My pain from the loss of my lovely grail is bad enough. And now *you* show up here in Zurich. What does the American idiot woman want with Devereaux when there is no more antique chalice—no more holy Sion Grail to worship? The golden beauty was mine. I am the collector. You are only a silly American woman with no connection to it. You or your friend did not deserve to have such a piece of antiquity in your possession." He spit the words out as though clearing phlegm from his mouth.

Maggie's temper flared. "Just watch your mouth! I'm proud to be an American, and you will find I'm not silly! You dare to call me names, you . . . you . . . vile Euro-trash. You're the thief, you vicious, inhumane monster! You bastard! Your selfishness and deceit have killed the most honorable, the most generous, and the most caring man I know. You are evil—arrogant—shameful! Do you know how many lives you spoiled by killing Nick Payne? Just everyone that ever came in contact with him—and that's probably thousands." The tears were there, tempting her, but she brushed them back. Damn! Maggie told herself, I will not succumb.

A blank look came over Devereaux's haughty face when she said, "killing Nick Payne."

"Wait. Stop!" Devereaux rose from the bed and walked toward Maggie.

Israel immediately moved in front of Maggie. "Stay back!" he said forcefully.

Devereaux asked, "What do you mean 'killing'? I have not killed anyone. What is this killing business about?"

"Nick!" Maggie sobbed. "Your servant or housemate or lover or whatever he was killed my dear friend Nick, and he tried to kill me and others as well. None of us had done anything harmful to you or Guillaume."

"Guillaume? Guillaume did this? I did not know. He was always so rational. He sometimes acted a bit spoiled—a bit jealous of others and of me. But killed someone?" Devereaux retreated to the bed and slumped there.

This was not the reaction Maggie had expected. He must have known about the murder. Was this some kind of subterfuge? "You know what you did! You commanded Guillaume to assassinate Nick because he knew you had the chalice, didn't you? You *were* involved weren't you? I know you were!"

Israel had come up behind Maggie and was holding her by her shoulders. His touch gave her strength.

Devereaux looked up, but he did not look at Maggie. "No. I don't think I—I don't remember ordering that. The last time I talked to Guillaume . . ." He stopped in midsentence again. Then, he asked, "When did this happen?"

Israel answered, "Wednesday—in the afternoon—in the apartment above yours. The police arrested Guillaume the next morning. They told us he had two suitcases with him. He was evidently planning a trip somewhere."

Maggie continued to stare at Devereaux.

At this, Devereaux dropped his head into his hands. "Oh, no!" he sobbed. "I'm sure he took some of my precious . . . my divines . . . my darlings . . . my beauties." He looked forlorn, as though he had lost a dear friend. Then, suddenly, he shrieked, "The alabaster jar! Guillaume knew how much it meant to me. He wouldn't take that. Oh, dear God! Not the alabaster jar!" He looked wildly from Israel to Maggie and back.

"Murderer!" Maggie yelled at him. "Who cares about your alabaster jar? Damn the jars and the chalices and the trinkets! A man's life has been lost because of you—a man who fawns over *things*—a man who has no consideration for human life. A very special human life is lost forever."

Devereaux no longer responded. Maggie shook her fist at Devereaux. She wanted to go over to him and shake him. He still didn't seem to get it. How could she make him understand the terrible thing he had done? "You know what you did!" she shouted.

Israel grabbed Maggie by the arm and pulled her to the room's only two chairs. They seated themselves, waiting for some response. Just the act of sitting had a calming effect on her. She felt so conflicted. She wanted to say more, but something inside was telling her she might have said enough. Perhaps something else was at work here.

The entrance of a white-jacketed waiter followed a quick knock at the door. He nodded at the three and set a dome-covered dinner tray on the table closest to the door.

"I didn't order that!" Devereaux yelled.

Several other knocks followed—loud, sharp raps, and Israel hurried to the door and reached it just as Devereaux yelled, "It's open, you fools. *C'est ouvert!*"

Two police entered the room. Judging by their uniforms, one was Swiss and one French. The female officer spoke. "I am Inspector Mercédes Corbet of the Paris police." She looked at each of them, then focused on Devereaux. She asked, "Marcel Devereaux?"

"*Oui.*" Devereaux growled from the bed.

"*Ah. Bon soir, M. Devereaux.* And you are?" The inspector looked at Maggie and Israel.

Maggie answered, "Mary Magdalena Forsythe."

"Israel Hawkins, *un ami de Mlle. Forsythe,*" Israel replied.

The inspector turned back to Devereaux. "M. Devereaux. We have wanted to make your acquaintance for a long time. You have quite a reputation with the police, no?"

Devereaux did not respond.

"And now you are involved in the murder of Nicholas Payne."

"No! I know nothing about that. I was here in Zurich."

"Liar!" Maggie shouted. "You are the person behind Nick's death! The Sion Grail was more important to you than Nick's life!"

"This stupid woman lies. She's made up a story about me," he said, pointing to Maggie. "I can prove I was here," Devereaux shouted.

Inspector Corbet continued, "I remember that in 1998, we suspected that you, M. Devereaux, were involved in a robbery at l'Orangerie. Unfortunately, there was not enough proof at that time to arrest you."

Devereaux's despondent air vanished. He was alert now. "I was not there, and I can prove it! Leave me alone."

"Ah, indeed, M. Devereaux! The l'Orangerie affair was very daring. And what did you gain from it?"

Devereaux sat belligerently silent.

Inspector Corbet continued, "A Monet? A valuable antique silver statue of Isis? An antique ruby and diamond necklace that I am told sold for close to one million euros? We have traced these items. The items may have found new owners, but all went through your hands. How very lucky for you to have gained such riches! But there are other unfortunate aspects of this affair that we would like to discuss with you." She paused dramatically.

Maggie hoped the inspector's method would bring a confession from Devereaux. She wanted so to hear it.

"*Et alors!* Now, we have the incident of a very valuable antique chalice being kept for its owner by a man from the US in your apartment building, Monsieur. Today, the caretaker no longer has the chalice, and he no longer has his life. He did not gain a thing, did he? But someone else did." Her look was sardonic and sly.

Devereaux's increasingly pale face was a mask.

After a pause, Inspector Corbet asked softly in French, "*Ou est la calice? We would like to know.*"

Devereaux finally spoke, "I do not have it. It's gone—stolen. The stupid Zurich police can't find my chalice. *They* couldn't find a razor blade in a cake, even if they bit into it! Now you accuse me of a robbery when I wasn't even there! You have nerve, Madame. I will not say more until I speak with my attorney."

"*Bien.* Marcel Devereaux, until we can determine exactly what role you played in this event, we are placing you under arrest." The Swiss policeman, who had been standing close by, moved toward Devereaux with handcuffs in his hand. Inspector Corbet added, "Certainly, we can press charges on the earlier theft—the l'Orangerie caper. Your associate, Guillaume Joinville, has been arrested, and he has told us a great deal about your affairs. He was also carrying some very interesting pieces that may have come from that heist." She pointed to the telephone. "Your attorney can meet you in Paris. You will not be free until a judge hears your plea, and perhaps not then either."

The pain of Nick's death was still gnawing at Maggie's heart, and she wanted Devereaux to pay for it, but the irony of what had just happened hit her. Maggie stepped in front of Devereaux, laughing. "Ha, ha, ha, ha. The joke is on you, Devereaux. They're gone now; your lovelies have all disappeared. No more Holy Grail. No more alabaster jars. Gone! You'll never see your precious things again!" She continued laughing as she backed away from him.

Devereaux looked back at Maggie with a glassy stare. Suddenly, his head jerked as he crumpled to the floor. Maggie screamed and jumped back. Inspector Corbet leaned over Devereaux. His eyes stared upward from an ashen face. Israel pushed a frozen Maggie back, away from Devereaux's body. The inspector took Devereaux's pulse. "He is alive," she said.

Israel grabbed the small pill bottle from the table. The label read nitroglycerine. He said, "Maybe these will help." He pried open Devereaux's mouth and placed two pills under his tongue. The other policeman phoned for medical aid.

Maggie, shaking, sat down. She was horrified. Had she caused Devereaux's sudden attack? Was he dead? Was she as guilty as Guillaume in taking a life? "I didn't mean to h-hurt him," Maggie said haltingly.

Israel turned to Maggie. "You didn't cause this, Maggie. Devereaux deserves this—whatever it is."

Maggie said, "Perhaps Justice *is* being done here.

"*Oui, Madame,*" said Inspector Corbet. "I have seen this happen before. Justice comes often outside of the courts. Justice is like a woman—she will act on what she knows to be right and true." Then, pointing at Devereaux, Inspector Corbet said, "This looks like some kind of attack—heart problems most likely. If he survives and is tried, we'll hope that Justice is there, too."

Maggie nodded. She wiped away the perspiration from her neck. She knew Nick could never be avenged, but she'd had her say. She felt that the cloak of pain that had enveloped her since his death was being lifted. She saw Israel approaching. Thank God he was here with her. She sensed that was a part of God's plan for her, too.

Israel sat down next to her and pulled her into his arms in a comforting embrace. He looked into her sad, drained face and said, "Maggie, you were wonderful. Now let's put this behind us."

CHAPTER FIFTY-EIGHT

Sanctuary

THE FOLLOWING DAY, with Devereaux in police custody, Maggie and Israel drove to see the Black Madonna at Einsedeln as Henri Diamond had recommended. They found the village of Einsedeln nestled amid rolling hills. The monastery—the focal point of the small village—stood high above the town.

You couldn't miss the shrine to the Black Madonna near the entrance of the monastery church. Maggie and Israel stood directly in front of it, scanning the intricate woodwork, the Madonna's golden gown, the floral tributes set before her. And then Maggie saw it. The Sion Grail sat on a narrow shelf high above the Madonna's altar—too far for hands of visitors to reach and enclosed behind a glass and steel shield. Two sprigs of lily of the valley peeped out from under its domed top, and a tiny electronic red security light blinked.

Maggie couldn't believe her eyes. The tremendous shock buckled her knees, and she sank silently to the floor.

"What's wrong?" Israel asked, bending to help Maggie. He began tugging at Maggie's arm worriedly as he tried to pull her to her feet.

She shook herself free and rose, shouting, "Israel! Look there!" She pointed at the gem-encrusted chalice in its new place of honor. "The Sion

Grail. It's there!" Then she muttered, "Oh my god! This is too much! I don't believe it!"

Israel's gaze followed Maggie's finger. "*That's* the grail? This is too weird! After all our trouble flying here to Zurich to find Devereaux, the missing chalice turns up here in a church? It doesn't make sense." He paused to stare at the golden vessel. "Well, finally, I get to see what all the intrigue has been about. The grail *is* really something, isn't it?"

"Yes," Maggie murmured, "I am *very* happy to see it again, no matter how it got here." Tears of relief began to flow. "But it's such a shock. I'm stunned. I feel like I must be dreaming. Yet I know it's the same chalice Nick and I hid in his Paris flat. Oh, welcome home, my lovely one!" She laughed at herself. "Now I sound like Devereaux!"

"You would recognize it, I'm sure. My question is, what is it doing here? How did it get here?"

Maggie shook her head, bewildered and incredulous. "I have no idea." She paused and said thoughtfully, "But what a wonderful place for it. I can't think of a more perfect spot. Here hundreds of people can look at it every day and enjoy its beauty. And it's with the Black Madonna."

"Do you think it's safe here?" Israel asked.

"I don't know. But sometimes hiding something in plain sight is safer than finding a perfect secret place for it."

Israel chuckled. "I hope it's finally safe from covetous types like our friend Devereaux. I noticed, as I presume you did, that even he didn't fare well while it was in his possession."

"Right, and more importantly, since the Sion Grail is isolated here, it cannot bring its legacy of danger and harm to anyone anymore."

Israel commented, "But it's ironic that it should end up in a Catholic Church after all the cruelty and death the church bestowed on the Cathars and other early Christians who may have possessed the grail. I'm not sure the church deserves it."

Maggie nodded. "Yes. Sometimes it seems that life is irony itself. But having it with the Black Madonna makes it feel right to me. I can accept that—a symbol of the divine feminine spirit that the church had ignored for centuries. I can't wait to tell Hércule and Alain." She turned and hugged Israel.

Over the past few days, Maggie had begun to understand that her experiences here weren't just about the Sion Grail and the trauma of losing it. She had become a woman. She had finally experienced love. A dear beloved person had died. Past lives she couldn't have previously imagined were shown to her. And it was all a part of her now.

Neither Maggie nor Israel noticed the short gray-haired woman in a bright floral dress standing to the side watching them. She approached them warily. She asked, "*Aimez-vous le nouveau calice?*"

Maggie turned to Israel with a questioning look. "Gypsy," he said under his breath.

Maggie responded, "*Oui, bien sûr, Elle is trés belle.*"

The woman said proudly, "*Je le lui en donne.*"

Ilona proceeded to tell them about how she got the grail away from Devereaux and to its new destination.

Ilona looked shyly at Maggie and asked, "And your name, *ma chérie?*"

Maggie looked straight into Ilona's eyes and said very firmly, "Mary Magdalena Forsythe."

"*Tiens!* I knew it! You are here for a reason. You are." She grabbed Maggie's right hand and looked at her palm. "There is much here! I could read your life to you. You know this chalice—this grail? Eh?"

Maggie nodded, "Yes, I know it. I have held it in my hands, and it spoke to me just like it must have spoken to you."

"Eeeeee! *Oui, oui, oui. Il me parle.* It says, 'Get me away!' You know this chalice is old? Is maybe old enough to be Holy Grail? It could be. And you were probably there then. You were there. I can see you there." Ilona grew more excited with each phrase. "You were a daughter of Zion, like the Magdalene, like she who was predicted to be the watchtower for the Christians. I think so."

Ilona looked at Israel. "And you, Monsieur. Your name?"

"Israel."

Before he could get the Hawkins out, Ilona was squealing, "Ayyyyyy! And you are together? Such a combination—connecting the holy feminine way and the old land by its new name! What power you can have together. This was truly meant to be."

Maggie could feel Israel's shoulder pressing on hers. Why so hard? Did he feel this too? She turned quickly and looked at him. His smile was the broadest she had ever seen. He nodded encouragingly. Could this little gypsy woman be right? Or was she being foolish to even consider it? But in the cave at St. Maximime, she had also felt that she had been with Mary Magdalene in another time. And her connection with Israel was incredibly strong. Anything was possible.

Maggie smiled at Ilona and hugged her quickly. "Perhaps you're right about my having lived during Christ and Mary Magdalene's time."

"You think about it . . . better yet, dream about it. See what you can remember. Scenes will come to you. You will remember. Sometime you will know," Ilona assured her. "But I must go back to Zurich now. The train leaves soon. *Au revoir, Mlle. Mary Madeleine et M. Israel.* Blessings on you."

They stood and watched as Ilona's brightly flowered dress disappeared in a sweep out the monastery's heavy door. Maggie and Israel stood for some time staring at the grail. Maggie felt Israel's arm close around her shoulders. She didn't look at his face, but she knew he was smiling. His voice was little more than a whisper when he leaned down to her ear and said, "Everything is one. It all works together if you let it." Golden-winged cherubs seemed to wink down at them from the Romanesque church pillars. Israel turned Maggie to face him and bent to kiss her.

"Here?" Maggie asked.

"Here in front of the Sion Grail. It brought us together." Israel's kiss was deliberate and intense.

The End